Why are you cast down, O my soul, and
why are you disquieted within me?

PSALM 42:5

Let tomorrow come tomorrow. Not by your
will is the house carried through the night.

WENDELL BERRY

Be Not Anxious

Pastoral Care
of Disquieted Souls

Allan Hugh Cole Jr.

WILLIAM B. EERDMANS PUBLISHING COMPANY

GRAND RAPIDS, MICHIGAN / CAMBRIDGE, U.K.

Published 2008 by
Wm. B. Eerdmans Publishing Co.
2140 Oak Industrial Drive N.E., Grand Rapids, Michigan 49505 /
P.O. Box 163, Cambridge CB3 9PU U.K.
www.eerdmans.com

Printed in the United States of America

14 13 12 11 10 09 08   7 6 5 4 3 2 1

Library of Congress Cataloging-in-Publication Data

Cole, Allan Hugh.
Be not anxious: pastoral care of disquieted souls / Allan Hugh Cole Jr.
p.   cm.
Includes bibliographical references.
ISBN 978-0-8028-6310-2 (pbk.: alk. paper)
1. Church work. 2. Pastoral psychology. 3. Anxiety —
Religious aspects — Christianity. I. Title.

BV4470.C56 2008

253 — dc22

2008022117

For Tracey, who understands

Contents

Acknowledgments

I am grateful to Donald Capps, professor of pastoral theology at Princeton Theological Seminary, who gave generously of his time and energy to read the entire manuscript for this book and helped me improve it in several ways. It has been my privilege to know Don for sixteen years now, having met him first as a seminary student and then enjoying the opportunity to study with him in a doctoral program. He continues to be a mentor and friend, modeling the finest qualities in teaching, scholarship, and friendship, and garnering my admiration, appreciation, and affection.

Other persons read portions of the book's manuscript. Their responses deepened my thinking about the subject of anxiety and helped refine my arguments. Robert C. Dykstra and Deborah van Deusen Hunsinger, both of whom are fine pastoral theologians teaching at Princeton Seminary, read portions of Chapters 4 and 1, respectively. Now colleagues and friends, they continue to teach me much. David Lee Jones, a trusted colleague and friend at Austin Seminary who keeps me laughing, graciously read Chapter 1 and offered helpful remarks. David J. Gouwens, professor of theology at Brite Divinity School, Texas Christian University, read a portion of what became Chapter 4. I have long admired him from afar, believing that he is among the finest Kierkegaard scholars we have. Having never met him, however, I wrote to him out of the blue asking if he would read the sections on Kierkegaard. He graciously consented. As I have since discovered, those who know him will not be surprised by this kind gesture.

I am also thankful to twenty-one students at Austin Presbyterian

Acknowledgments

Theological Seminary, where I have the pleasure to teach, for their engaging discussions on the topic of anxiety in a course I offered some years ago, "Pastoral Care with Anxious Persons." I remain grateful, too, to the many students I have been honored to teach and learn from in the various pastoral care courses I have offered at Austin Seminary over the last five years. The insights provided by these students' questions, reflections, and personal stories are found throughout this book. Furthermore, the four persons who provided the "portraits" of disquieted souls in Chapter 2, who told me their personal stories so candidly and courageously, have added a depth of insight to this book that otherwise would be missing.

I also want to thank my colleagues at Austin Seminary, including professors, administrators, and staff persons, who help make my vocation meaningful, pleasant, and rewarding. Furthermore, I deeply appreciate Ted Wardlaw, Austin Seminary's president, and Michael Jinkins, our academic dean, for their gifts of administration, faculty support, and encouraging scholarship that serves the needs and ends of the church.

I would be remiss if I did not also express my deepest appreciation to Jon Pott, vice president and editor in chief at William B. Eerdmans, who graciously listened over several months' time to my advocating for this book. I admire his vision and am grateful to have had the opportunity to work with Eerdmans on two books now. I also want to thank Linda Bieze, managing editor at Eerdmans, for her support of, and contributions to, this project. Furthermore, it was a true joy to work with Mary Hietbrink, who edited this book. Her insights, sensitivity, and gifts for clear expression enriched it in significant ways.

Finally, I am blessed with a generous family that inspires me to do the best I can in life, vocationally and otherwise, and yet never ceases to love me when I fall short. My parents, Allan and Jeri Cole, are generous souls. They have long encouraged me to dream large dreams and believe that they can come true with hard work. Such generosity is one of the true gifts that parents may offer their children. I thank them for all that they continue to give me and my family. My wife, Tracey, makes untold sacrifices in order for me to have the time and energy to write books and feed my creative passion, and she believes in me when I begin not to believe in myself. Tracey and our daughters, Meredith and Holly, provide me with life's greatest joys and adventures. This book is dedicated to Tracey, who after sixteen "odd" years of marriage is still the love of my life, in thanksgiving to God.

Preface

Several years ago, while I was the pastor of a congregation, I experienced a rather severe episode of anxiety that, while ebbing and flowing somewhat, nevertheless lasted for several months' time. I was aware that it was manifesting itself not only in an unusual degree of strife between my wife and me but also in physical symptoms — in such things as headaches, an inability to sleep well, and a handful of episodes when I nearly fainted while teaching, leading worship, or conducting meetings in a public forum. So I decided to get some help.

After making an appointment with a psychologist in town who had been recommended by one of my closest friends (who happens to be a psychologist himself), I arrived for the first session only to bump into one of my parishioners and her daughter in the waiting room! I remember opening the door and seeing the daughter, who also saw me, and then quickly shutting the door and walking back to my car. My heart pounding, I felt an encompassing heat that spread first across the back of my neck and then throughout the rest of my body, a bodily warmth that comes with deep embarrassment and shame. My initial thought was simply to forego the appointment. I would tell the therapist that something came up, pay him for the missed appointment, and then reschedule . . . probably with someone else so as not to have to risk bumping into my parishioners again.

But I had been seen. While my parishioner's young daughter would not know why I was there or that my problem had to do with anxiety, she *would* know that I stuck my head in and that I quickly left. Consequently, her mother and brother would almost certainly know too. I would have some explaining to do whether I went back into the waiting room and kept the appointment or not. Eventually it became clear to me that, for all sorts of reasons, it would be best to go back, to face my parishioners and face my feelings of shame. Entering the waiting room once again, with what I am sure was a sheepish expression on my face, I greeted my parishioners, engaged in some uncomfortable small talk, and sat there, embarrassed, for what seemed like hours but was only about five minutes. My parishioner's son eventually exited the psychologist's office. He looked surprised to see me and may have thought that his mother summoned me there as his pastor. This family left quickly, however, and I went into my own session with the therapist.

The next time I saw this family, which was just a couple of days later at church, the mother asked me what I thought of this psychologist. I responded with something like: "Oh, this was my first time. You know, sometimes pastors need to talk with someone too . . . and actually I needed to consult with him about how to help someone with a problem!" I am embarrassed to admit that I misled her. I did not own up to the fact that I was struggling with anxiety and needed to talk with someone about it; instead, I said I needed advice to help someone else. But at the time it was just too painful to be that honest and vulnerable. I was not only anxious, but anxious about others knowing that I was anxious. Among my biggest fears was that others would know and, consequently, would think less of me. Like many anxious persons, I became an expert at concealing it. . . .

Chapter 1

ANXIETY

The Disquieted Soul

Pastors encounter anxious persons. Those serving in pastoral ministry and most anyone paying close attention to congregational life will attest to that, particularly when they know more about how anxiety reveals itself and become more skillful at recognizing and working with it. Suggesting the "disquieted soul" as the apt metaphor for anxiety, I seek in this book to enhance that knowledge and skill by helping pastors with at least three things: (1) identifying anxious persons in their congregations; (2) understanding what may make them anxious; and (3) suggesting ways for supporting and nurturing them in ministry.

Anxiety's Pervasiveness

The term *anxiety* shares the same Latin root, *angere,* with the terms *anger* and *anguish.* Peter L. Steinke notes that *angere* "is translated 'to choke' or 'to give pain by pushing together,'" with its noun form, *angustus,* meaning "narrow."[1] Anyone who has experienced anxiety knows that a choking sensation, an apparent narrowing of one's throat and tracheal passage, and a painful "pushing together" of multiple thoughts, emotions, physical sensations, and behaviors often come part and parcel with it, particularly in more severe forms.

The *Oxford American Dictionary* uses words like *worry, concern, solici-*

---

1. Peter L. Steinke, *How Your Church Family Works: Understanding Congregations and Emotional Systems* (Herndon, Va.: Alban Institute, 1993), p. 14.

tude, uneasiness, apprehension, nervousness, disquieted, earnestly wanting or trying, longing, yearning, aching, and *stress* in depicting what anxiety involves. The sheer number of synonyms for anxiety alone indicates the condition's pervasiveness in human experience. Who among us has not experienced most, if not all, of what the dictionary lists? These various descriptions also point to the fact that anxiety appears in many forms. Some we may typically associate with the condition; others we may not. But regardless of how it appears, anxiety can make life difficult and painful, particularly in its more chronic and severe expressions. This holds true both for anxious individuals and for those around them. In fact, one of anxiety's qualities is that anxious people tend to raise others' anxieties.

The National Institute of Mental Health confirms how prevalent anxiety has become. Over forty million American adults, approximately one in every eight over age 18, suffer from an anxiety disorder.[2] Some experts have gone as far as to say that 25 percent of the population, at some point in their lives, will experience an anxiety-related problem significant enough to meet the criteria for a psychiatric illness, thus putting anxiety on pace with serious medical diseases and severe depression in frequency.[3] A survey conducted in the late 1990s of primary-care physicians in the United States supports this claim. It found that "at least one-third of office visits were prompted by some form of anxiety."[4]

Research shows that women are affected by most forms of anxiety at nearly twice the rate of men. Of course, men are not immune to anxiety; and to some extent, gender disparity in anxiety disorders almost certainly reflects the fact that men tend to report their struggles and seek help for them less frequently than women. Thus, the disparity between men and women experiencing anxiety is probably not as great as

2. National Institute of Mental Health, *Anxiety Disorders,* NIH Publication No. 06-3879 (Washington, D.C., 2007).

3. Michelle Craske, Ph.D., "Circuits of Fear: Anxiety Disorders" (Discovery Communications, 2001; Films for Humanities and Social Sciences, 2004). Information on criteria for fourteen different types of anxiety disorders may be found in *The Diagnostic and Statistical Manual of Mental Disorders,* 4th ed. (Washington, D.C.: American Psychiatric Association, 1994), pp. 393-444.

4. Edward M. Hallowell, *Worry: Hope and Help for a Common Condition* (New York: Random House, 2001), p. xi.

the research indicates. Men live anxiously too, perhaps more often than we know.

Older adults (aged 65 and beyond) are at least as likely as younger ones, and probably more so, to have an anxiety disorder. Depression and anxiety frequently occur together, and rates of depression among older adults tend to exceed those of younger populations.[5] Furthermore, anxiety often follows declining health, functioning, and independence, economic instability, role loss, and substantial interpersonal losses, all of which aging persons typically experience. Thus, the two largest groups in American congregations and the most frequent recipients of pastoral care — women and older adults — experience anxiety with substantial frequency. Current data suggest that in the typical congregation of 150 members a pastor may expect to find at least twenty people with anxiety serious enough to qualify clinically as a disorder, plus numerous others whose struggle with the condition is less severe but painful nonetheless. In a word, pastors regularly encounter anxious people.

A number of factors in contemporary life correlate with anxiety. These include an ongoing threat of terrorism, both domestic and international. For most Americans, terrorism was something that happened at a great distance until April of 1995, when Timothy McVeigh and his accomplices bombed the Murrah Federal Building in Oklahoma City. Even more profoundly, the events of September 11, 2001, touched American life in unprecedented ways. International terrorism and its threats now affect foreign and domestic policy decisions, presidential elections, constitutional concerns for privacy, immigration, the way we think about the display of American flags, and the manner that religion impacts the national scene. Moreover, since September 11 media coverage of terrorism has saturated daily living, with newspaper stories, magazine profiles, talk radio commentaries, and television news footage detailing the threats of violence at the hands of terrorists. We are bombarded with talk about nuclear proliferation, dirty bombs, weapons of mass destruction, and terror cells infiltrating the United

---

5. National Institute of Health, *Older Adults: Depression and Suicide Facts*, NIH Publication No. 03-4593, rev. ed. (Washington, D.C., 2003); National Institute of Mental Health, *Anxiety Disorders* (2004). See also www.adaa.org/AnxietyDisorderInfor/ AnxietyElderly.cfm.

States, Canada, and Mexico. We hear great concern expressed about world stability, national security, porous borders, and personal safety. For some, such saturation has a numbing effect. For others, who may already live anxiously, it adds to the soul's disquiet.

A great irony accompanies all of this. As Richard Restak, a medical doctor, has noted, now "may be the only time in our history when we are not only warned that we should be afraid, but told exactly how afraid we should be (red, orange, or yellow alert), and yet, regardless of how afraid we should be, we are given no advice about what to do, except perhaps be wary of strangers and stock up on duct tape and bottled water."[6] The current climate of fear, and the feeling that we cannot do much about it, exacerbates the already disquieted soul's predicament. Any anxious person can tell you how quickly being afraid of something or someone, whether the fear is "reasonable" or not, intensifies anxiety.

Life's fast and even frenetic pace, resulting in what James Gleick calls "hurry sickness," also contributes to anxiety in the present age, exacerbating it in ways similar to those of fear.[7] This sickness has to do with the stress that accompanies the fast pace of contemporary life. To be sure, living hurriedly may serve, to some extent, to insulate the anxious person from her pain, at least temporarily. Staying busy has long served to divert us from distressing thoughts, feelings, and behaviors. But, even so, anxiety certainly contributes to stress. Anxious persons often describe their lives by saying they feel "stressed out," "flustered," or "overloaded." In the same way, stress will almost always exacerbate anxiety. This becomes evident when already anxious people get more so as they assume additional responsibilities or take on added tasks, which, ironically, they may hope will ease their anxiety. Consequently, relief from anxiety brought about by staying busy is temporary. The point to underscore here is that anxiety is qualitatively different from stress. Although anxious people experience stress, and various stressors (like a frenetic pace) typically increase one's anxiety level, anxiety is more fundamental, pervasive, and potentially debilitating than stress, as unwelcome and harmful as stress may be.

---

6. Richard Restak, M.D., *Poe's Heart and the Mountain Climber: Exploring the Effect of Anxiety on Our Brains and Our Culture* (New York: Harmony Books, 2004), pp. 183-84.

7. James Gleick, *Faster: The Acceleration of Just about Everything* (New York: Vintage Books, 2000), p. 9.

The anxiety that lies at the heart of this book is deeper than the difficulties associated with life's pace and other stressors. It lies centrally in the "core" of our being, of our very souls. As Søren Kierkegaard described it, this anxiety involves "inner strife and disharmony."[8] It has less to do with the situations that we encounter and what could happen to us, and much more to do with who we are and to whom we belong. Even so, we should not discount the effects of stress on anxious lives, particularly in light of today's rampant "hurry sickness." We are more technologically advanced than any previous generation. While that may help us do more, we often do it with less efficiency than before. A popular way of speaking about this is to say that we become expert at "multitasking," an ability widely praised and rewarded despite its detrimental effects.

Consider too that many of us take relatively little time for relaxation, recreation, and rejuvenation. We work longer hours for comparatively less pay than in previous generations. We spend more time commuting between work and home than ever before, most of us alone in our own vehicles and on congested, slow-moving highways that, ironically, were built for speed![9] We also take on more personal debt than in previous decades, consuming more products, saving less money, often exhausting both our fiscal and our emotional reserves in the process. When we find time for vacation, many of us take along our cell phone, laptop computer, personal digital assistant (PDA), or other means for working at any hour, in any place, and in the presence of almost anyone. For many people, this frenetic pace results in less time with spouses, children, close friends, and colleagues, and the quality of these relationships suffers. If we are not careful, they deteriorate altogether. While not necessarily causing the soul's disquiet, these "consequences of haste"[10] do little to contribute to the soul's nurture and well-being.

Several years ago, as the new millennium dawned, a popular book diagnosed the problem. In *Finding Serenity in the Age of Anxiety*, Robert Gerzon aptly identified anxiety as "one of the most mysterious and

---

8. Søren Kierkegaard, *The Sickness unto Death*, ed. and trans. Howard V. Hong and Edna H. Hong (Princeton: Princeton University Press, 1980), p. 22.

9. Gleick, *Faster*, p. 123.

10. Gleick, *Faster*, p. 13.

profound aspects of the mind" and "humanity's most perplexing problem since the dawn of consciousness."[11] Agreeing with those who posit that anxiety now affects one in four American adults — or 65 million people — Gerzon called the condition an epidemic that must be brought under control. The book's success indicates how perceptive he was. Undoubtedly, the epidemic is real, and many are in search of "serenity." In fact, the NIMH study cited earlier, as well as much additional data, point to what three more recent books term "American mania,"[12] "hypomania" or "exuberance,"[13] and "status anxiety."[14] Evidence that anxious persons are legion, therefore, is overwhelming. Some of these persons are in congregations that pastors love and serve. Some may be pastors themselves.

Anxiety in the Bible

Though an increasingly common experience today, living with anxiety is hardly new. As early as the fifth century B.C.E. we find the Chinese philosopher Confucius (551-479 B.C.E.) commenting on the condition, declaring in his *Analects* that "A man should not be ignorant of the age of his father and mother. It is a matter, on the one hand, for rejoicing and, on the other, for anxiety."[15] Similarly, the ancient Roman poet Ovid (43 B.C.E.-17 C.E.) observed, "There is no such thing as pure pleasure; some anxiety always goes with it"; and "[even] love is full of anxious fears."[16] Likewise, the first-century Roman philosopher and statesman Seneca (c. 4 B.C.E.-31 C.E.) is said to have remarked that "There are more things to alarm us than to harm us, and we suffer more often in apprehension than reality," and to have ob-

11. Robert Gerzon, *Finding Serenity in an Age of Anxiety* (New York: Bantam Books, 1998), p. 7.

12. Peter C. Wybrow, *American Mania: When More Is Not Enough* (New York: W. W. Norton, 2005).

13. Kay Redfield Jamison, *Exuberance: A Passion for Life* (New York: Alfred A. Knopf, 2004).

14. Alain de Botton, *Status Anxiety* (New York: Pantheon Books, 2004).

15. Confucius, *The Analects*, Book 4, No. 21 (New York: Viking/Penguin, 1979), p. 75.

16. Tradition attributes these two quotes to Ovid, though no written citation is available.

served that "The mind that is anxious about the future is miserable."[17]

The Hebrew and Christian scriptures also attest to the long-standing presence of anxiety in human lives. To the dispersed people of Israel yearning for return to Zion, the prophet Isaiah declares, "Say to the anxious of heart, 'Be strong, fear not; behold your God! Requital is coming, the recompense of God — He Himself is coming to give you triumph'" (Isa. 35:4, *Tanak*). Recalling his distress in the wake of troubling dreams and visions, which led him to seek counsel from another who would "disclose . . . the interpretation of the matter," the prophet Daniel laments, "As for me, Daniel, my spirit within me was anxious and the visions of my head alarmed me" (Dan. 7:15-16, RSV). And extolling complete dependence on God for life's basic provisions while explicitly noting human tendencies to work hard to provide for ourselves, the psalmist declares, "It is in vain that you rise up early and go late to rest, eating the bread of anxious toil; for he gives sleep to his beloved" (Ps. 127:2, NRSV). While reflecting on the gift of life and its fleeting nature, Koheleth urges his readers to "Banish anxiety from your mind, and put away pain from your body; for youth and the dawn of life are vanity [i.e., ephemeral or fleeting]" (Eccles. 11:10, NRSV).[18] Furthermore, the book of Proverbs points out that "Anxiety in a man's heart weighs him down, but a good word makes him glad" (Prov. 12:25, RSV).[19] On the other hand, the book of Proverbs makes a positive case for anxiety when it involves openness to God's direction and reproof: "Happy is the man who is anxious always, but he who hardens his heart falls into misfortune" (Prov. 28:14, RSV).

The New Testament recounts anxiety too. To the Corinthian Christians Paul writes, "There is the daily pressure upon me of my anxiety for all the churches," and when discussing the Christian's "present affliction" and "future glory" he notes, "While we are still in this tent, we

17. Tradition attributes these two quotes to Seneca, though no written citation is available.

18. W. Sibley Towner, *The New Interpreter's Bible*, ed. Leander E. Keck (Nashville: Abingdon, 1997), pp. 353-54.

19. My choice to cite the Revised Standard Version of the Bible (RSV), as opposed to the New Revised Standard Version (NRSV), stems from the former translation's choice to use "anxiety" instead of "worry" or "fear." However, I regret the RSV's lack of gender-inclusive language, which the NRSV appropriately corrects.

7

sigh with anxiety; not that we would be unclothed, but that we would be further clothed, so that what is mortal may be swallowed up by life" (2 Cor. 11:28; 2 Cor. 5:4, RSV). Moreover, in his letter to the Christians in Philippi he urges, "Have no anxiety about anything, but in everything by prayer and supplication with thanksgiving let your requests be made known to God. And the peace of God, which passes all understanding, will keep your hearts and your minds in Christ Jesus" (Phil. 4:6-7, RSV). Similarly, the author of 1 Peter implores his audience to "Cast all your anxiety on [God], because he cares for you" (1 Peter 5:7, NRSV).

Jesus pays particular attention to anxiety. He insists that being anxious, living with a disquieted soul, runs counter to what God would have for us, especially when it occupies a central, controlling place in one's life. Jesus exhorts his followers, "Do not be anxious about your life," and asks, "Which of you by being anxious can add one cubit to his span of life?" He urges, "Do not be anxious about tomorrow, for tomorrow will be anxious for itself"; and recognizing that fear is anxiety's close associate, he adds, "Fear not, little flock, for it is your Father's good pleasure to give you the kingdom" (Matt. 6:19-21, 25-34; Luke 12:22-34, RSV).

Like the prophets and sages of old, Jesus recognized that many people lived anxiously. They struggled with hearts, heads, spirits, and toil infused with this painful and at times debilitating condition. On several occasions, Jesus took the opportunity to encourage those with "ears to hear" to live in a different way.

Distinguishing Anxiety from Related Experiences

Unfortunately, when it translates the Greek word *merimnan*, the NRSV sometimes uses *worry* or *fear* for the better term *anxiety*. This is particularly true of its translations of the Gospels. Although this follows the common practice of melding these terms, they are not interchangeable. While anxious people may indeed worry and tend to do so frequently, to suppose that worry fully captures an experience of anxiety is like suggesting that difficulty sleeping depicts the essence of depression or that strong sexual desire exhausts what it means to be in love.

Furthermore, fear differs from anxiety. Fear centers on a particular, identifiable locus of danger: an object, a person, a situation, or a circumstance. Anxiety is more pervasive, diffuse, and lacks a specific, identifiable locus. Fear thus seems more easily managed than anxiety. Because it has an identifiable location or source, fear gives one a greater sense of power over undesirable feelings or circumstances than anxiety, which feels like being unable to exercise control over what is happening. To put it another way, we may avoid, attempt to avoid, or compensate in some way for what we are afraid of — fear of flying, of spiders, of being in closed spaces, or of a particular person or circumstance. Such avoidance or compensation provides some measure of power over our fear, and this tends to lessen our struggle. We find it more difficult, however, to avoid or compensate for what we cannot identify or locate, the threat or cause of our uneasiness, so anxiety is an emotional state over which we have comparatively less power or control.

Even the attempt to describe or account for anxiety is not all that easy. The psychologist Rollo May described it this way: "The special characteristics of anxiety are the feelings of *uncertainty* and *helplessness* in the face of danger," an "objectless" or "vague" threat to one's well-being.[20] He held that anxiety stems from "apprehension cued off by a threat to some value . . . [an] individual holds essential to his existence as a personality," so that "anxiety is the basic, underlying reaction — the generic term; and fear is the expression of the same capacity in its specific, objectified form."[21] Aaron T. Beck and Gary Emery view anxiety differently. Embracing "a cognitive perspective" on anxiety, they locate the condition in the person's sense of vulnerability, that is, in "a person's perception of himself as subject to internal or external dangers over which his control is lacking or is insufficient to afford him a sense of safety."[22] Also, for them, anxiety differs from fear in that the former finds its basis in an emotional response while the latter is based in a cognitive one.[23] Offering a still different view, the psychoanalyst Barry E. Wolfe suggests that the anxious person perceives a profound threat to her "core self-beliefs." This threat may involve feelings of vulnerability, but it extends beyond this to the sense that she (in her core personhood)

20. Rollo May, *The Meaning of Anxiety,* rev. ed. (New York: W. W. Norton, 1996), p. 205.

21. May, *The Meaning of Anxiety,* pp. 205, 224.

22. Aaron T. Beck and Gary Emery, with Ruth L. Greenberg, *Anxiety Disorders and Phobias: A Cognitive Perspective* (New York: Basic Books, 1985), p. 67.

23. Beck and Emery, *Anxiety Disorders and Phobias,* p. 9.

is actually in "immediate, catastrophic danger."[24] This extension brings Wolfe's view closer to May's view that there is a perceived threat to some value that is essential to one's existence as a personality.

Each of these views on anxiety has merit, both for understanding the condition's roots and for helping to relieve it. In Chapter 4, I will discuss Beck's view in depth, along with several other psychological perspectives on the condition. Aspects of these perspectives will inform my own view on how pastors may care for disquieted souls. But for now I simply want to emphasize that anxiety has multiple sources and various expressions (which we might refer to as "types" of anxiety). Furthermore, anxiety may arise for different reasons, appear in various ways, and be joined to a variety of intrapersonal, interpersonal, and systemic dynamics. Pastoral caregivers need to keep its multiple features in mind. Anxiety is not one-dimensional, and we should never view it as if it were.

That being said, the concept of "angst," sometimes referred to as *existential* or *primordial* angst, best captures the type of anxiety that will receive our primary attention in this book. Though often translated into English as *fear, worry,* or *anxiety,* words like *anguish* and especially *dread* are closer to the meaning of *angst* and thus best denote the kind of anxiety I seek to highlight here. This anguish or dread has less to do with what may *happen* to us or those we love, and therefore has less to do with concern, worry, or fear about particular dangers that may, to some degree, be identified and avoided. It has more to do with *who one is or wants to be,* especially in relationship to others of supreme value and importance. To put it another way, the type of anxiety that concerns us here, and the type I believe pastors tend to encounter, has less to do with circumstances or situations and more to do with personhood and relationship, though circumstances and situations surely may affect one's anxiety. Thus, the type of anxiety or angst I have in mind shares commonalities with anxiety as various psychological perspectives have described it while also remaining different.

The point to underscore here is that existential anxiety or angst entails more than fear or worry — much more. The soul's disquiet re-

---

24. Barry E. Wolfe, *Understanding and Treating Anxiety Disorders: An Integrative Approach to Healing the Wounded Self* (Washington, D.C.: American Psychological Association, 2005), p. 106.

mains qualitatively different from more ordinary fears or worries, as much difficulty and pain as those may cause. I believe that this has always been the case. Matthew's and Luke's Gospels portray Jesus as having recognized as much, as did Paul and the authors of Isaiah, Daniel, Proverbs, 1 Peter, and the Psalms. Jesus thus seems to have something more intense and pervasive in mind than fear or worry when choosing to address his audience. This leads me to embrace the Revised Standard Version's choice to use *anxious* instead of *fear* or *worry*.[25]

Anxiety as a Condition of the Soul

I now want to say more about how and why I understand anxiety — particularly of the sort that persons with religious hunger experience and thus a kind that pastors tend to encounter — to be a condition of the soul. By "soul" I mean something like Jürgen Moltmann has in mind when thinking about the concept of immortality — namely, "the relationship of the *whole person* to the immortal God."[26] The soul is not a "thing" to be isolated and preserved, but rather a locus for relationship that requires cultivation and sharing. Implicit here is the idea that we should not think of either one's body or one's soul as substances, constituent parts, or discrete ingredients of personhood. Most of Western Christianity, influenced by Platonic idealism on the one hand and Cartesian dualism on the other, has mistakenly done just that. It has embraced a necessary separation, and sharp distinction, between body and soul or, more recently, body, mind, and soul, the mind serving as the bridge between the other two, presumably incongruent, entities.

As this line of thinking goes, the body, being mortal, does not endure. It eventually loses its capacities for health and functioning, and it

25. Again, my regret in using the RSV is its lack of gender-inclusive language, which I have chosen not to alter.

26. Jürgen Moltmann, *In the End — The Beginning: The Life of Hope* (Minneapolis: Fortress Press, 2004), p. 105 (my emphasis). I am aware of various debates about precise meanings, in Scripture and elsewhere, of the concepts of soul and spirit, particularly as these relate to the concepts of body and mind. Suffice it to say here that I share Moltmann's rejection of Platonic dualism, which splits soul and body, and thus that I use "soul" to speak of the relationship of the human being, *in toto,* to the living God.

ultimately dies. Some have concluded further that the body is tied in-trinsically to evil. Hence, the body always remains imperfect. For all of these reasons the body is thought to have little value and importance, and the soul, on the other hand, is different from, and superior to, the body. As immortal and the presumed locus and means for one's eternal relationship with God, it has potential for perfection, if not in this life then surely in the next. In various forms and expressions, the domi-nant belief has been that the immortal soul must ultimately be deliv-ered from the mortal body, so that the soul may live forever with God in heaven. Thus, whereas the soul has been highly valued and has re-ceived the most attention, both in theological reflection and in the Christian life, the body has been devalued if not discounted altogether. In popular Christian parlance, "If your soul is right with God, nothing else matters all that much!"

But as Moltmann observes, the creation story tells us something else about souls. It says that "God breathed his breath into the lump of the earth," so that the first human being, "Adam," "became a living soul" (Gen. 2:7, KJV). That means "he does not *have* a living soul. He *is* a living soul."[27] Similarly, as Luther understood, a person who dies "can lament: 'I am encompassed by death, I am flesh,'" which means "He does not possess his flesh. He *is* flesh."[28]

The writer Wendell Berry holds a similar view. He says that this kind of dualistic thinking that grounds the modern mind is "the most destructive disease that afflicts us" and that the body-and-soul dual-ism is the most "dangerous" and "fundamental" version of it. He writes, "God did not make a body and put a soul into it, like a letter into an envelope. He formed man of dust; then, by breathing His breath into it, He made the dust live. The dust, formed as man and made to live, did not *embody* a soul; it *became* a soul. 'Soul' here refers to the whole creature. Humanity is thus present to us, in Adam, not as a creature of two discrete parts temporarily glued together but as a single mystery."[29] Unfortunately, such dualistic thinking is very common. The main character in one of Berry's novels, a young man by the name

27. Jürgen Moltmann, *God in Creation* (San Francisco: Harper & Row, 1985), p. 256.

28. Moltmann, *God in Creation*, p. 256.

29. Wendell Berry, "Christianity and the Survival of Creation," in *Sex, Economy, Freedom, and Community* (New York: Pantheon Books, 1992), p. 106.

of Jayber Crow, comments on how the religious leaders he knew drew such sharp distinctions between body and soul:

> I took to studying the ones of my teachers who were also preachers, and also the preachers who came to speak in chapel and at various exercises. In most of them I saw the old division of body and soul I had known at The Good Shepherd [a religious school]. . . . Everything bad was laid on the body, and everything good was credited to the soul. It scared me a little when I realized that I saw it the other way around. If the soul and body were really divided, then it seemed to me that all the worst sins — hatred and anger and self-righteousness and even greed and lust — came from the soul. But those preachers I'm talking about all thought that the soul could do no wrong, but always had its face washed and its pants on and was in agony over having to associate with the flesh of the world. And yet these same people believed in the resurrection of the body.[30]

Jayber then queries, "And what about our bodies that always seemed to come off so badly in every contest with our soul? Did Jesus put on our flesh so that we might despise it?"[31]

Sympathetic with these observations, I view the soul as the whole person, in his or her entirety, in *relationship* to the living God. Such a view posits several things about human life and experience, including means for personal formation and transformation and also how God and faith communities take part in this formation and transformation. I discuss these matters at length later in the book. Here I want to stress two things. First, personhood should be thought of as the body, mind, and soul existing in "reciprocal relation" and "mutual interpenetration," together constituting who a person is and will become.[32] Second, and related, the term *soul* thus denotes *not* part of a person that relates to God but rather the whole person, *in toto*, in relationship to the living God in both life and death. A person *is* a soul. A soul *is* a person. As such, the soul is the central focus of pastoral care.

Let me foreshadow my discussion in Chapter 3 by saying here that I

---

30. Wendell Berry, *Jayber Crow* (New York: Counterpoint, 2000), p. 49.
31. Berry, *Jayber Crow*, p. 50.
32. Moltmann, *God in Creation*, p. 257.

hold anxiety, the soul's disquiet, to be a condition influenced chiefly by the following concerns.[33] The first involves one's beliefs and assumptions about who God is, meaning God's attributes, powers, and manner of being — God's nature or character. I call this the *theo-centric* concern. The second concern stems from an impression that one's life lacks appropriate relationship to God, fidelity to God, or clarity about God's claim on one — in other words, one's standing before God. I call this the *theo-relational* concern. The third, connected concern involves a sense that one's life requires (but lacks) a core foundation, basis, or grounding, and thus meaning or purpose. I call this the *vocational* concern. The fourth concern stems from what modern psychology has often identified as the root of anxiety — namely, one's fear of death; and that has important theological implications. I call this the *mortal* concern.

Given that anxiety relates to one's struggle with any or all of these concerns, the disquieted soul is at base a *spiritual* condition. I make this claim in light of the ancient Jewish understanding that the soul *(nephesh)* is enlivened by the spirit *(ruach),* so that soul and spirit, though technically distinct, nevertheless remain inseparable. I therefore take those who use the term *spirit* to have similar interests to mine despite the fact that I prefer to use the term *soul*. Most importantly, the soul's care and relief require *spiritual* attention.

Soul Care: A Pastor's Distinctive Offering

Anxiety, particularly in its more chronic and severe forms, may very well call for medical or psychological attention, or both, along with pastoral care. Treatments proffered by psychology and psychiatry may assist pastoral work and even prove indispensable for quieting the soul. Those who mistakenly posit an impassible chasm between the sacred and the secular regarding pastoral care and human need do so at great expense to those they serve. Persons are simultaneously religious, spiritual, biological, psychological, emotional, relational, behavioral, and

33. Here I draw somewhat on the rubrics put forth by Paul Tillich in his classic book *The Courage to Be* (New Haven: Yale University Press, 1952/1980). However, the content of my view on anxiety and also my approach to relieving it differ from his.

cultural beings. Anxiety may be related to any and all of these life qualities. So, like other experiences or conditions (e.g., depression, addictions, and marital problems), anxiety may be tied to and informed by multiple aspects of life. Consequently, psychotherapy, behavior modification, and medication provided by psychologists, clinical social workers, and psychiatrists may offer valuable means for soothing the disquieted soul. Indeed, these may be instruments of grace. Pastors should devote themselves to building relationships with various helping professionals so that pastors may, in appropriate ways, tap their offerings and support their work with parishioners.

Even so, a pastor's care for anxious persons differs from the care that others may offer in at least two significant ways. First, pastors can recognize persons struggling with a particular type of anxiety — namely, the disquieted soul whose disquiet is rooted in spiritual struggles. Second, pastors can attend to anxious persons by offering ways for quieting their souls that are central, even distinctive, to the Christian life. Such ways come from the Christian faith and its practices. These practices are informed by particular beliefs and understandings concerning human beings and their relationship to God (a point I will discuss later in the book). They include membership in the church, regular participation in its worship, Scripture reading, regular prayer, serving others in mission and outreach, and engaging in public and private confession.

I am purposefully making a claim here for pastoral care's distinctiveness alongside other kinds of care. What pastors distinctly have to offer those who come to them for care is a pastoral perspective or point of view. Pastors may think about life, experience, the human condition, behavior, relationships, and personal and corporate problems principally from a perspective or point of view that other helping persons do not have or may not employ as explicitly and routinely.

The pastor's distinct perspective is bound to a particular story, the Christian story, which is the story of God's creative, transformative, and redemptive acts throughout history, which Christians have most frequently recognized in the history of Israel; the life, death, and resurrection of Jesus; and the ongoing work of the Holy Spirit.[34] Knowledge and experience in helping in the care and cure of souls within the context of

---

34. I wish to thank Jon L. Berquist and Thomas G. Guarino for helping me craft this description.

that story comprise the pastor's expertise and distinguishing contribution among those of other helping persons, whom we typically call professionals. The pastor is also a professional, but more importantly, the pastor is a *professor* — that is, one who professes. She professes the Christian faith. She professes belief in and embrace of a particular story, the Christian story. In so doing, she lives her life in accord with what it proclaims and the responsibilities to which it calls its adherents. She must, therefore, see herself — and be seen by others — as caring for souls within the context or framework of this story. She should claim this kind of care as her purview and do so without apology and exception. Why? Because she recognizes that her faith and its practices, which she embodies, represents, and shares with others, ground her calling and training *as pastor* and serve as a means for quieting the anxious soul.

The perspective or frame of reference we employ in looking at or thinking about anything, and particularly our experiences, inevitably informs what we see, how we understand, and what we decide to do. A well-known example is the proverbial glass viewed as either "half empty" or "half full." Whether we "see" the former or the latter when peering upon that particular glass will shape our primary frame of reference, which we typically call a pessimistic or an optimistic view of life. That primary frame of reference (that perspective or worldview) goes a long way in influencing how we live, what we expect in life, and what we invest in and value. To say it another way, where we begin with respect to thinking about our lives, understanding them, and deciding how we will live them has a lot to do with where and how we travel in our life's journey. Pastors, therefore, must consider, understand, and seek to relieve anxiety from within their primary perspective or frame of reference — namely, their faith and its practices. These constitute the pastor's expertise and unique offering in her vocation as pastor.

In my experience, pastors frequently lose sight of their unique vocation and training. They tend to doubt and subsequently yield their expertise and distinctive contributions to those provided by "the professionals," particularly when providing pastoral care. Because they do so less frequently with respect to preaching, Christian education, and administrative matters, pastoral care seems to pose special challenges that bump up against the pastor's store of confidence and comfort with respect to his perspective. Typically, this becomes apparent when the pastor too quickly defers to the expertise of others (e.g., the psychologist, social worker, psychiatrist, or psychotherapist) through a referral. Worse is when the pastor tries to imitate others' expertise without the requisite training, experience, and wisdom born of practice. This attempt correlates with the increasingly widespread familiarity in our therapeutic culture with popular psychology and various self-help movements, many of which claim grounding in one or more spiritualities. In varying ways, influential persons like Oprah Winfrey, Dr. Phil McGraw, and television preachers Joel Osteen and Joyce Meyer, among others, champion spiritual and related self-help causes, and this seems to perpetuate their esteemed place in both popular *and* church cultures.

In any event, the pastor may know enough professional and popular jargon to begin a conversation about what we could call "psycho-spiritual" matters and feel reasonably comfortable doing so, only to discover that such a conversation turns out to be rather shallow and short-lived. Why? The pastor discovers that he is working outside of his training, expertise, and perhaps vocation.

Far from being a new phenomenon, the tendency for pastors to genuflect at the altar of the mental-health professional has been evident for more than a half-century. The clinical psychologist Paul W. Pruyser recognized this tendency in the mid-1970s. Pruyser was a Presbyterian layman and elder. He worked closely with clergy and laypersons for many years, supervising them in graduate and postgraduate education at the Menninger Foundation in Topeka, Kansas. Recalling his experiences of regularly reflecting on case studies with ministers, Pruyser observed that they typically had difficulty drawing on their unique perspective and training: "To put my observations in a nutshell, these pastors all too often used 'our' psychological language, and frequently the worst selection from it — stultified words like *depression, paranoid, hysterical.* When urged to conceptualize their observations in their own language, using their own theological concepts and symbols, and to conduct their interviews in full awareness of their pastoral office and church setting, they felt greatly at sea."[35]

Although the reasons for pastors' difficulty in drawing on their unique perspectives and training vary, and a full discussion of the matter lies beyond the scope of this book, pastors would certainly do well to

35. Paul Pruyser, *The Minister as Diagnostician: Personal Problems in Pastoral Perspective* (Philadelphia: Westminster Press, 1976), p. 27.

take full advantage of pastoral care's distinctiveness as compared with what related professions provide, and to maintain a heightened awareness of the challenges and struggles involved in doing so. As William R. Clebsch and Charles R. Jaekle noted in their classic book on the history of the cure of souls, a lot is at stake here: "Pastors who in this age have imitated doctors, lawyers, psychiatrists, psychologists, counselors, and social workers, like pastors who imitated the current helping professions of other ages, frequently become merely incompetent amateurs or inexpert apprentices in arts properly belonging to others."[36]

Addressing this problem, Pruyser calls for an end to imitating the professionals, urging ministers to reclaim their unique offering to those in need — namely, a pastoral perspective on personal problems. Just as physicians counsel medically, pastors counsel about religion, theology, and the Christian life.[37] In fact, drawing on ancient understandings of the pastor's vocation, we could say that pastors are physicians for the soul. As Pruyser observes, individuals turn to a pastor because in some way and to some extent they want (or feel the need) to ponder, understand, and solve a problem within the very framework to which the pastor professes. "I am convinced," Pruyser says, "that a great many persons who turn to their pastor for help in solving personal problems seek assistance in some kind of religious or moral self-evaluation. They want to see some criteria of their faith applied to themselves."[38]

We should assume, therefore, that a person seeking out a pastor believes, on some level, that the pastor will not only have something helpful to offer but that her help will stem from her vocation as minister of the gospel. As Pruyser puts it, "Problem-laden persons who seek help from a pastor do so for very deep reasons — from the desire to look at themselves from a theological perspective."[39] This does not mean, of course, that Pruyser recommends an exclusively theological perspective. As Robert Dykstra points out, although Pruyser wants to "release pastoral theology from any exclusive attachment to psychology and the intrapsychic realm," thus advocating that pastors reclaim their distinct offering on personal problems, he is not "suggesting that ministers re-

36. William A. Clebsch and Charles R. Jaekle, *Pastoral Care in Historical Perspective* (New York: Harper Torchbooks, 1967), p. 68.
37. Pruyser, *The Minister as Diagnostician*, p. 57.
38. Pruyser, *The Minister as Diagnostician*, pp. 49-50.
39. Pruyser, *The Minister as Diagnostician*, p. 43.

turn to some pre-critical, pre-clinical, moralistic frame of reference of past eras."[40] Nevertheless, while care-seekers may know little else about the pastor, it is safe to say that they assume that the care received will be informed by understandings and commitments arising from the pastor's embrace of Christian faith and vocation as one of its professors. As Pruyser puts it, "In seeking a pastoral answer, even if recognizing that [it] may be only a first or tentative answer, are they not placing themselves voluntarily into a value system, and into an ambience of special tradition and communion which they consider relevant?"[41]

I suggest that pastors and those they serve benefit when pastors learn how to recognize the disquieted soul as a spiritual condition and remain open to treating it as such. In this way, pastors offer those in their care something distinctive. I am reminded here of the psychoanalyst Erik H. Erikson's claim that what he offered was "a way of looking at things."[42] In much the same way, I believe that looking at things through the lens of the Christian story must guide pastoral care with disquieted souls. By virtue of their calling, training, and office — all of which assume a larger community's endorsement — pastors bring something particular and distinctive to caregiving. They offer something that other kinds of caring, concerned, and helping persons do not. Pastors have a particular way of looking at things, and this way of looking at things informs, in very fundamental ways, their practice of care.

Obviously, pastors do not have a monopoly on caring. Nor, for that matter, do Christians. Many persons in our society care for people in need, and we should never minimize or take for granted what those who are not Christian pastors have to offer. But pastoral caring entails a particular kind of care, a distinctive offering located in and arising from a particular perspective or central idea that provides its primary frame of reference. That frame, as I have suggested, is first and foremost the story of God's creative, transformative, and repemptive acts throughout history, which Christians have most frequently recognized in the history of Israel; the life, death, and resurrection of Jesus; and the ongoing work of the Holy Spirit. As Dietrich Bonheoffer put it in

40. *Images of Pastoral Care: Classic Readings,* ed. Robert C. Dykstra (St. Louis: Chalice Press, 2005), p. 153.

41. Pruyser, *The Minister as Diagnostician,* p. 45.

42. Erik H. Erikson, *Childhood and Society* (New York: W. W. Norton, 1950, 1993), p. 403.

his classic book *Life Together,* "It is not that God is the spectator and sharer of our present life, howsoever important that is; but rather that we are the reverent listeners and participants in God's action in the sacred story, the history of the Christ on earth. And only insofar as we are *there,* is God with us today also."[43]

Other helpers and what they offer may continue to serve as valuable, and at times indispensable, adjuncts to pastoral care. Pastors do well to make use of those in appropriate ways. Nevertheless, as Pruyser points out, the best "pooling of resources" among various helpers and their respective ways of looking at things takes place when we remain aware that "the specificity of each discipline is a great asset."[44] This book advocates for the specificity of pastoral care, and particularly care for disquieted souls for whom other helpers, their perspectives, and their resources remain insufficient. The Christian faith and its practices have the power to foster more peaceful, quieted lives that nothing else can provide, and the pastor professes their power and acts accordingly.

There is nothing all that novel in this proposal that pastors must concern and involve themselves with soul work. In fact, the early church understood what we now call pastoral care and counsel foremost as the care (or cure) of the soul: *cura animarum.* Such care explicitly involved healing, sustaining, guiding, and reconciling individuals and groups of believers in relation to one another and, principally, to God.[45] Throughout the vast majority of the church's subsequent history, pastors have taken seriously the charge to care for souls and have done so faithfully. They have sought to foster among those in their care a deeper, richer relationship of the whole person to the living God.

I want to support pastors as they continue to live into their important charge to care for souls. I have a particular interest in demonstrating how pastors may draw on the mine of spiritual treasures provided by the Christian faith and its practices en route to understanding *disquieted* souls and offering them pastoral care. Therefore, I write first and foremost for typical parish pastors, who likely do not have advanced training in psychological or therapeutic interventions, but who

43. Dietrich Bonhoeffer, *Life Together: The Classic Exploration of Faith in Community,* trans. John W. Doberstein (New York: Harper & Row, 1954), pp. 53-54.
44. Pruyser, *The Minister as Diagnostician,* p. 59.
45. Clebsch and Jaekle, *Pastoral Care in Historical Perspective,* pp. 32-66.

certainly know a great deal about Christian beliefs and faith practices. They have dedicated their lives to the task of relating what they know to the needs and aspirations of the persons in their care. And, as already noted, those persons tend to expect that their pastors will draw explicitly on what they know so well in their ministry of care.

Why This Book?

Jesus said, "Be not anxious." Taking seriously his entreaty, I write this book because I believe that pastors, as caregivers, have something to offer disquieted souls that no one else does. I also believe, however, that although pastors frequently encounter anxious individuals and groups in their ministries, they typically know less than they should know about anxiety, its prevalence, and how to care for anxious persons. My years serving as a pastor and my experience in seminary teaching confirm that most pastors and seminarians lack education on this subject. This stems in part from too little attention being given to anxiety over several recent decades in pastoral-care literature. While of central concern from the 1950s to the 1970s, much less has been written on the subject since.[46] Consequently, less attention has been given to it in seminary courses. When the subject *has* been broached, comparatively little focus has been given to anxiety as a spiritual condition and to guiding pastors in ministry with anxious people. Finally, no resource of which I am aware argues for specific faith practices as remedies for anxiety.

At least two things follow from this failure to focus on anxiety as a spiritual condition. First, the pastor loses his distinct perspective and approach to healing — namely, paying explicit attention to what the Christian faith may have to say about one's anxiety and what it offers the disquieted soul. Second, the pastor may recognize the value of drawing on contributions from psychology and psychiatry and of integrating them in her pastoral practice, but many pastors find this difficult because they are not trained in the art of integration. The end re-

46. A recent exception to the trend in pastoral-care literature involves two books by Donald Capps: *Social Phobia: Alleviating Anxiety in an Age of Self-Promotion* (St. Louis: Chalice Press, 1999) and *A Time to Laugh: The Religion of Humor* (New York: Continuum, 2005). While these are excellent resources for ministry with anxious persons, Capps's foci and resources differ from those I advocate in this book.

sult, in both instances, is that pastors are ill-equipped to provide disquieted souls with what they most want and need.

It should be clear by now that I am advocating for something other than pastors becoming therapists or engaging in long-term counseling with anxious persons. Other vocational professionals, including pastoral counselors, social workers, psychologists, and psychiatrists, are best equipped, in terms of training and time resources, to provide longer-term counsel and therapy. They are the *specialists*. They tend to be proficient with a comparatively narrow set of needs, concerns, and available resources that they make use of in their practice. They also engage in a different sort of relationship with those they serve than pastors do, a more formal relationship in which interaction takes place only within the context of the counseling session or "therapeutic hour."

Pastors, on the other hand, are *generalists*. They tend to be proficient with a broader, more encompassing set of needs, concerns, and resources than specialists. Generalists focus on the larger whole while specialists focus on one or a few parts of the whole. Often this will mean that generalists attend to a greater variety of needs, concerns, and interests than specialists, who tend to work on a given need or problem over a longer period of time and in a more focused manner than generalists. Furthermore, pastors live much more closely, even intimately, than specialists do with those to whom they offer care, such that pastors and parishioners tend to know a great deal more about one another than is the case with mental-health professionals and patients or clients.

Let me illustrate further the relationship of generalists to specialists. A medical doctor who practices "general" medicine, what we traditionally have called the general practitioner or GP, and who is now referred to as the primary-care physician or PCP, attends to various bodily systems and their needs. One may see one's GP to have blood work analyzed, basic cardiovascular assessments performed, reflexes checked, eyes, ears, nose, and throat examined, and to have numerous other needs met. These days the general practitioner or primary-care physician may even be involved in dispensing medication for psychiatric conditions like depression and anxiety, as long as those are relatively mild in intensity and duration. For many persons, the GP serves as the primary medical doctor and remains the first source of assessment and treatment of illness. We call on the specialist, like the cardiologist, oncologist, orthopedist, ophthalmologist, or otolaryngologist, only if and when necessary.

We find a similar relationship between generalists and specialists when considering other vocations or professions. In some cases we even use titles to identify those whose purview is the broader, farther-reaching, more encompassing and thus "general" one. Such titles include "general manager," "attorney general," "postmaster general," "surgeon general," and even "generals" in the armed forces, though the last thing Christianity needs is another military metaphor! At any rate, each of these focuses on the larger whole, the gestalt, of their respective interests and professions.

Pastors see and work with the whole of Christian faith and life. Pastoral care may provide for keeping a person's "larger whole" — the soul — foremost in mind. My proposal, a modest one, is thus twofold. First, I seek to educate pastors on the subject and experience of anxiety, including both theological and human scientific perspectives on the condition. Second, viewing the disquieted soul as principally a spiritual condition that calls for spiritual "solutions," I attend to what pastors may feasibly provide disquieted souls in their care. All of this entails drawing on the faith community's rich offerings, particularly faith practices, for living less anxiously in what seems to be an increasingly anxious age.

The Outline of the Book

The book proceeds as follows. In Chapter 2 I draw from narrative portraits depicting disquieted souls so that we may peer into the lives of anxious persons in order to recognize what characterizes anxiety and to empathize more deeply with those who struggle with it. Anxiety takes on numerous manifestations. Some are more obvious than others, but all impact not only anxious persons but also those with whom they live, work, and serve in ministry. Chapter 2 provides pastors with various illustrations of what anxiety looks and feels like, both to anxious persons themselves and to those in their presence. I seek to help pastors identify disquieted souls with more accuracy, confidence, and sensitivity. Such identification is a necessary first step for responding to them pastorally.

In Chapters 3 and 4 I consider the question of why we are anxious. In each chapter I introduce several perspectives on the condition. Specifically, in Chapter 3 I focus on theological perspectives and in Chapter 4 on psychological ones. Though not exhaustive, these discussions map the terrain of views on the experience of anxiety and, in turn, prepare the way for my suggestions and proposals for what pastoral care may offer anxious persons. I suggest that theological perspectives on the disquieted soul must inform pastoral reflection, understanding, and practice that remain located explicitly in the Christian story, even when the pastor also draws on psychological or psychiatric perspectives and their resources. Theological figures I discuss include Martin Luther, John Calvin, Francis de Sales, Søren Kierkegaard, Dietrich Bonhoeffer, Karl Barth, Reinhold Niebuhr, Paul Tillich, Hans Urs von Balthasar, and Jürgen Moltmann. Some of these thinkers appeal to existential experience as their starting point for understanding anxiety. Others begin their reflections from doctrinal commitments. Nevertheless, each recognizes anxiety as the soul's condition, and, furthermore, each provides a basis for pastoral responses to it tied to the Christian faith and its practices.

Because other views on anxiety may be valuable, for broader-based understandings of the condition and for providing additional ways to improve it, I also present perspectives on anxiety and its relief put forth by psychology and psychiatry. Those perspectives include Sigmund Freud's psychoanalytic theory, Harry Stack Sullivan's interpersonal theory, and Aaron T. Beck's cognitive approach, which has been applied therapeutically to anxiety disorders in recent years by Gary Emery. These thinkers' views do not exhaust the ways in which psychologists and psychiatrists have thought about and treated anxiety. Nevertheless, these three views provide a sound basis for understanding and assessing anxiety and its treatment grounded in psychological perspectives, including how these may converge with and diverge from more explicitly theological or pastoral ones.

In Chapter 5 the figures and perspectives I've discussed previously serve as a basis, and in some cases as conversation partners, for constructing my own view of anxiety and how pastors and care-seekers may understand and seek to relieve it. Briefly stated, like Beck, I base anxiety largely in a kind of thinking disorder. It arises from distortions in one's sense of reality based on erroneous thoughts, ideas, and concepts. Nevertheless, going beyond Beck's view and having in mind particularly the

person of faith who struggles with a disquieted soul, of central importance are one's assumptions about God, perceptions of oneself standing
before God, and the difference those make in how one's personal life
story takes shape and is lived. More specifically, one's anxiety may follow
from the belief that one's life lacks relationship and fidelity to God or to
God's claim on oneself; that one's life is deficient in grounding, meaning, or purpose; or that one's mortality is something to fear. Perhaps
one's anxiety stems from thinking about some combination of these beliefs. As philosopher Martha C. Nussbaum has claimed with respect to
all emotions, one's struggle with anxiety may also involve judgments
about one's well-being and status in relationship to things one values
but does not fully control, and thus include acknowledgment of one's incompleteness and neediness.[47] In any case, anxiety's improvement — enhancing the soul's quiet — requires at minimum reconstructing or relearning one's way of thinking, particularly thinking about God.

In Chapter 6 I detail the narrative qualities of human life and experience, including how the stories that we learn, tell, and live out serve
to form us, shape us, and make us who we are. That sets the stage for a
subsequent discussion, in Chapter 7, of how engaging various faith
practices fosters relearning, particularly those that allow one to formu-
late and internalize less troubling ways of understanding, being in relationship with, and thus thinking about God, others, and life as it is
lived. This includes, of course, the way one thinks about one's own
death. In making my case for the power of faith practices, I draw mostly
on narrative approaches to theology and cognitive therapy.

Narrative theology suggests that we "story" our lives in relationship to God and others through shared practices in community, all
within the narrative of the Christian story. I have described it as the
story of God's creative, transformative, and redemptive acts throughout history, which Christians have most frequently recognized in the
history of Israel; the life, death, and resurrection of Jesus; and the ongoing work of the Holy Spirit.

Cognitive approaches to therapy, and particularly what is called
cognitive-behavioral therapy, hold that one's behaviors (which include
practices) shape and alter one's thoughts, and that both of these, ac-

---

47. Martha C. Nussbaum, *Upheavals of Thought: The Intelligence of Emotions* (New York:
Cambridge University Press, 2004).

cordingly, affect one's emotions. In other words, certain practices (be-haviors), particularly those that are embraced by Christian faith com-munities and are embedded in their members' lives, have the potential, when routinely engaged, for helping to alter one's thinking. This, in turn, has the potential for changing the way one feels about and experi-ences life, including a condition like the disquieted soul.

My approach to pastoral care with disquieted souls presupposes this very relationship between practices, thinking, and emotions. By promoting in its practices assumptions about God, the world, human existence, and relationships that *differ* from those prompting anxiety, the pastor and faith community may help a disquieted soul find rest. Biblical and theological perspectives on God and human beings in rela-tionship to God — perspectives whose discovery and reinforcement fol-low from engaging the community's faith practices — may (indeed should) shape the believer's own worldview. In so doing, such perspec-tives shape the way one ponders, conceptualizes, and comprehends one's life and experiences, especially in relation to God and other per-sons. The anxious person's location in the faith community and partic-ipation in its practices help him learn to think and live differently, in ways more consistent with the peace God offers. This alters the sources of his disquieted soul and thereby reshapes his personal story. The faith practices that I detail in Chapter 7, which disquieted souls do well to engage and which pastors do well to encourage, include membership in the church, habitual worship, Scripture reading, prayer, service, and confession.

Note here that Christian practices are ends in themselves, not re-sources for achieving something greater or more important. As Deborah van Deusen Hunsinger notes with respect to how prayer and Scripture may be utilized in pastoral care, these "are the means by which we come into communion with God. They need to be valued for their own sake, not simply for what they can do for us. Communion with God — enjoying, knowing, and loving God, witnessing to God, and participating in God's work in the world — is the central purpose of human life."[48] Hence, no Christian practice should ever be seen fun-damentally, or merely, as a means to some other, perhaps more valued

---

48. Deborah van Deusen Hunsinger, *Pray without Ceasing: Revitalizing Pastoral Care* (Grand Rapids: William B. Eerdmans, 2006), p. 33.

end — even if that end is caring for the soul. We seek membership in the church, participate in its worship, read Scripture, pray, serve others in mission and outreach, and practice confession because these practices are faithful responses to God's grace in Jesus Christ. That is their principal purpose or end. Even so, precisely because the disquieted soul is fundamentally a spiritual condition, and given that the Christian practices I cite help alter and enrich our souls precisely *as* they glorify God and draw us closer to God, which includes shaping our understanding of God and thus our sense of our standing before God and others, Christian practices provide appropriate *means* for enhancing the Christian life and its fruits. When I speak of the value of faith practices, I have in mind that they provide means for enriching our communion with God. In this sense, they serve as "means of grace."

I also hold that when rethinking both what anxiety entails and how better to live with it, we may in fact come to view this condition differently. Specifically, we may come to see it less as an affliction to survive and more as a kind of gift from God that serves to enhance our life of faith. Consequently, we will consider how pastors may minister with those whose souls remain, in effect, disquieted, never finding the measure of peace and quiet they desire even as they seek continuously to do so. Such ministry may very well center on helping the anxious accept this condition and even recognize its potential gifts.

Therefore, I am not suggesting that anxiety can be relieved in every person, or that it can be alleviated entirely in any one person. Rather, I claim first that the Christian faith has something powerful and distinctive to offer the disquieted soul which may alleviate anxiety in many persons *and* which is found nowhere else. Second, I propose that we may help anxious persons consider that a measure of anxiety as described herein is actually appropriate for their faith as lived. When understood and appropriated in more positive ways, anxiety may become empowering for a life of faith. After all, it encourages participation in the faith community's formative and transformative practices, which, consequently, holds potential — and thus reason to hope — for eventually soothing the disquieted soul.

Chapter 2

FIVE DISQUIETED SOULS

The Many Faces of Anxiety

"Early in life I was visited by the bluebird of anxiety." So filmmaker Woody Allen has commented on his personal lifelong struggle with this condition. Many of Allen's films have one or more characters present as anxious people, as disquieted souls. We might describe them by saying that they have "hangups" or exhibit "quirkiness," or we might call them "neurotic" in the popular understanding of that term. They demonstrate in a variety of ways obsessive thoughts, compulsive behaviors, relational difficulties, and a sort of generalized restlessness, all of which mark anxiety and tend to complicate their own lives and those of others.

Though apparent to even the casual observer and wearing for most, the anxiety experienced by Allen's characters nevertheless seems largely benign and even endearing. These characters tend to entertain their audience when negotiating life with their condition. Their struggles typically draw humorous, lighthearted responses from the anxious characters themselves and from those who live and work with them. Although quirky and eccentric, they present as reasonably well-adjusted and lovable people. One thinks of these memorable Woody Allen lines, among others: "Eternal nothingness is fine if you happen to be dressed for it"; "What if everything is an illusion and nothing exists? In that case, I definitely overpaid for my carpet"; "Nietzsche says that we will live the same life, over and over again. God — I'll have to sit through the Ice Capades again"; and "I don't respond well to mellow, you know what I mean, I — I have a tendency to . . . if I get too mellow, I — I ripen and then rot." Allen's films have

28

provided a vehicle for working out how to live with "the bluebird's" offering. But his anxious characters seem to live out their anxiety with an ease and etiquette for which most disquieted souls and their associates can only hope.

Anxiety's Forms, Expressions, and Degrees

Whether visiting early in life or later, the bluebird's anxiety can assume various forms, expressions, and degrees. Anxiety looks and feels different among persons and situations. But rarely does it show itself as positively as Allen's characters might lead one to believe. Pastors should remain aware of the tendency for anxiety to manifest itself in deeply painful and destructive ways as they become increasingly attuned to the disquieted soul's expressions. This awareness becomes especially important in a congregational context, where even a few anxious persons will have a significant impact on the larger community. Anxious persons tend to make other people anxious.

Perhaps the disquieted soul's condition appears in the overly eager-to-please board member, playing out in her vigilance to complete not only her assigned tasks but additional ones she initiates and takes on, typically without consulting others. Maybe anxiety shows itself in her close associate, the perfectionist, who tends never to be satisfied with his own, the pastor's, or others' contributions to the congregation's ministry, and who may hinder making decisions, completing projects, or otherwise stalling, if not detracting from, community life. Included in this may be his attempt to control people and process in congregational matters, along with a penchant for assigning responsibility or blame to others when failing to achieve desired results.

The disquieted soul may emerge in the man who criticizes frequently and in earnest what most consider relatively unimportant details. Though some may view him as having a share of redeeming qualities, others tend to avoid him because he is less tolerant than expected and requires "high maintenance." It may be that anxiety appears in the person who seems overly sensitive to criticism or who tends to take things too personally. Perhaps that fosters less thoughtful or reflective responses on her part — we might call them reactionary or defensive — as well as overly aggressive attitudes or behaviors.

Maybe the disquieted soul shows itself in the bright and typically articulate young woman who freezes, stammers, or seems otherwise clumsy in her speech, particularly in more public settings. The condition may come through too in the talented but underachieving young man, the identified "non-performer" who routinely disappoints himself and others as he refrains from trying to achieve something he values and could realize. Anxiety also may be revealed in one's incapacity for making decisions or taking action — that is, in constant procrastination. An anxious person may present herself as one who tends to separate from and avoid other people. This response comes from beyond what we may think of as a case of shyness. It follows from a profound fear of having to be in others' presence, which, for the anxious person, often includes a presumption of their negative evaluations.

Anxiety may materialize in still other ways too, like in the person who listens inadequately, who moves from topic to topic abruptly and unpredictably in conversation, or who seems unable to focus, concentrate, or stay on track. It may appear in the chronic worrier for whom "doom and gloom" remains ever "just around the corner." Similarly, anxiety may come to light in the person who seems fixated on the negative in life, embodying the proverbial "glass half empty" outlook that he extends readily to others.

Anxiety also may be joined with various physical symptoms. These include tightness in the chest, a rapid heartbeat or palpitations, excessive perspiring, nausea, a lump in the throat or a knot in the stomach, trembling or shakiness, wringing of one's hands, excessive foot-tapping or leg-shaking, shortness of breath, chronic headaches, back and neck pain, sleep disturbances, and eating disorders. In extreme cases, one may experience difficulty seeing or, worse, temporary blindness or paralysis. Anxiety also may loom in various addictions and compulsive behaviors. While these may provide a temporary measure of relief from the pain of anxiety, they are, of course, destructive in nature.

Anxiety may appear too in individuals and groups of people who resist change and seek fervently to maintain the status quo. It may be evident in the person who plans excessively, elaborating minute details and insisting on each one being honored. Perhaps the condition surfaces in fractures or factions among church members, staff, or both, as conflict is bred, trust undermined, and relationships lay tattered if not destroyed. Maybe anxiety exists in a persistent, if diffuse, feeling across the broader congregation that church life is unpredictable, unstable, or inadequately understood. Pastors encounter disquieted souls, perhaps more frequently than they realize. As recent studies indicate, its frequency is on the rise.

The following list provides a summary of the various ways the disquieted soul may present itself, particularly within the context of the faith community:

- Overzealousness to please people, particularly church leaders
- Earnestness to complete tasks that disregards appropriate process and/or consulting with others
- Perfectionism that may result in rigid decision-making or, alternatively, result in procrastination
- Propensity for assigning blame or responsibility to others when desired results are not forthcoming
- Fixation on a particular project, event, concern, plan, or other matter to a point of obsession
- Hypercritical responses to relatively insignificant matters
- Aggressive attitudes or behaviors, particularly when criticized
- Intolerance for receiving appropriate criticism, which is often received as a personal affront
- Nervous speech or behavior, particularly in more public settings
- Addictive and compulsive behaviors: substance abuse, gambling, eating disorders, and sexual dysfunction
- Avoidance of others or isolating oneself from others
- Poor listening, abrupt and/or unpredictable pace and tone in conversation
- Inability to focus, concentrate, or otherwise stay on task
- Chronic worry, which includes persistent "what ifs?"
- Generally negative view of life, with belief that "catastrophe" is ever looming
- High degree of resistance to most forms of change, with a corresponding fixation on maintaining the status quo
- Conflicted relationships among church members, staff, or both
- Lack of trust joined with suspiciousness of others' motives, aims, and actions
- Feelings that congregational life is unpredictable, unstable, inadequately understood

31

Other ways to describe what anxiety looks and feels like, some of which are noted in a helpful book on how to support anxious persons,[1] include the following:

- Difficulty relaxing; being constantly "on edge"
- Poor sleeping patterns, which often include ruminating about concerns
- Hypervigilance with respect to planning for and anticipating outcomes
- A nervous stomach, perhaps to the point of nausea
- Tightness in the chest
- Increased heart rate and breathing patterns, especially shortness of breath
- Experiencing of hot or cold flashes
- Clamminess, chills, feeling sweaty, dizzy, or faint
- Wringing of hands, clenching of teeth (especially during sleep), rocking, shaking of a foot or leg while sitting
- Inability to concentrate or focus; a racing mind
- Vulnerability to distraction from thoughts or tasks
- Intense feelings of vulnerability
- Pessimistic outlook on the future
- Lack of confidence
- Feelings of childishness or immaturity
- Feelings of isolation and aloneness
- Questioning of one's identity: Who am I?
- Fear that one is a disappointment to others
- Lack of clarity about where anxiety comes from or why it happens, even when it has been experienced often for extended periods of time
- Emotional and physical fatigue
- Sexual dysfunction, including a lack of desire or an inability to perform
- Erratic behavior: anger, indecision, insistence, persistence, avoidance
- Fear that one is "going crazy" or "losing one's mind"

---

1. Claudia J. Strauss, *Talking to Anxiety: Simple Ways to Support Someone in Your Life Who Suffers from Anxiety* (New York: New American Library, 2004), pp. 59-64.

Let me add here that anxiety's intensity and duration may vary widely from person to person but also within the same person. One may feel mildly to substantially anxious for long periods of time, having a kind of low-grade but chronic anxiety experience, and then enjoy marked periods without significant anxiety. Or one may feel severely anxious for comparatively brief but also fairly regular periods of time. Likewise, one may on occasion suffer from full-fledged panic attacks, which go beyond generalized or chronic anxiety in their severity and which almost always require medical intervention. During any given day, week, month, or year, an anxious person may move back and forth with respect to both intensity and duration on an anxiety continuum. As a result, two anxious persons sitting side by side in a congregational meeting may very well appear different with respect to their anxiety because they are in fact experiencing their anxiety differently. We want to avoid thinking in "one size fits all" terms about this complex, multifaceted, and often rapidly changing human experience.

Anxiety from Different Points of View

One way to consider anxiety is from the point of view of a person perceiving it in someone else. For example, a pastor detects it in a church member. The pastor may say to herself:

> "Sally seems anxious to me."
> "Pepé appears unsettled or bothered by something."
> "Rachel gives the impression that she's uptight on Sunday morning."
> "Tyrone seems so high-strung, always cutting folks off before they finish speaking."
> "Robert is so wishy-washy with his choices — afraid to make a decision and stick with it."
> "I wonder if Joan's difficulty getting along with people stems from some kind of anxiety. She attracts conflict so much of the time."

Each of these scenarios illustrates what could be called the *interpersonal* point of view on anxiety. One considers anxiety principally by way of observing how *others* appear to experience life.

Another way to consider anxiety is from an anxious person's *own* point of view. Whether he would call it anxiety or something else, and regardless of how aware he is of the condition, he would self-identify his state in some way. He may say something like the following:

"I can't relax or settle down."

"I'm always dreading something, on edge most of the time; and that gets in the way of my relationships."

"I want more than anything to find peace in my life."

"I just can't make decisions I need to make; as much as I want to, I just freeze up."

"Without warning my chest tightens, my breathing becomes labored, and I feel waves rolling in the pit of my stomach. It's a terrible sinking feeling."

"My mind just won't slow down. It takes off and races out of control."

These comments on anxiety stem from what could be termed the *intrapersonal* point of view. The anxious person considers anxiety principally by way of appealing to his *own* experience with the condition.

We can think of people experiencing anxiety in intrapersonal ways, interpersonal ways, or both. We capture each point of view when we consider anxiety *experientially.*

We also may consider anxiety *conceptually.* We do that by drawing intentionally on concepts associated with the Christian faith on the one hand, and concepts associated with psychology and various therapies on the other. Concepts inherent to the Christian faith relate to biblical and theological sources, and also to lived practices within the faith community. We might term all of these, collectively, the *tradition.* Likewise, concepts inherent to psychology and various therapies relate to the theories, empirical research, and practice wisdom that the fields of psychology and therapy embrace. In the next two chapters I will give sustained attention to both of these conceptual approaches to thinking about, understanding, and responding to anxiety. Looking ahead, I want to comment further on my use of the phrase "the Christian faith."

It would be difficult to reach agreement on what exactly constitutes "the Christian faith." This descriptive term connotes different things to different people, including those who adhere to divergent traditions or denominations *and* those claiming the same ones. Both history and the contemporary religious climate confirm that Baptists may clash with Roman Catholics, Methodists may have a bone to pick with Lutherans, and Presbyterians may quibble with Episcopalians over what the Christian faith involves and requires. At the same time, any one of these groups may struggle to reach agreement *within itself* concerning the same matters. One need not look far to see an abundance of rifts and ruptures among both individuals and groups identifying themselves as Christian. Many of those divisions stem from disagreement on what the Christian faith involves.

For our purposes, the previously mentioned understanding of Christian faith will suffice. The Christian faith entails embracing as one's guiding framework for understanding, meaning-making, and conduct in life a particular narrative or story: the story of God's creative, transformative, and redemptive acts throughout history, which Christians have most frequently recognized in the history of Israel; the life, death, and resurrection of Jesus; and the ongoing work of the Holy Spirit. I hope that such an understanding will be specific enough to resonate with large numbers of persons who claim that faith as their own, while at the same time remaining broad enough to include adherents to a variety of traditions and theologies that presumably would not see eye-to-eye on all matters having to do with that faith. In subsequent chapters I demonstrate why the Christian story has something helpful to offer disquieted souls, and also how locating or relocating one's own story within it may provide the kind of quiet for which anxious persons clamor in their souls.

Experiential and Conceptual Perspectives: Value and Limits

Pastors charged with caring for disquieted souls should consider anxiety experientially, seeking to enhance their awareness of how the condition looks and feels to anxious persons themselves but also to those who live, work, or serve with them. As with any life struggle, more familiarity with anxiety promotes a caregiver's ability to recognize it in various forms, expressions, and degrees. Familiarity also breeds greater sensitivity to what disquieted souls require in order to live more quietly. Greater awareness and sensitivity enhance one's capability for supportive pastoral care that may not only relieve the condition's effects but also address its underlying causes.

Pastoral care of disquieted souls also requires that pastors go beyond the experiential perspective. Any particular experience with anxiety, profound, painful, and instructive though it may be, offers insufficient information for the pastoral caregiver called upon to minister with numerous persons whose disquieted souls may look and feel considerably different from one another. We need a way to reflect on anxiety that goes beyond subjective experience. This requires an interpretive framework from which to consider the disquieted soul and its needs. Such a framework must provide at least two things. First, it must account for uniqueness of experience but also for commonalities across varied experiences. Second, it must draw on insights provided by multiple sources, including conceptual understandings or ways of thinking, in an attempt to understand and work with a variety of needs.

We could think about anxiety in terms of a psychiatric disorder, using psychiatry and psychology as the guiding conceptual framework. We could also think of anxiety as a spiritual condition, using the Bible and Christian tradition as our primary guides. We could also draw on both frameworks to inform pastoral care. My point is that conceptual frameworks are essential because an experientially based consideration of anxiety, by itself, does not provide the caregiver with enough in the way of either knowledge about the condition or resources for alleviating it. I tell my students that seeking to provide pastoral care without grounding it in clear, appropriate, and internalized conceptual frameworks results in "flying by the seat of the pants," the risks of which remain too high for us and for those for whom we are privileged to care. I thus want to sensitize the reader to the need to reflect on anxiety both experientially and conceptually in one's caring ministry.

Considering anxiety *experientially* remains our focus in the balance of this chapter. Having noted some of the disquieted soul's varied manifestations in congregational life, among individuals and groups, I turn next to additional ways that people may experience this condition. Before doing so, let me caution here against using this material in a simplistic or rigid fashion. Sound pastoral care requires more than a "cookbook" approach, wherein a few descriptive accounts of anxiety serve as sufficient ingredients for formulating our ultimate recipe for relieving the soul's disquiet. Anxiety grows from various roots and manifests itself in multiple forms and severities. The art of caring begins not with formulaic diagnoses but with a wide degree of openness to another person and her experience. At its heart this entails making an intentional effort not to assume too much too soon about another person's experience or need, whatever her condition and however much we presume we know about it.

To facilitate the kind of openness required, we adopt what some have called the "not-knowing" position. We simply do not know another person's experience and cannot know before he tells us about it. Our care begins, therefore, as we intentionally open ourselves up to observing, listening, and conversing with a care-seeker as fully as possible on his terms and from his *own* point of view. This requires us to bracket our assumptions, which we inevitably bring to any caring situation, as we listen as closely and intently as we can to what is shared. Some of our assumptions may be informed by previous experiences with anxiety, whether that anxiety was our own or belonged to someone we have cared for. Other assumptions we make may follow from conceptual commitments, including theological, psychological, and therapeutic frameworks. Nevertheless, we seek in pastoral care first to experience the world as the other person experiences it: on his terms, from his perspective. Only then do we understand as fully as we could what he struggles with and requires in the way of help.

We want to learn from the person with a disquieted soul what he is experiencing — how it feels, looks, and seems. We also want to learn about the things he has tried for quieting his soul. Making these our first considerations when ministering with a disquieted soul, we increase our likelihood of coming to know more about the condition from the perspective of the one who struggles with it, who remains the best conveyor of that experience, who is the expert on describing what it is like for him, and thus who serves as an invaluable — even essential — partner in offers of care.

Even so, the "not-knowing" position alone remains insufficient. The pastoral caregiver needs to incorporate something more in her ministry. As Nancy Gorsuch points out, we must balance "not-knowing" with "appropriate knowing." The latter describes "a pastoral perspective that knows and claims the wisdom of faith and its practice and appropriately proclaims the gospel."[2] Balancing "not-knowing" and "appropriate knowing" means that, in openness to our partner that informs listening to her describe her experience in *her* terms, we nevertheless wonder about how her experience may parallel or diverge from what we already know about anxiety and the disquieted soul. Some of what we know may stem from previous experiences with the condition, our own and others'. Some of our knowledge may follow from what various conceptual perspectives provide. In any case, extending Gorsuch's point, we remain particularly interested in the wisdom found in the Christian faith and its traditions, including its claims, norms, and practices. Growing from roots deep within the Christian story, this wisdom guides what we "appropriately" know about disquieted souls and caring for them pastorally.

For instance, we know that disquieted souls share similar experiences, including those listed previously and additional ones recounted below. We know too that faith communities attract disquieted souls seeking quiet. Furthermore, we know that the Christian faith and its practices have something to say about the disquieted soul, including what informs it and what may quiet it, which I will detail further in subsequent chapters. As a result, we make qualified assumptions about caring for anxious persons. Those assumptions inform our appropriate knowing. Of course, those assumptions may change or be dismissed altogether in light of what care-seekers reveal or exhibit, precisely as we yield to their stories and points of view ("not-knowing"). But I want to stress that the pastoral caregiver, by virtue of her knowledge of anxiety and experiences with it in ministry, may observe the qualities of anxiety in another person. When that happens, the caregiver appropriately wonders about what may lie behind the anxiety and employs one or more conceptual perspectives that hold promise for enriching her understanding of the person's anxiety and how to care for it pastorally.

Recalling Paul Pruyser's observation, the person who comes to a pastor for help, as opposed to seeking out another helping person or professional, does so with the hope and expectation that his problem and solutions for it will relate to the faith the pastor professes. In Gorsuch's terms, the caregiver offers "a pastoral perspective that knows

2. Nancy Gorsuch, "Collaborative Pastoral Conversation," in *Strategies for Brief Pastoral Counseling,* ed. Howard Stone (Minneapolis: Fortress Press, 2001), p. 31.

and claims the wisdom of faith and its practice and appropriately proclaims the gospel." The observations of Pruyser and Gorsuch should inform how the pastor makes use of the conceptual perspectives available to her as she artfully moves between the "not-knowing" and "appropriate knowing" positions in her ministry to disquieted souls.

Portraits of Disquieted Souls

The rest of this chapter presents narrative portraits of persons with disquieted souls. These narratives depict what that condition is like for those who live with it and those who care for them — the experiential perspective. As I will detail in the next two chapters when discussing conceptual perspectives on anxiety, the condition is often rooted in spiritual struggles or concerns. These roots may be obvious or explicit, both to the anxious person and to the pastor. One may say, for example, "I can't seem to get right with God" or "I just can't find the peace and calm that I need so desperately for God to provide." Or, in the case of the pastor observing it in the parishioner, "You seem like a restless soul." In each of these cases we quickly see the connection between anxiety and spiritual matters.

In other cases, however, the spiritual nature of the disquieted soul's struggle may be less clear. Someone may make one or more of the following statements: "I can't figure out what I'm all about and what I'm supposed to be doing"; "I'm not a very good person. I've done some really awful things that bother me"; "I can't put my finger on it. I'm just not content with life, and I worry if I ever will be"; "I always feel like there's something bad about to happen, like this dark cloud is looming over me most of the time." Or, in the case of a pastor commenting on what he's observed in his parishioner, "You seem so often to be looking over the horizon for something you think you may be missing." Remember that spiritually rooted anxiety follows less immediately from one's concern over what may happen to oneself or to those one loves, though that may be part of it, and stems more immediately from concern about who one understands oneself to be or who one wants to be. Such concern relates especially to one's view of God, one's sense of life purpose or vocation, and also one's confidence about God's claim on oneself, both in this life and beyond. Whether the pastor observes anxiety in another person or listens to an anxious person describe his own experience, she may decide to make a qualified assumption that the struggle has spiritual roots or concerns. People who seek out pastors for care often want to understand their needs from a spiritual or faith-oriented perspective and expect pastors to address them accordingly. However, pastors must also remain open to having their assumptions changed or proven wrong as the caring process unfolds.

We now consider five personal accounts of anxiety, presented in the form of verbal self-portraits. The first four portray those struggling with their own disquieted souls. The last one depicts a pastor's experience in ministry with a disquieted soul, an elder serving in his congregation. The accounts presented by "Karla," "José," "Charles," "Leticia," and "Pastor Jones" and "Darrell" (the pseudonyms I have used) together become a chorus of voices that communicate how anxiety is experienced. In doing so, these accounts promote deeper awareness not only of how anxiety looks and feels, but also of how it affects anxious persons themselves as well as others around them. Greater awareness fosters deeper insight and understanding. These are essential for compassionate and skillful pastoral care with disquieted souls. Each of these accounts, except those of Pastor Jones and Darrell, comes from a real person sharing actual experiences. I want to thank each of them for their generosity, honesty, and courage in sharing their stories, which will help those who care for disquieted souls gain a richer understanding of what anxiety entails and demands.[3]

KARLA   "The anxiety comes from having to divulge something about myself. . . ."

I never really thought I was anxious because I'm pretty easygoing and kind of a laid-back sort of person, but I have realized that I am anxious, a lot. It always has to do with interactions with other people; and it's worse if the interaction is more . . . is something that has to come from me, something that has to come from inside me. So I've identified that I'm not anxious if I have to get up in front of a group

3. These portraits have been drawn from interviews with four self-described anxious persons. The words depicting anxiety are their own. The portrait of "Pastor Jones" and "Darrell" is a composite taken from my experiences in ministry.

and do something that's not really me, to act out or say something that isn't really of a personal nature. That's no problem. The anxiety comes from having to divulge something about myself; those types of situations really become a problem. They cause anxiety way in advance of the time that it's actually going to happen. I'll think about it and play through it in my mind from the time that I learn about it until the time that it happens, and that's not good. During all that time it just kind of builds more anxiety, and then what happens at the time of the event is that no matter how much preparation I've done for what I'm going to say and what the whole thing's going to be like, I go in thinking, "Okay, this is what it's going to be like," and it never is like that. And then it always — whatever it is — seems not to work, and I fail at whatever I'm trying to do. It doesn't matter if I've told myself, "You know this. It's going to be okay. It's no big deal. They're just people." All of that kind of talking to myself doesn't help when the time to do whatever I dread actually comes.

I think I've always felt that way. I don't remember a whole lot about my childhood, but I can remember in second grade — I remember show-and-tell in second grade, for some reason being anxious about doing that. And in kindergarten — I know it goes way back, and this is something that I'm trying to figure out with my therapist, but I remember two things about kindergarten. One is playing on the playground, and the other is this encounter with my teacher. I remember it vividly, because I wanted to talk to her and I didn't have anything to say. She had this piece of paper, and she was cutting it, like this, in circles, and I knew that she was making a calendar. And I knew that it was March and she was cutting a lamb. But I wanted to talk to her, and I went up and asked her what she was cutting. And she said (in a tone that suggested I should have known what she was making), "I'm making a lamb for the calendar." And then I just felt so stupid, because I already knew what she was making. It was the first instance I remember of something like that, where I wanted to have some kind of an interaction and it didn't work out the way I thought [it would]. Anyway, I don't think I ever said anything to her [about it], but I know that was the first time I talked to her, because she called my mother. My mother told me just two years ago that my teacher had called her and said, "You know, Karla talked to me today." And my mom said, "What? She hadn't talked to you before?" Anyway, so I guess it's that old.

There are different kinds of anxiety, I think. There's the situational type like I just described, and then there's just the underlying, "all the time" type of anxiety. I'm not sure they're related, but I think they probably are, because I think the undercurrent type is there based on others' perceptions of me, and so I always

41

*have tried to . . . and this probably goes way back with my mom — you know,
"You have to be this way and do this and that kind of thing." So I'm always
aware of what other people think, including my husband. And so I've always put
everyone else's thoughts first and haven't really done anything with what I
think. So if . . . I've really kind of been a non-person, I guess. So now I'm becoming a person.*

*Since I didn't think I was anxious, I never asked God to help me not be anx-
ious, because I thought that was just the way that I was. If you're anxious but
you haven't identified it as that, then you just think that's you. So I just thought
that's the way it was supposed to be. I just thought I was quiet. My dad was quiet,
and my mom always said, "You're just like your father." I guess I didn't go off
the deep end or whatever with the anxiety because I've always had faith. I knew
that God was with me, so it didn't matter what happened. God would always be
there.*

*Fairly recently it dawned on me that being in a sanctuary — all the sanctu-
aries I've been in — feels like I'm at home. And interestingly, I've never had a
problem talking in front of people in a sanctuary. I know — I'm weird. But I
think it's because I figure if there's any place you can be who you are and mess
up, it's the church, because I assume that there's acceptance there. I know there
isn't always, but that's my perception of what should happen there. I think if you
are who you are, you have a lot better chance of acceptance than if you're trying
to be who you're not.*

*It's possible that if you're anxious about everything that's going on around
you because you want things to be right or don't want conflict or whatever, you
tend to notice everything that's going on around you so that you can avoid anxiety. So that may be a way that anxiety is good or helpful. I think it's possible. I
don't know if that's why sometimes I'm more in tune with everything going on
around me. If that sort of sense is developed, it can be a positive thing. If you look
at a room and see who's there and doing what, and also gauge what's happening, and if you don't look at that through anxious eyes but through caring eyes,
then that can be a plus.*

*I don't know why [this realization has] come at this time in my life. What
would have been really good is if I could have recognized it a long time ago.
When you think that's just the way you are, and you don't identify it as anxiety,
then you can't change it.*

JOSÉ   "I have a big fear of death and disease. . . ."

I'm always a little anxious, with a kind of generalized anxiety; and then I can instantly be thrown into something and become very anxious. For example, if I'm called on in class, sometimes my heart rate will just race. So I'm always a little anxious, and then I guess the anxiety manifests itself as fear. I have obsessive fears, like being hypersensitive to my body. If I have a headache that lasts awhile, I think I have a brain tumor. I obsessively worry, and worry, and worry about it.

I remember sitting in a lecture on bereavement and grief, and hearing about how when you're going through a period of anxiousness you can't concentrate, you can't read. I remember hearing that lecture and I thought, "My goodness, this is exactly what I'm going through right now. This is horrible, and I'm having the hardest time taking notes and concentrating." It's the anxiety.

I'll end up going to a general practitioner all the time, and there's nothing the matter with me — but it's a "what if" mentality in my brain. I know it's not logical, but emotions are tied up in it, so I just obsessively worry. You know, it just depends on where I am in my life. I went through a two- and three-year period of feeling really good. My anxiety level was still above the average person's, but I didn't have the obsessive worrying. But I still couldn't speak in class. It's so hard to give a speech. I gave one for a class recently. I took Lorazepam. I'm given that and Ativan. I carry them in my pocket so that if I need to I can take them. I can then usually push through having to speak publicly.

I suspect that people with anxiety become experts at concealing it, hiding it. I know that I sure have become very good at hiding it. People don't really know. But you can tell when my voice cracks during a speech or I'm shaking and stuff. As far as my anxiety [goes], I was at my therapist's office the other day, and I was curious because I knew I was going to come and see you and be interviewed for this book. I asked my therapist, "Where am I in my anxiety?" He said, "You're in the severe category; however, you're actually moderately severe." He then told me some stories of some individuals he treats who are a lot worse than I am. I realized, "Oh, I'm not as bad off as that!" But you know, it's tough. I'm not going to lie. It's a tough deal.

I think I have a genetic predisposition for anxiety. My mother has signs of it. My sister, every once in a while, has signs of it, and apparently my grandmother had it too. So I suspect that's where it comes from. And I think it may have manifested itself [when I was] a kid by me being shy. I remember every day as a kid being nervous about going to school, which I think is common, but I think I had more anxiety than the typical person. And then I went through college and social events. You know, I'd get kind of nervous but I didn't know what it was. I think I actually ended up self-medicating with alcohol, as so many people do. You know, a couple of beers will take the edge off, and I'm fine. So I think people with anxiety have to be careful with alcohol. I really do.

Anyway, so I think I had it through college. I studied psychology, and I think . . . I kind of thought, "Hmm. I might . . . I think I probably have this," but I didn't worry about it that much. And then . . . let's see . . . I had a variety of jobs, and one job was in advertising. I was an account executive, and we had a Monday-morning staff meeting, and I just couldn't. . . . I didn't know the industry because I was new and naturally there's a learning curve. Oh, at the Monday-morning meeting we had to talk about our accounts, and I just . . . I would freeze up in those meetings and get so scared. I thought, "This isn't too normal," but I thought, "I'll get over it." And then I remember applying for a job with the police department. I got into the academy and was driving there for an orientation. I couldn't find the place, and it was getting late, and I started to panic — and that's the first time I ever dealt with my fight-or-flight response kicking in. And it kicked in. I think for me it manifested itself differently than it did for other people. For me it was nausea. I wanted to throw up, and had to use the bathroom. It was miserable. I panicked. It was a panic attack but an induced panic attack, you know? I don't really have panic attacks out of the blue like I think some people do. Mine come from situations like throwing me in front of a group, having to give a speech or something like that. But they're panic attacks, and they're scary. They're scary as hell.

So I went to the police academy fighting. We'd have criminal role-plays at night where other officers were acting as criminals, and I was so nervous — not because of the situation, but because I was being graded. You can get kicked out if they don't like your performance. So, I just fought the anxiety. I was able to hide it. No one knew. I got out on patrol, and during every single shift I had incredible panic attacks. I was just fighting my body, and my field-training officer never knew, so I hid it well. I ended up having to take Lorazepam, and that got me through it. Even with that you can still get yourself in a panic. So I came home and went to a doctor in a city over an hour away from where I was working, because I didn't want anyone to know about my condition. There's a stigma with anxiety, especially with police officers. My doctor told me what was happening to me, and that was the first time I'd known for sure. He said, "You have generalized anxiety disorder, performance anxiety disorder, and social anxiety disorder."

Well, okay. So he gave me some medicine. I can't remember what it was. It made me sick. I took it one night and I thought, "Oh, I can't do this." So I re-signed from the job because of the disorder, and then that's when I realized, "Hey, this disorder has gotten to the point where I can't do the job I was always wanting to do, my whole life."

I have a big fear of death and disease. It's an unnatural fear. I know that logically, but the anxiety feeds off of that, or the anxiety created that, and then I can't get it out of my head. I think it's . . . maybe the worry is physiological. I can't think of any other thing. I think other people go through the same events, but they bounce back or just blow it off, and I . . . maybe there's an element of obsessive-compulsive disorder in there, but . . . I don't know. The fear of death in college — that was a big one. I had like . . . my sinuses or something felt infected, and I felt like I had a brain tumor. I worried for five years. I was scared to death. I wouldn't go to the doctor because I was too scared to know. I just thought, "Whatever — I'll get through this." I kind of knew it probably wasn't bad news, but I didn't know for sure. It affected my studying.

I let it go too long. Five years. You know, that stress will do something to your body. I finally went in to the doctor and said, "I think I have a brain tu-mor," and he said, "Um," and he tested my blood for all the cancers and what-ever, and he said, "You're okay." And I said, "Well, I need an MRI. I have to, or I'm not going to feel good." And he was real understanding and said, "Well, I'm going to do whatever it takes to get you better." I went and got the MRI and was absolutely fine. It was five years . . . it really was hell. I can talk about it now. But I didn't share this with my parents until I was done with testing, you know, and knew I didn't have a brain tumor. I can't . . . I don't know where that comes from. One can say, "Well, it's lack of faith in God." I don't know. Whatever. All I know is I was worried about it but at the root I was afraid of death or living with a terminal illness, and it affects . . . it grows and it affects you. My doctor said, "Well, medicine's not the answer."

A lot of it, I think, is that my personality is such that I care what people think about me, whereas other people don't care as much. When I give a speech, I'm so nervous because I care what people think. My mother's like that. I don't think a lot of . . . I remember in the police academy they did a lot of psychological tests, and mine showed that I cared what other people thought about me while other people cared more about being an authoritative figure. I was different than everyone else in that group in that way, and it made me think. And perhaps I care too much. I don't know what else to say on that, but yeah — absolutely, there's a component there. I think I had it as a kid, too. I cared, you know? I wanted to be liked by people in school and stuff. You know?

My belief in God has helped me through the struggles. Some years back, Scripture reading would help. I think reading, you know, some poem . . . or there was a psalm, "Be anxious" — or no, "Be still and know that I'm God." I came across another, where Paul says, "We're perfect in our weakness." Those would bring me some comfort. Through this I've never doubted God, his sovereignty. I just look at it kind of like: We all have our struggles, absolutely, and this is one that I have. I don't want to come across as "Poor me," you know.

I wish I could say that prayer and Scripture reading and turning to God has helped me, but I can't say it has, to be honest; and in times of high anxiety it's hard to pray and it's hard to read Scripture because it's hard to concentrate. Your mind's focused on something else. Your ability is another thing that suffers. I don't want to be bothered by little insignificant things when I'm trying to deal with my anxiety with something big. So I have to be careful.

Is [the answer] faith? Perhaps it helps to worship and to do things for others. I had the opportunity over Christmas to go down to a mission I'm familiar with, with a friend. There, you worship and help individuals who are drug addicts and stuff. A wonderful thing — I would love to do that. But I just was so anxious that day. My feeling was I can't give what I don't have, and so I didn't go. Perhaps that's what I should have done, and it would have helped me, but I was just too anxious. I couldn't . . . I couldn't do it.

But helping others has brought some comfort. Exercise helps a lot too. Long jogging helps, definitely. I drink green tea and decaf coffee. No Cokes! I stay away from alcohol. Not because it doesn't help — two beers will calm me down easy — but the next morning it tends to make it worse. But studying theology, religion, and about God has helped.

CHARLES   "I was so scared about not getting it right. . . ."

I can remember all the way back to . . . even before middle school, and it would evolve . . . at that point in time it would come about through a guilty conscience. I have a really strong conscience, and as a kid I felt like I had to constantly tell my parents what I had done wrong. I'd have a lot of anxiety build up until I could vent it . . . get out of my mind what I was carrying, the guilt I was carrying. Then that started to play itself out in middle school with a really strong concern for what others thought about me . . . trying to hear what people were saying, thinking they were talking about me; and I wanted to know what they were talking about. It really brought itself on in a kind of bullying experience

46

*in seventh grade, where I was at a small private school and there were only —
gosh — maybe fifteen seventh-grade boys in a class, and it just happened that it
was my year! I was going to be picked on for the year.*

*I was small for my age. I was pretty immature for my age too; and there was
just a huge amount of anxiety around that, just fear and being a . . . just a lot of
verbal stuff, not too much physical bullying, but relentless all through the school
year. I was always driven competitively, especially in sports, needing to win. I
had a really bad temper too, and I'm not sure if that would play itself out or not
due to my anxiety. I should say that anger is a natural tie to anxiety, but now,
looking back, it all had to do with my self-esteem and how I felt, how good a person I was and whether I won or lost. If I was making mistakes in a game that I
was playing, I would go off and get very angry and have a very bad temper.*

*Like if I double-faulted in tennis. I played a lot of tennis competitively.
And there was a lot to do also with competition [with] my father. I always felt
very self-defeated in that I could never win a game off of him or . . . and he
was the kind of guy that wasn't going to give me a "gimme." He played the
most competitive tennis, and ping-pong down in the cellar. You know, he'd
play me left-handed. He's right-handed, and I still couldn't beat him . . . and
that just set me off.*

*The anxiety would also come in relationships as I matured and started get-
ting interested in girls. One of the things that would happen is I would find someone that I thought I was attracted to physically, and I would see whether or not I
could get them to like me. Then, once that would happen, I'd get scared about it.
I'd say to myself, "All right, now that that's happened, what do I do now?" And
I'd have this anxiety around: "Oh no, you mean I've got to get closer in this relationship and be in this kind of deeper commitment?" And that would . . . I'd go
running . . . and I played the anxiety out through college that way too.*

*Test anxiety would come into play beginning in middle school. Anything I
had to memorize, where I had to sit still and memorize and spit [material] back
out, was the worst. So languages were difficult for me, and science and math
were very difficult for me. I'd have test anxiety around those things — so much so
that I had to drop chemistry my sophomore year. I remember having special consideration given to me, so I could get out of chemistry and be reassigned into an
easier science class for my high-school diploma.*

*I was so scared about not getting it right that I couldn't concentrate to study
and I couldn't . . . I hated just sitting and studying too. For instance, the SAT; I
just tested horribly on the SATs and the PSATs, whereas if you asked me to write
a paper or get up and speak in front of a group, it was no problem. So I was*

47

highly relational from that standpoint, and also creative in my writing and in researching for papers. But anything that had to do with being tested — that would get me into a room either to do well or not do well, [and] that would cause me a lot of anxiety.

I started self-medicating. Looking back, what I was doing was partying, and I was self-medicating in that way. By the time I got to college, I was way . . . I would just not care — I would blow it off. My grades weren't important. Once I got into a fraternity — you hear those stories a lot, but I was . . . I was doing it a lot to be in the in crowd, but I was also partying because it took the edge off. I was good at it, you know . . . I was the life-of-the-party kind of [guy]. But the anxiety would still be there when taking exams and in terms of relationships, getting closer to people.

Then it manifested itself in the workplace, once I got out of college. I was in a very competitive and prestigious management-training program in Manhattan, and I was given a lot of responsibility at a young age and can still remember certain times being introduced to clients for the first time and just really starting to have physical manifestations of the stress that was affecting me — sweats and things like that. The physical symptoms got worse as I moved into my mid- to late twenties and I was still working hard and playing hard. That was kind of my motto. I had no real pursuit of a relationship with God. I was not attending a church. I was all about climbing the corporate ladder and playing hard along the way. I started to really have more physical problems . . . and I didn't realize what was going on. I didn't realize it was anxiety. I remember coming down in an elevator at a big meeting in Chicago where we were going to have to confront some clients about errors that they had made. And coming down the elevator at the hotel, I just kept getting dizzy and [had] to stop myself and wondered what that was. Then stomach pains — real, real bad stomach stuff — came up. And I just kind of blew it off . . . cramping . . . and I just would get through it and not think twice about it. It just continued on and on, and it wasn't until I hit some major failures that the anxiety then triggered into depression when I was thirty-two.

I was a senior vice president of a well-known firm in my field. I was on a big, big account, a multimillion-dollar account, and I was young to be given that responsibility. I had equity in the firm, and there were five people at my level — it was a medium-sized firm. And they had a layoff because they lost a big account, and at my level, out of the five, I was the one chosen to be laid off. That was the first time I ever really had a failure. You know, I've lost games, obviously, and stuff like that, but this one hit hard. I'd always succeeded.

I was married at the time, and shortly after getting fired my marriage started unraveling. . . . In my job search, I landed a job quickly with another company. But my resume had floated out, and it found its way to [a much larger company]. So, six months into my new job I get a call asking if I'd interview with [this other] company for a marketing position. Well, you know, . . . working for a large company in marketing was kind of . . . I looked at it as . . . a much larger responsibility that requires more skills. I wasn't sure I was equipped. But I interviewed, and they offered me the job. It meant moving, and my marriage was really starting to come apart at that point in time, and I couldn't decide whether or not to move. I was fearful of change, and that was when self-doubt and fear of change and, you know, another failure on the horizon with my marriage, triggered another bout of both anxiety and depression.

Sleeplessness is what started to hit on the anxiety side, and the constant spiraling of thoughts, not being able to settle my mind — and just fear. And also happening were the slides into the depression of "Nothing's going right" — you know, looking at everything with dark glasses on. That was in 1989, the first time it was so bad; and in 1990 I saw a therapist and psychiatrist and got medication, and I really started to understand what it was I was dealing with. Back then, psychiatrists also did therapy, and so I was just seeing one person, and I pretty much decided on my own that I was over it. And so I took the job, and about a year into seeing this doctor I said, "Thanks for everything that you've done for me. I'm okay." Well, my behavior hadn't really changed a whole lot, and I continued to do the work-hard-and-play-hard thing. I was divorced, and I . . . basically was self-medicating again with the partying . . . but I wasn't. . . . From an anxiety standpoint, the only fear was getting back into a relationship again, and that started to manifest itself when I met my current wife and we started getting serious and talking about whether or not we were going to get married. I was really . . . what happened was having to make a choice whether or not this relationship was going to go forward and [I was going to] remarry or not. And then my parents divorced after thirty-nine years, and it was not a pretty divorce. I was taking sides, and that sent me — those two things sent me — back into anxiety and then depression again. Two or so years later, I saw a psychiatrist again and got diagnosed as manic-depressive, and the medication he gave me was Prozac. I did therapy with him for three years.

I remember going through some real testing with him — you know, filling out some things. . . . I don't remember the tests, but they were helpful for him and for diagnosing; but I don't remember all the ones that we did. What started to happen was that between therapy and swimming, and making the decision to marry, and being engaged in the life of my church, and volunteering with the prison ministry, and really beginning to get focused on my walk with the Lord and being called back into that relationship — it was all of those things coming together in that ten-year period. But still, when I would go to facilitate a class at Sunday school and was unsure of myself, the sweats would come. That's when the anxiety was still there . . . so much so that I'd have to excuse myself and towel off in the bathroom and come back. That's the only place where it would surface.

I know now that how severe my anxiety will be is a function of what stressors I have in my life, but also a function of how clear a sense of purpose I have and how much structure I have in my life. Those things help a lot. They reduce the level of anxiety that I carry with me, and the medications handle the depression.

But I think . . . I was always real sensitive as a person, always concerned about what other people thought about me. And a part of that sensitivity, I know, was coming from two things. One was that it took me a long time to mature, to actually hit puberty. Number two: I was living in a "WASP" environment with an [obviously foreign-sounding] last name . . . in an affluent world; and I was teased a lot about my name, and I never quite felt comfortable with how I fit in. I always carried that chip on my shoulder. I was real sensitive to that. So I had to prove myself, and there was always this kind of inner circle of — you know, the preppy nature of New England and the kind of blue-blood world. The expectations were that you go to a prep school and then to an Ivy League college and then to Manhattan to work in the banking business or investment business; and you would be going to the Dartmouth club, the Harvard club, the Yale club. . . .

There was all this status evaluating going on. And I just remember having friends in that world but never quite feeling that I was accepted in that world, that somehow I was different and I don't . . . so that was a contributor to how competitive I was and how I felt like I needed to prove myself. . . . But it was also just watching my father and how he approached life and how hard he worked and how competitive he was and . . . that was the way he did things.

And so there's a perfectionism that comes with the anxiety, where I have very high expectations of myself and earnestness. There's a good side of me, which is that I'm very earnest about doing the right thing, about doing the task well and being able to be counted on. I have high integrity, accountability. I'm upright in how I deal with people. I'm very conscientious — all those things. But at the same time, because of that, it's . . . I'm hard on myself, and it's very difficult for me to lighten up and say, "Hey, I'm just human."

The other by-product is you get very self-absorbed because you're analyzing yourself so much, and when you start getting into deep anxiety, having trouble functioning and getting . . . sliding into depression, your world is about this small — you really just are focusing on yourself at that time. "How do I get healthy?" "I need to get out of this." "What are other people thinking about me?" You think it's noticeable. So all of a sudden, you slide into this very self-absorbed manner of thinking, and that's why, if you can . . . one of the best things you can do is just start helping other people . . . to break the cycle and to think outside of yourself. It's one of the things I did that helped me. I decided to take a risk in terms of what I was choosing to do to help other people, and that became the prison ministry I got involved in.

I still have to catch myself on being a performer in church and being so fo-cused on doing well. I'm not good at practicing inner silence and being alone. I've come to understand that about myself. So I do create anxiety still, even within the walls of the church, in terms of worrying about what my reputation is and being concerned with that as opposed to just trusting God — and I still grap-ple with that. I mean, one of the things on the negative side of the faith is that when you start really battling anxiety again, you start doubting and have this fear of failure. You start doubting your faith; and it's like "Wait a minute — what kind of person am I? Why can't I trust in God? Why can't I just take it one day at a time and trust that God's in control, he's sovereign? How can this be go-ing on right now? This makes no sense. What am I? Is my faith real?" You really start to . . . I start to question myself significantly in that way. I have grown over the last several weeks, like I was telling you about earlier, in understanding more things about myself, and the triggers pertaining to my worldview and my view of myself that set off the pattern in my thinking and my choices . . . my behavior that sets me up for greater levels of anxiety. Also, I understand that there's got to be a chemical-imbalance part of this, and that I need to allow myself the ability to say, "You know what? God gave me this anxiety for a reason, and I'm not sure why, but let's look at it as a way to draw closer to him."

And I'm trying to do that. As painful as it is, I'm trying to give myself the permission to do that, to really sink my teeth into it and believe in it — that God made me for a reason uniquely in this way. I look for every opportunity I can — in small-group situations, at retreats, when asked — to give my testimony. I in-clude the anxiety and depression, and I do it for a reason. It's to combat the stigma on mental health that's out there and because I know there's somebody out there who needs to hear what I have to say. Each time I share my story, some-one will come up to me afterwards and seek counsel and seek advice and tell me how glad they are to hear me share, because they suffer from the same thing.

Leticia   "It's like I'm holding on by a string. . . ."

*I come from a long line of worriers. That's what I call it. My mom is like the
quintessential worrier. If somebody dies, and is close to my age, she'll call me and
tell me be to careful, just watch out, and so part of it is this underlying . . . I'm
used to people worrying. When the anxiety . . . when I really realized kind of
what it was, was when I had a miscarriage; and afterwards I don't think I slept
for about three months. I would just have these really vivid dreams where things
were totally out of control and I couldn't figure it out. I would wake up and
couldn't breathe and it just . . . it was a horrible experience. So I went to counseling and, you know, I worked through some of that. We tried different methods,
and we talked about medication to help me to deal with it, but I wanted to try
not doing that first. So we tried different behavioral stuff, and that worked for
me. I can't remember all the ones we tried because some of [them] didn't work.
But the one that works for me is actually the image of a crossing guard, like a
school security guard, with a stop sign. So I can actually stop my thoughts before
they get to where I can't stop them, and that works . . . that worked then and it
still kind of works now. And now I know what triggers it, so I can try either to
avoid it or. . . . A friend of mine has anxiety too, and she found the thing that
helped her was breathing exercises.*

*There was this one book . . . it was by a Buddhist, and it was . . . the mantra
was "Breathing in, I calm my body. Breathing out, I smile." And so when I start
feeling myself going down that path, I can use that first, before I even have to get
to the whole visualization of the stop sign.*

*When I was in counseling — it was probably the worst time with the anxi-
ety. I felt completely out of control. There was nothing I could do to stop the . . .
the . . . I don't know if they're called attacks . . . but I couldn't make myself get
out of it, whereas now I can do that a little better. I can . . . I'm more self-
aware, and I can know if I'm in a good place. Like, for example, my anxiety
has to do with losing control. So when I travel to a hotel, I have to read all the
emergency signs on how to get out in case of fire or tornado or earthquake, you
know, so I feel like I know what to do in case of an emergency. When hurricane
Katrina hit . . . it's that kind of stuff that creates anxiety for me, the losing control. When Katrina hit, I was in a good place, so I said, "Okay, you can obsess
about this for two days, and after two days you have to stop." I was able to do
that, so for two nights I didn't sleep, and I worked through it: "Okay, if I were
in a hurricane, what would I do?" and "If this were to happen, what would I
do?" and "If this happened. . . ." And once I work through what I theoretically*

could do if in that situation, I'm fine; but until I can get there, it's just like it consumes me.

When we moved to a new house, I knew, like if there was a robbery, I knew five different ways to get me and my children out of the house. It's kind of like I have to know if I can allow myself to think about it or if I have to put the stop sign up and say, "Okay, now is not a good time . . . to deal with that." I find that I don't watch the news. I can't . . . I try not to put myself in situations that will trigger "Oh, my gosh! If that were me, what would I do?" type responses.

As a child, I worried about almost everything. If I didn't do well in school; if something happened to my parents. We moved a lot growing up, so it was like, "What if I don't make any friends?" Lots of those kinds of things. I think I worried about almost everything.

But I don't remember it as much as a kid as I do since I've gotten older, into adulthood. Like when I went away to college and after, I really remember the scenarios really well. When I'm in a moment of sanity — that's what I call it — I can look back and say, "Why would I even think that?" But when you're in it, it feels like "It's going to happen, so you better prepare for it" type scenarios.

With respect to how it feels, well, it's physically very hard. It's like I can't breathe, [and] I feel just really tense, like at any moment I'm going to lose control, lose my sanity. It's like I'm holding on by a string. And then I get really tired because I'm not sleeping; it's at night when the scenarios just play over and over and over and over. So it's just kind of a really downward spiral.

During the day I can stay busy enough to where I can feel . . . it's like it's in the background but it's not terrible. I can invest myself in my three kids, but I can still feel it in the background. It's right there, and it's going to come out. I can deal with it then; but then at night, when you don't have anything to occupy yourself — that's the worst.

And stress. Like right now. I was doing really well, anxiety-wise. Actually I was talking to a friend, and I said when I offered to do this, to talk to you for the book, I was in a good place and could talk logically about it. Now it's more stressful. I think a lot of it has to do with my faith, actually, because when I had the major anxiety attack I was very mad at God because of the miscarriage and all that. And before that I believed God controlled everything. If I made a stoplight or didn't make a stoplight — that was determined by God. God controlled every single little detail of my life, so when things got out of control, it was God's fault. So I had to struggle with that for a while, to try to figure out "What does God control?" I'm still struggling with that, and it's like . . . if I knew the answer. . . . If God did this and I did this, I think life would be much easier to deal with and . . . part of it is I don't necessarily trust God anymore. And so if I [could] trust God, I think I wouldn't have anxiety, because God would be taking care of me. So I think faith is a huge part of my anxiety.

After I had the miscarriage, I basically quit praying. I mean, I was like, "That's it — I'm done." But I still went to church, and so I think that helped me reconcile over time. It wasn't like in a moment I went, "Oh — aha," but I think continuing to go to church kept me in the relationship, even though I didn't want that. And there were times when I said, "Oh, I don't have the energy to go to church" and then afterwards thought, "Oh, I'm so glad I went." So there are times that it is helpful.

People say that I ask good questions about God. I say to them, "I know, but I don't have the answers!" That's the problem. I've got the great questions, but. . . . So I think . . . I think that does play into it . . . and it does help, for me being an anxious person, to help other people. At least I know where people are coming from when things aren't going right. It's funny, because I'm great at giving other people advice. It's just really hard for me to take it, you know, to apply it to my own life. It's kind of like intellectually I say to others, "You need to do this" or "Have you thought of that?" whereas for me it's like I can't apply the same thing.

The anxious moments are more like . . . there's this shadow over me. And in non-anxious moments I don't have that lurking sense of something's about to happen. I guess the moments of non-anxiousness are when I don't feel that. I can just enjoy life and not feel like I have to be very careful about what I think or what I say or what I watch on TV or anything like that. When you are anxious, you just know something's about to happen.

You know, that's the logical side. I know I can't totally prevent it, but yet I'll spend a week trying to figure out "If the fire starts in this room, then I can do this. If the fire starts here . . ." So it's really a safety or natural-disaster type of thing. So that's why the hurricane got me going. There's no control there. You can't plan what's going to happen at all. One of my good friends — she and I are kind of helpers of each other with anxiety; hers is medical. She can't watch ER. If she watches ER, within the next week she's going to have the symptoms [she saw]. She's called 911 several times for heart attacks.

If somebody came to me with anxiety, I don't know what I would say. I mean, I think for me, getting help meant getting somebody who could give me different tools and exercises and a free place to talk about it. That was really helpful. My girlfriend that I was telling you about — she is still in counseling and she's on medication, so I think that for some people . . . you know, that's a good option. And to be aware that more people have it than may realize they have it. I mean, as I've experienced it and been able to talk to other people about it, I find I'm really surprised at the number of people that actually struggle with different issues but have the same reaction and responses. I had never heard about [anxiety] until I went to counseling. I'd never heard that there was actually a thing, a name for my experience. I thought it was only what I was going through — you know, that I worried too much. I just needed to snap out of it. I didn't know that there are actually things that I had to do to get better.

"Pastor Jones" and "Darrell"

This last portrait depicts both the interpersonal and the intrapersonal points of view, as Pastor Jones meets with Darrell, a parishioner, out of concern over difficulties that Darrell has encountered with other church members. Pastor Jones has served Grace Church for four years. Darrell, aged thirty-eight, along with his wife, Kelly, and their three children, has been an active member of the congregation for twelve years. Having held numerous leadership positions, he typically garners his peers' respect, and most view him as responsible, motivated, and a dedicated "doer." In fact, not only is he a person that both staff and others frequently ask to take on important tasks, and especially during "crunch time," but he is a person who relishes these and other opportunities to serve, especially in a lead role. For the most part, others in the congregation appreciate his motivation and earnestness, though he can come across as intense, demanding, and impatient at times. His relationships with other church members, especially those with whom he works closely on projects, have on occasion become noticeably strained, particularly as deadlines approach and he becomes increasingly concerned about getting the job done.

In planning for a recent church function, when he served as chair of the coordinating committee, Darrell experienced conflict with two other church members. Upon learning of this conflict from Jane, another person on the committee with whom Darrell has not had problems, Pastor Jones requested a meeting with him. Pastor Jones began the meeting by telling Darrell of his concerns, saying,

Darrell, you are such an asset to ministry in this place; and I know I speak for many others when I say thank you for how much you give of yourself in our

shared ministry. I hope that you'll always feel comfortable here and sense that God is calling you to use your gifts in such significant ways. But I'm concerned about you. I have the sense that it may at times get difficult for you to work with people on projects here, especially as deadlines approach. And I'm wondering if we can talk about that?

In the conversation that followed, Darrell revealed some of his pain and struggles.

I find myself taking on too much — at work, at home, and even here in the church. I take on so much because I just can't say "No." Saying "No" for me means the possibility of angering those I care about, which really bothers me. So I just say "Yes" and then try to figure out a way to do what is asked of me. The problem is that this makes me really uneasy, even anxious. I guess you could say I analyze things way too much, and I do that because I seem always to be dreading failing at something. I often lie awake at night, or wake up in the middle of the night, and think, "I'm never going to get this done; why did I agree to do it?" Or I say to myself, "If I get it done, I won't do it well." Or I say, "Even if I think I do it well, surely there will be some who disagree." That leads me to wonder if you [pointing to Pastor Jones] will second-guess asking me to do something, meaning you'll regret it. And, if you don't, some others may. So what I find myself doing is working too hard at things, trying too hard to get it right, and thinking way too much about what could go wrong and what I'm going to do if that happens, and how embarrassed I'm going to be. I think people pick up on some of this. At least I sense sometimes that people around me, like other elders, think I'm way too intense, or that I need to chill out, and I understand that. Believe me, I don't want to be that way, but I just can't seem to rein things in. Or if I do, I feel like the damage has been done, that I've blown it. And so I begin to worry about that too — and the cycle begins all over again.

You see, I really love this congregation and feel like God wants me to be here and to serve in whatever ways I can. Ever since I was a boy, I felt like God wanted me to be active in the church. I even thought about going to seminary for a while. I didn't think I'd be a good pastor, though, because I'm not very peaceful inside. But I guess what I want to say today is that I don't like ruminating, worrying, feeling like I can never do things well enough, be faithful enough, or deserve the responsibilities given to me. It's like an endless cycle of uneasiness, questioning, and dread. I'm a nervous wreck most of the time, even when I'm able to hide it! And I've gotten pretty good at that.

Conclusion

In this book's final three chapters, I suggest how engaging the Christian story through various faith practices might help persons like "Karla," "José," "Charles," "Leticia," "Pastor Jones," "Darrell," and others who live with a disquieted soul. The Christian story and its practices may serve to alter a personal story where the disquieted soul lives so centrally. But first I attend to how anxiety has been viewed conceptually by considering various theological and psychological perspectives on the condition.

Chapter 3

WHY WE ARE ANXIOUS

Ten Theological Views

In this chapter I consider various theological views on anxiety. These views extend the Bible's commentary on the condition, discussed in Chapter 1, and serve to plot how Christian thinkers have pondered and understood the disquieted soul. I take a look first at how a concern for understanding anxiety theologically carried into the Middle Ages, through the Renaissance period, and into the Protestant Reformation in Europe. Next, I consider more modern and contemporary views on the condition by focusing on nineteenth- and twentieth-century perspectives. These reflections provide not a comprehensive account of theological views on anxiety, but rather a representative sample of the more influential perspectives on the struggle with a disquieted soul and its relationship to God and Christian faith. Nevertheless, knowing these views on anxiety helps us consider how they might inform pastoral care with anxious persons.

Three Reformation Period Views

In the sixteenth and seventeenth centuries, various religious thinkers, like the authors of the scriptures before them, attended to anxiety's roots and effects. Significant figures who paid close attention to the condition, each of whom lived with his own disquieted soul and relied upon faith in God for help in assuaging it, included Martin Luther, John Calvin, and Francis de Sales. Each located anxiety in one's relationship to God and observed how anxiety prompts profound spiritual pain and struggle. Moreover, each looked to faith in God as anxiety's palliative balm if not its remedy.

"Remember that Christ is near and bears your ills. . . ."
MARTIN LUTHER

Luther paid close attention to anxiety and its consequences, having both a theological interest in the condition and a longtime personal acquaintance with it. One could argue that his personal struggles with the disquieted soul gave rise to a concern for gaining clearer theological understandings of anxiety that spanned his career as a reformer. In his reflections on Psalm 127, Luther ties anxiety to our tendency toward self-sufficiency, particularly with respect to securing what we require in life. He notes that we tend to rely foremost on ourselves to get what we need to sustain us. Calling the tendency toward self-reliance "arrogance," he thinks that our attitude about work, which we tend to view primarily as the means to acquire things and shore up resources, provides evidence for this claim. To counter such "arrogance," Luther suggests that while it is necessary and appropriate, work should not be viewed primarily as something we do for ourselves in order to get what we need, desire, or believe that we are due. Human beings ought to work. This is in keeping with God's desires. Luther goes so far as to say that without our working, God gives us nothing. However, we work first of all *not* for ourselves, but for God; and the problem arises when, in our working, we begin to rely increasingly on ourselves and our abilities for securing what we need, as opposed to relying more upon God and the blessings God provides. Luther makes it clear that whatever provisions we enjoy in life come first from God, not from our own labor. Where we ascribe "the fullness of our house" to our own efforts, rather than to God's blessings and goodness, "there covetousness and anxiety quickly arise," and we hope to acquire much through our striving.[1] For Luther, then, we do not work to acquire things or to achieve whatever glory follows our gains. Rather, we work to glorify God, aware that what we secure in life comes not from our labors per se, but from God.

1. Martin Luther, "Exposition of Psalm 127, for the Christians at Riga in Livonia, 1524," in *Luther's Works*, vol. 45, American edition, ed. and trans. Walther I. Brandt, gen. ed. Helmut T. Lehmann (Philadelphia: Fortress Press, 1962), pp. 324-25.

Luther thinks that Psalm 127's opening verse substantiates this claim: "Unless the Lord builds the house, those who build it labor in vain." We build in vain when we perform work for reasons other than to glorify God. Relying on ourselves and our own sufficiency, we grow anxious about whether we will be able to secure what we need. That leads to us thinking about our labors in the following kind of way: "If my sustenance is all up to me, then I better make sure I plan for today, tomorrow, and beyond. Otherwise, if I happen to let my guard down and take it easy, I might not be in a position to get what I need, whether for myself, my family, or other close associates." Furthermore, relying principally on ourselves prompts anxiety over whether someone else has, through *their* labors and self-sufficiency, taken something that we may eventually want, need, or believe we are due! Growing anxious, we begin to covet. For Luther, Psalm 127 serves as a much-needed corrective to this tendency. It "so beautifully turns the heart away from covetousness and concern for temporal livelihood and possessions toward faith in God, and in a few words teaches us how Christians are to act with respect to the accumulation and ownership of this world's goods."[2]

Luther also linked our striving for self-sufficiency, and the anxiety it prompts, with our concern for physical health and safety, whether that of others or our own. Luther's wife, Catherine, grew increasingly anxious as Martin undertook more and more travel and experienced increasingly precarious health. In response to her concerns, he reminded her that we tend to worry about what should be left to God and God's care. During one of his travels he wrote to her and said, "You are worrying in God's stead as if he were not almighty. . . . I beg you to leave the worrying to God. You are not commanded to worry about me or yourself. It is written, 'Cast your burden upon the Lord, and he shall sustain thee,' and similarly in other places."[3]

As is evident here and in many other personal letters, Luther, as a pastor, was deeply concerned about those who struggle with anxiety, and he sought to help them with appeals to faith. Writing to a woman

2. Luther, "Exposition of Psalm 127," *Luther's Works*, p. 317.
3. Martin Luther, *Luther: Letters of Spiritual Counsel*, ed. and trans. Theodore G. Tappert, Library of Christian Classics (Louisville: Westminster John Knox Press, 1955/2006), pp. 105-6, 108.

he knew, Mrs. Elizabeth Agricola, Luther referred to her condition as one of the "body and soul" and encouraged her with reminders of the love and presence of Christ: "You must not be so fearful and down-hearted. Remember that Christ is near and bears your ills, for he has not forsaken you, as your flesh and blood make you imagine. Only call upon him earnestly and sincerely and you will be certain that he hears you, for you know that it his way to help, strengthen, and comfort all who ask him."[4]

Luther invited the woman to travel from Eisleben to Wittenberg, where he and his family lived, for a few days of respite. She accepted. Approximately one month later, he noted what he had observed during her stay in a letter to the woman's husband, John Agricola. Luther conveyed that her "illness" was "more of the soul than of the body," and that he had sought to comfort her as much as he could. He added that "her illness is not for the apothecaries (as they call them), nor is it to be treated with the salves of Hippocrates, but it requires the powerful plasters of the Scriptures and the Word of God. . . . I should dissuade you from the use of medicine and recommend the power of God's Word."[5] Luther recognized that this woman's struggle, rooted in her soul and thus a spiritual condition, called for something that treated her spirit — namely, Jesus Christ and the witness to him contained in the scriptures. Luther also corresponded over the span of many years with numerous other persons who struggled with a disquieted soul. In each of his letters he locates their struggles in relationship to God and urges them to cling to faith in Christ to sustain them and ease their plight.[6]

Throughout his life and career as a reformer, Luther focused his attention on how God's grace, through faith in Christ, assured the Christian of God's favor. This was his theological breakthrough, and it served as a remedy for anxiety, which Luther knew well both personally and pastorally. Recognizing its sinister nature, he rooted anxiety in the devil's doings. He had a deep personal concern with being overwhelmed by the devil. We could even call it a preoccupation. Luther also believed that the devil always sought to capitalize on his difficulty with trusting his own thoughts and actions, a common struggle for anxious persons.

---

4. *Luther: Letters of Spiritual Counsel,* p. 82.
5. *Luther: Letters of Spiritual Counsel,* p. 83.
6. See *Luther: Letters of Spiritual Counsel,* pp. 82-138.

He was convinced too that the devil wanted constantly to distract him from living obediently before God and likewise threatened him unceasingly with dire consequences.[7] Luther did not assume that his experience was unique, however, and claimed anxiety as a common, if not universal, condition. He also recognized anxiety's spiritual basis: "The devil never ceases to disturb and worry men so that even at night and in their sleep he vexes them with disquieting dreams and anxieties to such a degree that the whole body is suffused with perspiration from mental anguish" and "the human spirit cannot rest."[8] Drawing particularly on Augustine, who held that our hearts are restless until they find rest in God, Luther located anxiety at the center of our spiritual struggles. As a result, he set the stage for others to do the same.

> *"We cannot be otherwise than continuously*
> *anxious and disturbed. . . ."*
>
> JOHN CALVIN

Indebted to Luther's thought concerning anxiety, and also sharing with him a personal struggle with it, John Calvin, a next-generation reformer who lived in Geneva, Switzerland, would also locate the soul's disquiet in a lack of faith and trust in God.

Calvin was "unusually sensitive to anxiety, that of others as well as his own," says Calvin biographer William J. Bouwsma, and sought through his work as a pastor and theologian "to soothe a peculiarly anxious generation."[9] As Bouwsma notes, Calvin surely had his share of pastoral experience with the condition:

> He saw anxiety everywhere, in the episodes recorded in Scripture, the study of which occupied so much of his mature life, and among his contemporaries. He brooded about the place of

---

7. See Allan Hugh Cole Jr., "A Spirit in Need of Rest: Luther's Melancholia, Obsessive-Compulsive Disorder, and Religiosity," *Pastoral Psychology* 48, no. 3 (2000): 169-90.

8. *Conversations with Luther: Selections from the Recently Published Sources of the Table Talk,* ed. and trans. Preserve Smith (New York: Pilgrim Press, 1915), p. 161; Cole, "A Spirit in Need of Rest," p. 181.

9. William J. Bouwsma, *John Calvin: A Sixteenth-Century Portrait* (New York: Oxford University Press, 1988), p. 32.

anxiety in human existence, and he wrote about it, sensitively, compassionately, and at length. A vocabulary of anxiety pervades his discourse; it includes not only *anxietas* and its equivalent *solicitudo* in Latin, but in French, *angoisse, destresse, frayeur, solicitude,* and even *perplexité.* He generally treated it as a perennial and abominable affliction of sinful humanity, though he was also aware of its uses.[10]

Calvin's familiarity with anxiety, both personally and vocationally, informed his abilities to describe anxiety's qualities and effects with great accuracy, which he did multiple times in his commentaries on Scripture. He notes that anxiety begins at a young age: "Before men decline into old age, even in the very bloom of youth . . . they are involved in many troubles, and they cannot escape from the cares, weariness, sorrows, fears, griefs, inconveniences, and anxieties to which mortal life is subject." He observes too that "those who are anxious wear themselves out and become in a sense their own executioners," and also notes anxiety's paralyzing effects on the mind: "We can often escape from lesser evils, but when we are oppressed by anxieties, we can, in our despair, neither see nor judge." Calvin also calls anxiety "an aggravation worse than murder when we are consumed within by trepidation as by a lingering death." His close familiarity with this "aggravation worse than murder" led him to conclude that anxiety is a universal experience: "Amid the uncertainties of life, 'we cannot be otherwise than continuously anxious and disturbed.'"[11]

Like Luther, Calvin recognized anxiety's roots as religious in nature and located them specifically in the human struggle with distress over God's mercy. Anxiety stems from a lack of faith. Anxious souls lack sufficient trust in God's mercy and all that it entails. Two related concerns seem particularly linked to anxiety for Calvin. One is ambiguity about human existence, especially with respect to what lies in the future. The other is the nature of human finitude, evidenced most profoundly in death. Concerning the "dread about what might lie ahead," Calvin's experience with and understanding of anxiety was similar to Luther's. As Bouwsma remarks in quoting Calvin, "Although we are tranquil today

10. Bouwsma, *John Calvin,* p. 37.
11. Bouwsma, *John Calvin,* p. 37.

. . . 'doubt might steal into our minds about what will happen tomorrow and make us continually anxious.'" Calvin agreed with Luther too on anxiety's relationship to lack of faith, covetousness, and striving for material gain: "No one . . . is hungrier or more in want than unbelievers whose peace is destroyed by care for possessions," for "our covetousness is an insatiable abyss unless it is restrained."[12]

With respect to human finitude, Calvin shared his age's generalized anxiousness over death, which was commonly premature and unpredictable:

> Innumerable are the evils that beset human life; innumerable, too, the deaths that threaten it. We need not go beyond ourselves: since our body is the receptacle of a thousand diseases — in fact holds within itself and fosters the causes of diseases — a man cannot go about unburdened by many forms of his own destruction, and without drawing out a life enveloped, as it were, with death. . . . Now, wherever you turn, all things around you not only are hardly to be trusted but almost openly menaced, and seem to threaten immediate death.[13]

Although Calvin thought it impossible to live with complete absence of anxiety, he believed that only faith in God makes it tolerable. He suggested that "we benefit greatly when we put off this faithlessness, which clings to the very bones of almost all men," and also that "when that light of divine providence has once shone upon a godly man, he is then relieved and set free not only from the extreme anxiety and fear that were pressing him before, but from every care."[14] Furthermore, like Luther, Calvin hastened to add that faith in God "implies certainty" and thus remedies anxiety: "Those who, relying upon God, have once for all cast out that anxiety about the care of the flesh, immediately expect from him greater things, even salvation and eternal life. It is, then, no light exercise of faith for us to hope for those things from God which otherwise cause us such anxiety."[15] Tying anxiety to the soul — "salvation" and

---

12. Bouwsma, *John Calvin*, p. 38.

13. John Calvin, *Institutes of the Christian Religion*, 2 vols., ed. John T. McNeill, trans. Ford Lewis Battles (Philadelphia: Westminster Press, 1960), p. 223.

14. Calvin, *Institutes*, p. 908, p. 224.

15. Calvin, *Institutes*, p. 560, p. 908.

"eternal life" — and more specifically to a lack of faith, Calvin urges disquieted souls to find quiet in God's mercy and care, casting off anything that would get in the way of faith and the experience of God's peace.

At the same time, Calvin understands anxiety's use and value. He concurs with the perspective put forth in the book of Proverbs, as would Søren Kierkegaard three centuries later: "Happy is the man who is anxious always, but he who hardens his heart falls into misfortune" (Prov. 28:14, Tanakh). For Calvin, some measure of anxiety remains useful in that "it kindles in us the desire to pray" and thus to glorify God.[16]

> *"Sadness . . . produces anxiety, and anxiety*
> *in turn produces increase of sadness. . . ."*
>
> FRANCIS DE SALES

A half-century after Calvin's death, the Roman Catholic Bishop of Geneva, Francis de Sales, took up the subject of anxiety. In his classic work *Introduction to the Devout Life,* Francis too describes anxiety as a condition of the soul. Saying of anxiety "there is nothing worse," he characterizes it as "weariness of mind which in turn produces . . . coldness and numbness in your soul."[17] He thought that it derives first from a "sadness" over some malady we experience that is "contrary to our will," and second, from the soul seeking refuge from its troubles by means of its own abilities and strivings, as opposed to complete reliance upon God. Rather than overcoming its troubles, however, which Francis calls "evils," the self-reliant soul "grows very anxious and impatient," and "instead of removing the evil, it increases it and this involves the soul in great anguish and distress together with such loss of strength and courage that it imagines the evil to be incurable." In tying anxiety to "self-reliance," Francis echoes claims made by Luther and Calvin. Francis's additional insight centers on the relationship between sadness and anxiety: "That sadness, which is justified in the beginning, produces anxiety, and anxiety in turn produces increase of sadness. All of this is extremely dangerous."[18] Francis recognizes what many anx-

---

16. Calvin, *Institutes,* p. 853.

17. Francis de Sales and Jane de Chantal, *Letters of Spiritual Direction,* trans. Peronne Marie Thibert (New York: Paulist Press, 1988), p. 100.

18. Francis de Sales, *Introduction to the Devout Life,* ed. and trans. John K. Ryan (New York: Image Books, 1972/1989), p. 251.

ious persons can affirm, and also what psychological perspectives on anxiety observe, namely, that anxiety and pervasive sadness (depression) relate to one another as close cousins, and that anxiety may be self-perpetuating and vicious.

Francis ties anxiety explicitly to "self-love" and self-importance, which disquiet us in the face of "our misery, our nothingness, and our weakness." He advises anxious persons to do at least three things: seek first the honor and glory of God; do what little you can toward that end; and leave the care of everything else to God. Francis believes that by focusing our attention on God, we lessen our focus on ourselves, including our attitudes of self-importance and self-reliance, which serves to quiet the soul. Realizing that Christ is the Prince of Peace, and that "wherever he is absolute master, he holds everything in peace," disquieted souls may find relief.[19] Unlike Calvin and Kierkegaard, whom we turn our attention to next, Francis saw little benefit or redeeming value in living with a disquieted soul. In fact, rather than seeing anxiety as a spiritual gift that draws us to faith in Christ and the Christian life, Francis thought that it gets in the way of such a faith and life. In a personal letter to a woman who suffered with anxiety and had sought counsel from him, Francis calls the condition "useless" and "one of the greatest obstacles to devotion and real virtue," adding that "it pretends to incite us to good, but all it does is cool our ardor; it makes us run, only to have us stumble," and "that's why we have to be on guard against it at all times, especially during prayer."[20]

Nineteenth-Century Views

Widespread interest in anxiety continued in the eighteenth century and proliferated in the nineteenth century, as evidenced by its great thinkers' reflections on the condition. Anxiety occupied novelists and poets, philosophers and theologians. It also garnered attention from psychologists and psychiatrists as their respective fields of inquiry and understanding burgeoned.

The Russian novelist Fyodor Dostoyevsky took up the subject of

19. Francis de Sales and Jane de Chantal, *Letters of Spiritual Direction*, p. 119.
20. Francis de Sales and Jane de Chantal, *Letters of Spiritual Direction*, p. 100.

anxiety in several novels. In a manner similar to that of Søren Kierkegaard, who will be discussed below, he focused particularly on anxiety's tie to human freedom. In his deeply religious novel *The Brothers Karamazov*, Dostoyevsky writes, "Man is tormented by no greater anxiety than to find someone quickly to whom he can hand over that great gift of freedom with which the ill-fated creature is born."[21] Dostoyevsky's American contemporary, Ralph Waldo Emerson, depicted the kind of apprehensiveness that may be joined with this freedom. In his poem "Borrowing from the French," Emerson writes, "Some of your hurts you have cured,/And the sharpest you still have survived,/But what torments of grief you endured/From evils which never arrived!"[22] Another poet, the American Emily Dickinson, was known to have suffered personally with chronic anxiety. Her poetry, which also has deep religious overtones, considers the subject in various ways. In "It Was Not Death" she keenly describes what anxiety is like: "As if my life were shaven/And fitted to a frame/And could not breathe without a key,/And 'twas like midnight. . . ."[23] Also capturing the condition's power and precariousness in that age was James Russell Lowell, Emerson's colleague and devotee, who noted in a public address that "the misfortunes hardest to bear are those which never come."[24] These reflections not only point to the vexing qualities of anxiety; they also represent well the nineteenth century's concern for its prevalence and perils.

Religious thinkers of the time continued to associate anxiety with the soul and thus rooted the condition foremost in religious questions or struggles. However, influenced by those in other fields of study and practice, like psychology and psychiatry, some of these religious thinkers enlarged their view to link anxiety to broader religious concerns. These concerns included moral and ethical ambiguity or misstep;

21. Fyodor Dostoyevsky, *The Brothers Karamazov*, trans. Constance Garnett (New York: Macmillan, 1948), p. 261.

22. Ralph Waldo Emerson, "Borrowing from the French," in *Yale Book of American Verse*, ed. Thomas R. Lounsbury (New Haven: Yale University Press, 1912), p. 86.

23. Emily Dickinson, "It Was Not Death," in *The Complete Poems of Emily Dickinson*, ed. Thomas H. Johnson (Boston: Little, Brown & Company, 1961), p. 510.

24. James Russell Lowell, "On Democracy," Inaugural Address on Assuming the Presidency of the Birmingham and Midland Institute, Birmingham, England, 6 October 1884.

strained, damaged, or insecure relationships; confusion about life's meaning and purpose; and dilemmas relating to human freedom and its uncertainties.

"Anxiety may be compared with dizziness. . . ."

SØREN KIERKEGAARD

No one gave more sustained attention to anxiety, including its sources, effects, and solutions, than Søren Kierkegaard, the Danish philosopher and theologian who wrote extensively on the subject. He placed anxiety at the very center of human existence, such that one cannot escape its grip entirely. Why? Because anxiety inevitably comes with freedom, and human beings, whom God has created to be free, eventually awake to their freedom and the potentials that come with it. Kierkegaard compared anxiety to "dizziness" and claimed that "the possibility of freedom" lies at its core.[25] He believed that human beings find themselves anxious because they discover their freedom and the countless ways to use it. In *The Concept of Anxiety*, Kierkegaard's most sustained discourse on the matter, he reflects on freedom's discovery:

> Anxiety may be compared with dizziness. He whose eye happens to look down into the yawning abyss becomes dizzy. But what is the reason for this? It is just as much in his own eye as in the abyss, for suppose he had not looked down. Hence, anxiety is the dizziness of freedom, which emerges when the spirit wants to posit the synthesis [between body and soul] and freedom looks down into its own possibility, laying hold of finiteness to support itself.[26]

He identifies this dizziness as a kind of innate disorientation, one that stems from human beings becoming aware that they are free and likewise sensing what freedom offers — namely, infinite possibilities. This dizziness, or anxiety, becomes the precondition of sin.

Kierkegaard thinks that he stands on firm biblical grounds when suggesting that, before the first sin, Adam's initial state was one of in-

25. Søren Kierkegaard, *The Concept of Anxiety*, ed. and trans. Reidar Thomte (Princeton: Princeton University Press, 1980), p. 155.
26. Kierkegaard, *The Concept of Anxiety*, p. 61.

nocence and ignorance, and that his spirit was in a dreamlike state. Kierkegaard writes,

> In this state there is peace and repose, but there is simultaneously something else that is not contention and strife, for there is indeed nothing against which to strive. What, then, is it? Nothing. But what effect does nothing have? It begets anxiety. This is the profound secret of innocence, that it is at the same time anxiety. Dreamily the spirit projects its own actuality, but this actuality is nothing, and innocence always sees this nothing outside itself. . . . Awake, the difference between myself and my other is posited; sleeping, it is suspended; dreaming, it is an intimated nothing. The actuality of the spirit constantly shows itself as a form that tempts its possibility but disappears as soon as it seeks to grasp for it, and it is a nothing that can only bring anxiety.

Kierkegaard thus describes anxiety in terms of "freedom's actuality as the possibility of possibility," and notes its status as "altogether different from fear and similar concepts that refer to something definite."[27]

Kierkegaard's thinking is complex and difficult to decipher. But what he suggests here follows from his understanding of both human being-ness — we could call it his anthropology — and original sin. A lengthy discussion of these matters moves beyond this book's scope, but some explanation is in order.[28] Briefly stated, Kierkegaard wants to explain how God created human beings good, and yet we find ourselves in sin. How can this be? Kierkegaard places himself among those wanting to refute the error of body-and-soul dualism. He contends that "human beings are best understood as a synthesis of body and soul" united in the spirit.[29] He identifies the body with the term *physical* and the soul with the term *psychical*. Stating that human beings are "a synthesis" of the two, the psychical and the physical, he

27. Kierkegaard, *The Concept of Anxiety*, pp. 41-42.

28. For an excellent and wide-ranging discussion of Kierkegaard's religious thought, see David J. Gouwens, *Kierkegaard as Religious Thinker* (Cambridge: Cambridge University Press, 1996).

29. Gordon D. Marino, "Anxiety in *The Concept of Anxiety*," in *The Cambridge Companion to Kierkegaard*, ed. Alastair Hannay and Gordon D. Marion (Cambridge: Cambridge University Press, 1998), p. 315.

states further that "a synthesis is unthinkable if the two are not united in a third. This third is spirit."[30] Thus, sin cannot be explained by a body-and-soul dualism.

Rather, dreaming innocence awakens us to freedom, possibility, and the opportunity for sin. In the dreamlike state of innocence, which was Adam's initial condition, the human spirit that unites body and soul is "unreflective" or "unselfconscious." It knows only itself and its immediate state. It has no awareness of anything outside itself, and thus nothing outside itself exists. Eventually the spirit begins to project outward, to "look" beyond itself and its immediate state. While Kierkegaard is not clear about why this happens, the most plausible means for its occurrence is through the imagination.[31] The dreamlike spirit imagines beyond itself. In doing so, it awakens to what lies beyond. What lies beyond is possibility. Thus, as the spirit imagines beyond itself, several things happen. A new condition of being follows. It includes a distinction between the self and others, and also awareness of freedom and its potential. The self now lives in relationship to things outside itself, all of which can be related to and engaged in various ways. The self has become aware of what it can do, who it may be, and how it may live — its "possibility." Hence Kierkegaard's claim that anxiety is simply "freedom's actuality as the possibility of possibility."

This newfound freedom brings with it "a feeling of being able,"[32] which Adam experienced before all others. Importantly for Kierkegaard, when God forbids Adam to eat from the tree in the Garden and tells him that if he does so he will die, Adam does not understand what God is talking about. He does not understand because he does not yet know about good, evil, or death. All Adam "knows" is an experience of freedom, "a feeling of being able and forbidden" by one outside himself — namely, God; and that is the "last stop before the first sin."[33] In other words, in being cautioned by God against doing something he has an ability to do, Adam discovers his freedom. Joined to this discovery is anxiety over the capacity for choice. Adam desires something that he

---

30. Kierkegaard, *The Concept of Anxiety,* p. 43. Kierkegaard says often that the human being *is* spirit.

31. Marino, "Anxiety in *The Concept of Anxiety,*" p. 316.

32. Kierkegaard, *The Concept of Anxiety,* p. 44.

33. Marino, "Anxiety in *The Concept of Anxiety,*" p. 317.

can have but is forbidden to have. He may choose to satisfy his desire, or not. Either way, he exercises his newfound freedom. Kierkegaard describes Adam's condition:

> When it is assumed that the prohibition awakens the desire, one acquires knowledge instead of ignorance, and in that case Adam must have had a knowledge of freedom, because the desire was to use it. The explanation is therefore subsequent. The prohibition induces in him anxiety, for the prohibition awakens in him freedom's possibility. What passed by innocence as the nothing of anxiety has now entered into Adam, and here again it is a nothing — the anxious possibility of *being able*.[34]

In his innocent state, wherein he discovered the dizziness of freedom, Adam leaped into the abyss of possibility, which included the possibility of sin. In so doing, through his free choice, Adam actualized sin's opportunity. The conditions for sin were there, given particular choices, which Adam made. He was able to opt for freedom and its possibilities, and he acted accordingly. Thus, for Kierkegaard, the fall of humanity is viewed as "the leap into the abyss of ontological possibility as an intentional act of freedom."[35]

As one commentator observes, this suggests that "the first sin for every individual — whatever that might mean — is a product of weakness, as opposed to defiance. It could not be defiance, for it is only with the first sin that the categories of good and evil are posited."[36] We cannot defy what we do not yet know. Even so, no individual relinquishes responsibility for her error, her sin. In fact, Kierkegaard explicitly states that though the first sin follows from weakness and thus would seem to lack responsibility, "this lack is the real trap."[37] The freedom that comes with being able — that is, with possibility and the free choices accompanying it — is terrifying. With "being able" comes anxiety that

34. Kierkegaard, *The Concept of Anxiety,* p. 44.

35. David K. Coe, *Angst and the Abyss: The Hermeneutics of Nothingness,* American Academy of Religion Series, no. 49, ed. Carl A. Raschke (Chico, Calif.: Scholars Press, 1985), p. 71.

36. Marino, "Anxiety in *The Concept of Anxiety,*" p. 322.

37. Søren Kierkegaard, *Journals and Papers,* ed. and trans. Howard V. Hong and Edna H. Hong (Bloomington: Indiana University Press, 1976), vol. 1, no. 94; pap. III A 233, n.d. 1842.

leads inevitably — though not necessarily, Kierkegaard insists — to sin. As with Adam, so with us.

As Adam discovered further, our own "being able" corresponds with others "being able" too. This prompts Kierkegaard's view that the core of our greatest anxiety is awareness of the possibility that the Supreme Other — namely, God, who is able to choose us — will opt in the end not to do so. For Kierkegaard, as for Luther, Calvin, and Francis de Sales, one's perception of one's relationship to God is what prompts anxiety. Even though we may not be consciously aware of it, and while we may think that our anxiety relates to something other than God, our faith, or spiritual matters, anxiety in fact arises from the possibility of being rejected and abandoned by God and winding up alone. In other words, Kierkegaard believes that we are anxious about God whether we think that we are or not! Likewise, anxiety's scope remains universal in that all persons experience it: "Deep within every human being there still lives the anxiety over the possibility of being alone in the world, forgotten by God, overlooked among the millions and millions in this enormous household."[38]

Kierkegaard holds as one of his guiding principles the Latin phrase *unum noris omnis,* which translates "If you know one, you know all."[39] He believed, as another commentator has suggested, that this same principle lies at the core of Socrates' dictum "Know thy self!"[40] Kierkegaard held that one must, through a process of introspection, come to know oneself; for knowing oneself holds the key to knowing others. He was quick to recognize that we can deceive ourselves, however, such that we may "know" things about ourselves that prove false or inaccurate. Therefore, we must continue to examine our knowledge of ourselves, and that occurs precisely as we observe others who, presumably, operate with a similar basis for self-knowledge.

This concept "If you know one, you know all" becomes important with respect to original sin. Kierkegaard argues against merely seeing "hereditary sin" as beginning with "Adam's first sin." Such a view actually places Adam outside the human race in that it does not account for

---

38. Kierkegaard, *Journals and Papers,* vol. 1, no. 40; pap. VIII A 363, n.d. 1837.

39. Kierkegaard, *The Concept of Anxiety,* p. 79. See also Coe, *Angst and the Abyss,* pp. 45-87.

40. Reidar Thomte, "Historical Introduction to Søren Kierkegaard," in Kierkegaard, *The Concept of Anxiety,* p. xv.

the freedom that all who have followed Adam enjoy. As such, this view does nothing to clarify the origin of sin in all the rest of us. Kierkegaard appeals to psychology and anxiety in exploring original sin because he wants to make clear how original sin touches all of us, but in a different way than heredity. For Kierkegaard, Adam remains important in that knowing what lay at the heart of Adam's disquieted soul (the one) reveals what lies at the heart of our own (the all). As with Adam, so with us!

Rounding out this discussion requires explicit mention of another of Kierkegaard's observations — namely, anxiety's paradoxical quality. He uses the curious phrase *"sympathetic antipathy* and *antipathetic sympathy"* to describe anxiety as "a paradoxical form of desire, or if you will, a paradoxical form of fear."[41] Kierkegaard writes, "Anxiety is a desire for what one fears, a sympathetic antipathy; anxiety is an alien power which grips the individual, and yet one cannot tear himself free from it and does not want to, for one fears, but what he fears he desires. Anxiety makes the individual powerless."[42]

Another Kierkegaard commentator has described anxiety by saying that it "involves a deep ambivalence. We are divided against ourselves and want something that another part of us does not want."[43] We love our freedom, but it comes with a series of choices that need making. We simultaneously want and do not want those choices. The infinite possibilities that discovery of freedom and its choices brings are both attractive and frightening: "Attractive because any one of [our choices] can potentially be actualized; and frightening because when one *is* actualized, all others must be abandoned."[44] In other words, as the individual makes choices in her freedom, she foregoes other possibilities, at least for the time being. While she may find it feasible to actualize other possibilities at another time in the future, she cannot do so immediately — that is, as she makes her present choice. Thus, rather than subduing anxiety because we have other, presumably attractive options before us, the choices that present themselves actually increase it. We love our freedom and we hate it.

41. Marino, "Anxiety in *The Concept of Anxiety*," p. 321.

42. Kierkegaard, *Journals and Papers*, vol. 1, no. 39; pap. VIII A 363, n.d. 1837.

43. Walter Kaufmann, *Discovering the Mind*, vol. 22 (New York: McGraw Hill, 1980), p. 25; quoted in Coe, *Angst and the Abyss*, p. 68.

44. Coe, *Angst and the Abyss*, p. 71.

This kind of ambivalence relates to something that anxious persons know all too well. On the one hand, they do not want to be anxious. On the other hand, the harder they try to quiet their souls, the more disquieted they often become. Likewise, their anxiety often centers precisely on having to make choices, whereby they wonder if they have made the correct choice and whether in so doing they have foregone another choice that could prove to have been the better one. If these occasions for choice bring some degree of ambivalence for most everyone, anxious persons feel it more profoundly and painfully. Anxiety thus relates to something reminiscent of Paul's description of his own struggles: "I do not understand my own actions. For I do not do what I want, but I do the very thing I hate" (Rom. 7:15).

Kierkegaard spoke of anxiety and its despairs in terms of "spirit sickness," a condition that all human beings share to some extent. He claimed,

> Just as a physician might say that there very likely is not one single living human being who is completely healthy, so anyone who really knows mankind might say that there is not one single living human being who does not despair a little, who does not secretly harbor an unrest, an inner strife, a disharmony, an anxiety about an unknown something or a something he does not even dare to try to know, an anxiety about some possibility in existence or an anxiety about himself, so that, just as the physician speaks of going around with an illness in the body, he walks around with a sickness, carries around a sickness of the spirit that signals its presence at rare intervals in and through an anxiety he cannot explain. In any case, no human being ever lived and no one lives outside of Christendom who has not despaired, and no one in Christendom if he is not a true Christian, and insofar as he is not wholly that, he still is to some extent in despair.[45]

For Kierkegaard, who locates anxiety in the sick human spirit, the condition has a profoundly *spiritual* nature. It has to do with the spirit's

---

45. Søren Kierkegaard, *The Sickness unto Death,* ed. and trans. Howard V. Hong and Edna H. Hong (Princeton: Princeton University Press, 1980), p. 22. Note that Kierkegaard offers commentary throughout the book on anxiety and its despairs being fundamentally a "spirit sickness."

"presentiment," a kind of apprehension that "seems to precede every-thing which is to happen."[46] The disquieted soul constantly gazes rest-lessly into the future, and the future "is apprehended by reference to the past."[47] One's previous experience inevitably shapes one's appre-hensions — and one's apprehensiveness — concerning future possibility — that is, of what "might be." This apprehensiveness is felt especially by the Christian person, whose awareness of the choices before him — what Kierkegaard calls leaps into life's freedoms — increases his anxiety over making them.

Nevertheless, Kierkegaard viewed anxiety as playing an invaluable role in our lives. Though painful and prompting our most basic life struggles, it quickens us to faith. Anxiety thus remains useful, even nec-essary, for the Christian life. Living with it brings excitement and re-ward in that it has the capacity to prompt one to make choices appro-priate for a life that rests in Christ. In a sense, anxiety *is* a gift, one that reminds us of our need for Christ. Our faith leads us to seek a kind of "eternal blessedness" that would finally "resolve the dilemmas of anxi-ety and despair."[48]

Like Calvin, Kierkegaard considered anxiety to be a universal expe-rience, one that every person must endure, and also believed that its re-wards ultimately follow from its capacity for stirring within us the de-sire for a stronger relationship to God. Anxiety plays an invaluable role in life because it may eventually serve to bring us closer to the One who alone can relieve it. So convinced that anxiety has merit, Kierkegaard went so far as to call anxiety "an adventure" which, if mastered in the right way, becomes for the adventurer "the ultimate."[49]

Twentieth-Century Views

The twentieth century, particularly following the First World War, brought sustained attention to anxiety. In the words of poet W. H. Auden and composer Leonard Bernstein, this was "the age of anxi-

46. Kierkegaard, *Journals and Papers*, vol. 1, no. 91; pap. II A 18, n.d. 1837; Coe, *Angst and the Abyss*, p. 63.
47. Coe, *Angst and the Abyss*, p. 64.
48. Gouwens, *Kierkegaard as Religious Thinker*, p. 85.
49. Kierkegaard, *The Concept of Anxiety*, p. 155.

ety."[50] The potential and promise of human achievement, so central to the Renaissance and the organizing belief in the West since, became widely questioned. This period's experiences of wars, totalitarianism, economic depression, environmental neglect and disasters, and nuclear proliferation made for less certainty about life and more anxiety. These experiences prompted a broader cultural awareness that something was awry and needed attention. This awareness led to greater interest in solving the problems of human alienation and idolatry, along with suggestions for finding solutions to those problems through greater "connection" and "health."[51]

Like Kierkegaard, numerous theologians from Europe and the United States saw anxiety as a spiritual problem and attended to its sources and solutions. Representative of that group were Dietrich Bonhoeffer, Karl Barth, Reinhold Niebuhr, Paul Tillich, Hans Urs von Balthasar, and Jürgen Moltmann. As Renata Salecl described it when writing about European experiences with anxiety during this period, "Some . . . saw as the main cause of the overwhelming feeling of anxiety the death of all modern idols: it looked that man was very much alone, since he had lost belief in God. However, equally important was the loss of belief in science, progress, and reason."[52] The American experience was similar, and its effects continue into the present, in the West and beyond.

> *"The core of the 'problem' is*
> *flight from the Word of God."*
>
> DIETRICH BONHOEFFER

Dietrich Bonhoeffer located anxiety's roots in sin — that is, in one's alienation from Christ. Unlike Kierkegaard, who thought of anxiety as the precondition of sin as well as its product, Bonhoeffer believed anxiety to follow from sin. More specifically, anxiety links with the importance we place on "earthly possessions" — material things — that we suppose will provide security and freedom *from* anxiety. Describing "the

---

50. Leonard Bernstein titled his 1949 symphony *The Age of Anxiety*, basing it on W. H. Auden's poem (1948) by the same title.

51. See, for example, Erich Fromm, *The Sane Society* (New York: Henry Holt & Company, 1955).

52. Renata Salecl, *On Anxiety* (London: Routledge, 2004), p. 2.

simplicity of the carefree life," Bonhoeffer reflects on Jesus' command-
ment to his disciples in Matthew's Gospel: "Be not anxious" (Matt. 6:25-
34, ASV). For Bonhoeffer, the external things we look to for security are
precisely what cause us anxiety: "The fetters which bind us to our possessions prove to be cares themselves."[53] Like Kierkegaard, Bonhoeffer
recognized anxiety's future orientation. He observed that in constantly
looking ahead, we seek to shore up goods for our well-being. We thereby
become "helpless victims of infinite anxiety." Bonhoeffer writes,

> The way to misuse our possessions is to use them as an insur-
> ance against the morrow. Anxiety is always directed to the mor-
> row, whereas goods are in the strictest sense meant to be used
> only for to-day. By trying to ensure for the next day we are only
> creating uncertainty to-day. Sufficient unto the day is the evil
> thereof. The only way to win assurance is by leaving to-morrow
> entirely in the hands of God and by receiving from him all we
> need for to-day.[54]

For Bonhoeffer, one becomes anxious as one contemplates tomorrow
and grows concerned about its provisions. Rather than focusing on
what one has today, and thus on what is certain, when one seeks for assurance about tomorrow, one inevitably has to entertain uncertainty.
Anxiety has to do with a question about what the future holds and corresponding insecurities.

Bonhoeffer claims that we find assurance and security in life only
by leaving the future in God's hands. We grow secure by trusting, in
faith, that we receive from God what we need each day: today, tomorrow, and the days after. Citing Jesus' question, "Do you have little
faith?" (Matt. 6:30, my translation), Bonhoeffer points out that faith
(trust) is not a general life philosophy or "moral law"; rather, "it is the
gospel of Jesus Christ, and only so can it be understood." In other
words, placing our trust in God's provision, as Jesus himself did, holds
the key to living satisfied with today and less anxiously about tomorrow. A trust whose basis, or object, is God in Jesus Christ remains qualitatively distinct from a trust located in something or someone else. By

---

53. Dietrich Bonhoeffer, *The Cost of Discipleship* (New York: Simon & Schuster, 1995),
p. 178.

54. Bonhoeffer, *The Cost of Discipleship*, p. 178.

trusting in Christ, we glorify God, not through our labors and concerns but "by a daily unquestioning" of God's provision that remains the heart of the Christian gospel.[55] Through being "in Christ" we begin to trust in new and distinctive ways. Our goal then becomes living with an attitude that Wendell Berry has suggested: "Let tomorrow come tomorrow. Not by your will is the house carried through the night."[56]

The trust that Bonhoeffer describes may seem to have more to do with worry or fear and less to do with anxiety. His attention appears to focus largely on a type of discomfort related to something identifiable and concrete — namely, what could happen to a person with respect to her daily needs and available provisions. As we have noted, fear tends to link with identifiable threats we perceive, whereas anxiety relates to more ambiguous ones. Nevertheless, Bonhoeffer's comment on what counters anxiety indicates something crucial for disquieted souls to hear. In calling for trust in God's provision and for glorifying God, not through our labors but by accepting God's provision in an unquestioning (trusting) way, Bonhoeffer had in mind divine-human relationships. His appeal to Jesus saying "Be not anxious" has less to do with what one may be given in the way of material goods, and more to do with who one is in relationship to the giver — namely, God in Jesus Christ. As Bonhoeffer himself notes, for Jesus, "bread is not to be valued as the reward for work; he speaks instead of the carefree simplicity of the man who walks with him and accepts everything as it comes from God."[57]

Bonhoeffer's comment in another work, *Spiritual Care*, indicates further that he conceived of anxiety as having first and foremost to do with our relationship to God. Here again he locates the condition in our relationship to Christ, saying that in denying Christ, and particularly in failing to take responsibility for our sin through confession, we feel anxious. Noting that withholding from God "specific parts of our own nature, of our vocation, and of our social life gradually delivers us into tight imprisonment," Bonhoeffer claims that the pastoral question to ask is this: "Why do you deny Christ obedience at this particular point in your life? . . . The anxiety you express is in reality your sin."[58]

---

55. Bonhoeffer, *The Cost of Discipleship*, pp. 178-79.

56. Wendell Berry, *What Are People For?* (New York: North Point Press, 1990), p. 13.

57. Bonhoeffer, *The Cost of Discipleship*, p. 179.

58. Dietrich Bonhoeffer, *Spiritual Care*, trans. Jay C. Rochelle (Minneapolis: Fortress Press, 1985), pp. 33-34.

Withholding something of ourselves impacts our relationships. Holding back parts of who we are, whether from God or other persons, quickly becomes grounds for anxiety to flourish because relationships require personal authenticity. Recognizing that our alienation from Christ grows out of withholding parts of ourselves from God and others, as does our subsequent anxiety, leads to what Bonhoeffer names "the decisive starting point for spiritual care." Spiritual care begins with a focus on one's relationship to Christ. Consequently, "it must always be clear to the pastor that the core of the 'problem' is flight from the Word of God."[59]

For Bonhoeffer, the disquieted soul presents itself following two things: our failure to trust in God's provision and the lack of responsibility we take for our sin. In both cases, anxiety derives from being out of proper relationship to God. A disquieted soul thus has more to do with who we are (anxiety) than with what may happen to us (fear).

"Fear not!"

KARL BARTH

Karl Barth, who influenced Bonhoeffer deeply, thought of anxiety in terms of a fear of death, which he held is more appropriately understood as a fear of life. In part, Barth's perspective recalls Calvin's view on the condition. Barth understands that the gospel forbids us to fear death. He bases this claim on the Gospel of John, which conveys Jesus' promise that those who hear his word and believe have eternal life (John 5:24). Barth observes further that "in place of this fear we do not put a substitute faith which postulates a false beyond or a false present, or which effaces the distinction between them."[60] What he had in mind here were unbiblical beliefs about life, death, and the life to come. Such beliefs currently abound, and include everything from the immortality of the soul in the dualistic, Platonic sense, to more New Age beliefs about communicating with the dead, receiving "signs" from them, and related practices. Barth points out that the gospel offers something else in place of these kinds of false beliefs. Citing the scriptures, he

---

59. Bonhoeffer, *Spiritual Care*, pp. 34, 33.

60. Karl Barth, *Church Dogmatics*, vol. 3.4, ed. G. W. Bromiley and T. F. Torrance (Edinburgh: T&T Clark, 1961), p. 594.

makes explicit note of what Christ offers: "He has utterly destroyed death, i.e., not merely dying, but the nothingness which threatens and lurks behind it, and brought life and immortality to light (2 Tim. 1:10)." This leads to Barth's entreaty: "Fear not!"[61] The resurrected Christ has overcome death and all its attributes. This is the good news. Christ, who holds us in right relationship to God, removes our fear and uncertainty about death, which is the source of our anxiety.

Reminiscent of Luther, Calvin, and Francis de Sales, Barth grounds anxiety explicitly in self-will. He believes that we seek to delay death for as long as possible. This delay happens out of fear and, in a sense, becomes our attempt to overcome our mortality. Consequently, we engage in an act of self-will. The alternative, which overcomes this tendency for asserting self-will and its accompanying anxiety, becomes obedience to God and the hope joined to it. Barth grounds this obedience and hope in baptism, claiming that baptism's full meaning includes a true conversion. By conversion he means a "transition from an old path to a new," the old being a state of anxiety and the new being obedience to God.[62] Commenting further on Christ's power to free us from this "fear of life" and willfulness of the self, Barth writes,

> He removes the atmosphere in which our opportunity cannot be known or apprehended at all but can only be missed. He makes the recognition and apprehension of it the important, free, joyful, serious and responsible life work which it is as the required work of human obedience. He does this who by His dying and rising again is Himself our hope in the face of our dying — God for us where we can no longer in any sense be for ourselves.[63]

Like Luther, Calvin, Francis, and Kierkegaard, Barth holds up Christ as the answer to anxiety. Standing before Christ, who is "God for us where we can no longer in any sense be for ourselves," anxious persons who, incidentally, often feel like they can no longer "be for themselves," may find quiet for their souls. As Barth suggests, the one "who grasps his unique opportunity, who occupies his place, may be known by his con-

---

61. Barth, *Church Dogmatics*, vol. 3.4, p. 594.
62. Karl Barth, *Church Dogmatics*, vol. 4.4, ed. G. W. Bromiley and T. F. Torrance, trans. G. W. Bromiley (Edinburgh: T&T Clark, 1969), p. 136.
63. Barth, *Church Dogmatics*, vol. 3.4, p. 594.

stant readiness and joyfulness in the face of the fact which unambiguously characterizes his being in time as a limited being, namely, that he will one day die."[64]

> *"Anxiety is 'the internal description*
> *of the state of temptation.'"*

REINHOLD NIEBUHR

Reminiscent of Kierkegaard, Reinhold Niebuhr locates anxiety in the relationship between human finitude and freedom, the latter's misuse, and, similar to Barth, particularly in the sin of pride (self-will), for which anxiety remains the precondition. Niebuhr contends that not only did Jesus recognize anxious persons in his midst, but, just as Kierkegaard had suggested, he identified anxiety both as being central in human existence and as the precursor to our sin. Niebuhr cites Jesus' question in the Sermon on the Mount — "Which of you by being anxious can add one cubit to his span of life?" — and calls it "part of a general analysis of the human situation." Niebuhr thinks that Jesus acknowledges here that all of creation, human beings included, exists "by and in God's providence." Furthermore, Jesus' response — "I say unto you, be not anxious" — "contains the whole genius of the Biblical view" of the relationship between human finitude and sin: "It is not his finiteness, dependence, and weakness but his anxiety about it which tempts him to sin."[65]

Niebuhr alternates language of "insecurity" and "anxiety" when discussing the human condition. He claims that because of our involvement in "natural contingency," we are finite and thus limited in our freedom. We are free but not entirely so. We live with restrictions on our strength, endurance, and capacities for thinking, doing, and persevering. Furthermore, we get sick, become injured, and die. As a result, we constantly live with insecurity. Nevertheless, we remain free within the confines of our limits. This means that we have the capacity to act in ways that make us more secure.

However, a problem arises. As we respond to our limited existence

64. Barth, *Church Dogmatics*, vol. 3.4, p. 595.

65. Reinhold Niebuhr, *The Nature and Destiny of Man*, vol. 1 (Louisville: Westminster John Knox Press, 1996), p. 168.

by seeking greater security, we attempt to triumph over our anxiety by virtue of our own capacities and power. This "will to power" becomes sinful in that it is tied to at least two additional corresponding matters: first, our attempting to transcend our creaturely and limited state by our own means; and second, our losing awareness of our dependence upon God and God's providence. Both of these involve the sin of pride, which comes about when those who seek greater security do so at the expense of others' lives and a proper relationship to God.

Similar to Kierkegaard and Calvin, Niebuhr thinks of anxiety as universal in scope, and also as both a liability and a gift. Anxiety leads to sin (liability), but also informs creativity (gift). Even so, Niebuhr thinks we err when we posit a sharp separation between anxiety's destructive and productive facets. As the precondition of sin, or what he terms "the internal description of the state of temptation," anxiety causes sin and thus all kinds of pain and destruction. In fact, even though anxiety has value in that it informs creativity, "it is always destructive" to some extent, even if it has creative qualities. As Niebuhr puts it, "The destructive aspect of anxiety is so intimately involved in the creative aspects that there is no possibility of making a simple separation between them. The two are bound together by reason of man being anxious both to realize his unlimited possibilities and to overcome and to hide the dependent and contingent character of his existence."[66] Anxiety operates, then, by virtue of our being free and yet limited creatures, our "paradoxical situation." It exists because, in knowing that we live with limits and freedom, we find ourselves tempted to transcend both. Such temptation "resides in the inclination . . . either to deny the contingent character of . . . existence (in pride and self-love) or to escape from . . . freedom (in sensuality)," the latter of which results in "unlimited devotion to limited values."[67]

Niebuhr agrees with Kierkegaard too in claiming that anxiety and sin must not be equated. Furthermore, like each of the figures already discussed, Niebuhr locates anxiety's relief in faith. Anxiety does not *necessarily* lead to sin because ideally one may find it possible to "purge anxiety of the tendency toward self-assertion" through "faith in the ultimate security of God's love" that overcomes "all immediate insecuri-

---

66. Niebuhr, *The Nature and Destiny of Man*, pp. 182, 186.
67. Niebuhr, *The Nature and Destiny of Man*, pp. 182, 185.

ties." In other words, transcending our paradoxical life between freedom and finitude, wherein anxiety and its companion (the sin of pride) dwell, a "perfect trust in divine security"[68] serves to assuage our anxiety. Trust in God quiets the soul.

> *"Anxiety turns us toward courage*
> *because the other alternative is despair."*
>
> PAUL TILLICH

No other twentieth-century theologian attributed greater significance to anxiety within the human condition, or devoted more attention to helping persons live with it more faithfully, than Paul Tillich. In Tillich's view, anxiety sits at the core of human existence. Attending to it must therefore lie at theology's center. Largely indebted to Kierkegaard's thinking about the human condition, and especially the role of anxiety in it, Tillich's concern for anxiety permeates his works. He locates the condition in human ontology, in one's "being-ness," claiming that "anxiety is the self-awareness of the finite self as finite."[69] Going beyond Kierkegaard's view, Tillich distinguished between *existential anxiety*, which is a basic, universal kind of anxiety tied to the base of being, and *neurotic or abnormal anxiety*, which grows from basic anxiety and has particular features.

Tillich held that much of the confusion about anxiety follows from a lack of clarity on these distinctions. Existential anxiety, which all people experience to some degree, has its roots in our awareness of the possibility for us not to exist: "I exist but I easily could not exist and, in fact, could *never* have existed." Calling this awareness "the threat of non-being," Tillich observed what a substantial role it plays in our religious, psychological, and relational lives.

Embedded in our limited and dependent nature as human beings, existential anxiety moves to transform itself into fear. It seeks for something identifiable and concrete of which to be afraid, as opposed to remaining in its diffuse, more pervasive, and less identifiable state of uncertainty. Existential anxiety seeks to become fear because that expe-

---

68. Niebuhr, *The Nature and Destiny of Man,* pp. 182-83.

69. Paul Tillich, *Systematic Theology,* vol. 1 (Chicago: University of Chicago Press, 1951), p. 192.

rience causes comparatively less pain than anxiety. To say it another way, managing our fears tends to come more easily to us than managing our anxiety, because we seem to know more about the former than the latter as concerns its origins, qualities, and means for relief. We can name what we fear, touch it, perhaps, and consciously work to remove it from close proximity to our lives. Doing any of this with what makes us anxious proves more difficult and distressing.

Tillich notes further that, unlike anxiety, fear finds a resource for its care — namely, self-affirmation and the courage it births. Courage, which Tillich defines as self-affirmation of one's being "in spite of" the possibility of nonbeing, may compensate for fear and its perils. As Tillich describes it, "Anxiety turns us toward courage because the other alternative is despair. Courage resists despair by taking anxiety into itself."[70] So, anxiety seeks to become fear because fear finds relief in courage.

Anxious persons must therefore cultivate courage, what Tillich calls "the courage to be." This courage, which follows from securing ways to affirm the self in the midst of what threatens it, comes ultimately from God, whom Tillich calls "the Ground of Being." Chronic and severe anxiety, which he dubs "neurotic" or "pathological," essentially follows from an inability to avoid despair by taking on anxiety courageously. Abnormal anxiety may be thought of as a greater degree of existential anxiety that has not been curbed by courage and thus has turned to despair.

Existential anxiety, which all of us live with and which receives most of Tillich's attention, finds expression in three principal ways, what Tillich alternately calls "forms" and "types." These ways include the anxiety of death and finitude; the anxiety of meaninglessness; and the anxiety of guilt and condemnation — that is, the anxiety of sin. I want to offer a brief comment on each of these.

William James observed the role that awareness of death plays in our lives. He claimed, "Back of everything is the great spectre of universal death, the all-encompassing blackness."[71] Tillich understood this too. He

---

70. Paul Tillich, *The Courage to Be* (New Haven: Yale University Press, 1952), pp. 2-4, 66.

71. William James, *The Varieties of Religious Experience* (New York: Library Classics of the United States, 1987), p. 131.

identified anxiety tied to our fate and ultimate death as "the most basic, most universal, and inescapable" form of anxiety. Furthermore, anxiety about death serves as the basis for anxiety over other matters, "overshadowing" them all and "giving them their ultimate seriousness."[72] Life itself (our being-ness) remains always uncertain, for we can die at any moment and will certainly die someday. Death looms in daily living. This tinges whatever else we experience with a degree of despair. Important for Tillich's analysis here is the fact that awareness of our contingency — that we could just as easily not exist as exist — means that our lives have "no ultimate necessity." Anxiety thus remains inextricably linked with an awareness of our relative insignificance in the world. Consequently, anxiety pushes us toward securing a more significant place in it.

Noting this quest for significance brings us to the second form of existential anxiety — namely, that of emptiness and meaninglessness. Tillich contends that this type of anxiety centers on "the loss of an ultimate concern," by which he means what we hold most dear. He believes that all human beings require "spiritual self-affirmation" in the face of loss or its threat. This affirmation comes by virtue of "living creatively in the various spheres of meaning."[73] To be spiritually active, or spiritually alive, one needs to create. One needs to participate in and contribute to forming original ideas, crafting innovative things, discovering fresh truths, and finding new meanings. Such participation in matters of ultimate concern, our creativity, provides spiritual affirmation in the midst of the threat of nonbeing and the sense of insignificance (emptiness) that accompanies it. Tillich goes so far as to say that "we are human only by understanding and shaping reality, both [our] world and [ourselves,] according to meanings and values."[74] Being human depends on being creative.

Anxiety's third form, guilt and condemnation, has to do particularly with anxiety about sin and its ramifications. This form of anxiety derives from the fact that human beings must, when asked, provide an accounting of themselves and their lives. Tillich thinks that we all ask this of ourselves. We judge ourselves and need "moral self-affirmation" in order to fend off "self-rejection" and "condemnation," which be-

72. Tillich, *The Courage to Be,* p. 43.
73. Tillich, *The Courage to Be,* p. 48.
74. Tillich, *The Courage to Be,* p. 50.

comes the anxiety of guilt. This need flows from human beings existing in "finite freedom." By this term Tillich means that, within the bounds of our finitude and its contingencies, human beings are free to actualize their potential. Here he agrees with Kierkegaard and Niebuhr. We actualize our potential through our decisions, behaviors, and actions. When we can morally self-affirm any of these, we become who we desire to be. On the other hand, when our decisions, behaviors, or actions do not warrant moral self-affirmation, we contradict our "essential being," become who we desire *not to be,* and feel guilty. In a sense, we actualize our moral "nonbeing."

These types of anxiety interact with one another, such that they are not mutually exclusive. They often merge with one another and actually play off one another. Anxiety about death impacts anxiety about meaninglessness. Together those may impact anxiety about sin, and vice versa. Moreover, while Tillich follows Kierkegaard and champions the self and the significance of its individuation, Tillich simultaneously recognizes the necessity for the individual's participation in the world with others. He also states that any existential anxiety has to be overcome finally in relationship with God and others. He uses the term "collectivism" to get at the self's participatory and relational qualities. This suggests that living in isolation exacerbates anxiety, while living in community assuages it.

> *"God grants . . . participation in the anxiety of his Son on the Cross to no believer unless he has first granted to him the entire strength of the Christian mission and joy and the entire light of faith, love, and hope. . . ."*
>
> HANS URS VON BALTHASAR

Another twentieth-century theologian who took great interest in anxiety was the Roman Catholic Hans Urs von Balthasar. Arguing *explicitly* against Kierkegaard's view, he located anxiety's roots *not* in the relationship of human finitude and freedom per se, but rather in original sin and its legacy, which manifests itself foremost by alienating the human being from God. He held that in our freedom we sin, breach relationships, estrange ourselves from God (and others), and thus experience anxiety.

Balthasar frames his discussion of the condition in terms of the Word of God, by whom he means Jesus Christ, claiming that we do well always to remember his purpose in the world. That purpose is not, as we often assume, "to protect humanity in this world from suffering and death," nor "did the Word enter the world simply to remove anxiety or to preserve people from it."[75] Rather, the Word became flesh and dwelled among us to redeem us from our sin and restore us to right relationship with God. This happened in Christ's crucifixion and resurrection. Dying on the cross, Jesus experienced the magnitude of human sin, separation from God, and its accompanying anxiety at the greatest depth. He knew personally the pain and perils of the disquieted soul. In being raised from the dead and restored to full communion with God, he overcame the wages of sin and death, and with that he prevailed over the anxiety tied to both. Balthasar describes anxiety as "one of the authorities, powers, and dominions over which the Lord triumphed on the Cross and which he carried off captive and placed in chains, to make use of as he wills."[76]

Our own experiences of anxiety, painful though they may be, thus serve an invaluable purpose. On that point Balthasar can agree with Kierkegaard, though Balthasar disagrees with Kierkegaard's understanding of anxiety's basis and the nature of its subsequent value. Nevertheless, anxiety holds value to the extent that God utilizes it for redemptive purposes. Anxiety thus becomes a means for Jesus' restoration of, and ultimately God's absolution of, the fallen creation. One commentator goes so far as to say that, for Balthasar, anxiety serves as "the condition upon which the fulfillment of God's saving plan depends," for "the whole of human anxiety, concentrated in a single mass, closes in upon Christ, who alone can say Yes to God the Father in place of the sinner's resolute No."[77] By virtue of God's grace, Christ's followers receive "the gift" of anxiety, which bids them to participate in the Cross of Christ and the grace of God unto which it opens.

75. Hans Urs von Balthasar, *The Christian and Anxiety,* trans. Dennis D. Martin and Michael J. Miller, Foreword by Yves Tourenne, O.F.M. (San Francisco: Ignatius Press, 2000), p. 39.

76. von Balthasar, *The Christian and Anxiety,* p. 81.

77. von Balthasar, *The Christian and Anxiety,* p. 16.

"In anxiety we anticipate possible danger.
In hope we anticipate possible deliverance."

JÜRGEN MOLTMANN

Jürgen Moltmann has also taken an interest in looking at anxiety theologically.[78] While Moltmann does not maintain a sharp distinction between anxiety and fear, he recognizes that these experiences are so
closely related that seldom does one occur without the other. He also
recognizes anxiety's benefits, as Kierkegaard and others have.

With Kierkegaard, he holds that we must learn how to be anxious
appropriately. This assumes, first, that anxiety has value and, second,
that there are positive and negative ways of living with it. To make his
point, Moltmann cites Kierkegaard recollecting a fairy tale of the
Brothers Grimm:

> There is a story of a young man who goes in search of adventure
> in order to learn what it is like to be in anxiety. . . . I will say that
> this is an adventure that every human being must go through —
> to learn to be anxious in order that he may not perish either by
> never having been in anxiety or by succumbing in anxiety. Who-
> ever has learned to be anxious in the right way has learned the
> ultimate.[79]

Nevertheless, we require something more than anxiety to sustain us.
Drawing on the work of philosopher Ernst Bloch, Moltmann claims
that anxiety needs a partner — namely, hope. Learning to be anxious
in the right way necessitates learning also to be hopeful. Hope prevents anxiety from "numbing" or completely "engulfing" us. Moltmann notes that anxiety and hope share a future orientation in that
they have concern for "the possible," for "in anxiety we anticipate
possible danger. In hope we anticipate possible deliverance." Likewise,
both our anxiety and our hope impact how we live in the present. As
Moltmann recognizes, "In anxiety and hope we go beyond existing re-

---

78. Jürgen Moltmann, *Jesus Christ for Today's World* (Minneapolis: Fortress Press,
1994), pp. 50-57.
79. Kierkegaard, *The Concept of Anxiety*, p. 155. See also Moltmann, *Jesus Christ for Today's World*, pp. 50-51. Note that Moltmann has provided his own translation, which differs slightly from the one I have cited.

ality and anticipate the future, so as to make a correct decision about the present."[80]

For Moltmann, all human experience with anxiety stems from a fear of separation: from others, from life's meaning, and ultimately from God. He discusses the fear of separation and its corresponding anxiety by comparing our experiences with both to those Christ experienced. Moltmann claims that when we believe and trust in Christ, our anxiety draws us into closer communion with him. It does so because "in our anxiety we participate in Christ's anxiety; for in his suffering Christ went through the very fears and anxieties which men and women encounter too."[81] Moltmann cites as evidence for the consolatory effects of our identifying with (participating in) Christ's suffering, and he in ours, the historic faith practice of devotion to the crucified Jesus. Having experienced God's forsakenness in death, including a total separation from God, and having overcome that separation through his resurrection, Christ frees anxious persons from what they feel most threatened by and empowers them to live in a new, less anxious manner. Moltmann describes this new way of living as follows: "Believers are not just brought into solidarity with Christ's fate. . . . They also, and even more, enter into a relationship of gratitude freed from fear. For the knowledge that someone else has gone through everything that threatens me, and which I was afraid of, is for me a liberation. It liberates me from my fear of fear."[82] To say it differently, Christ liberates us from anxiety about anxiety. This happens because Christ has intervened on our behalf and we have been granted "an indestructible identity in him."[83] Consequently, remembering Christ's offering of himself for our benefit and seeking deeper communion with Christ remain the key to living with anxiety.

Conclusion

The ten views of anxiety presented in this chapter do not exhaust theological perspectives on the condition. Moreover, many of these views

80. Moltmann, *Jesus Christ for Today's World*, p. 52.
81. Moltmann, *Jesus Christ for Today's World*, p. 53.
82. Moltmann, *Jesus Christ for Today's World*, p. 56.
83. Moltmann, *Jesus Christ for Today's World*, p. 56.

differ in significant ways. Nevertheless, each understands anxiety to be a condition of the soul. Each holds that anxiety relates to one's standing before God in some form or fashion, including how one understands and approaches one's finitude, freedom, and potential for sin. As such, anxiety has to do with the core of personhood, with *who one is*. But anxiety also has a great deal to do with God. This is because who one is cannot be separated from who God is. Nor can who one is be divorced from one's relationship to God. In the case of both classical Christianity and psychoanalysis, "who one is" remains foremost a condition of the soul.

I present my own understanding of anxiety beginning in Chapter 5. In preparation for that, however, I should say that I find Tillich's rubrics for thinking about anxiety, his forms of anxiety, to be helpful. I give nuance to his three forms in my own view of the condition while also adding a forth form. Nevertheless, my suggested approach to quieting the soul differs from Tillich's thinking. Looking ahead, let me state again that I view anxiety as a condition of the soul influenced by four primary concerns. The first concern involves one's beliefs and assumptions about the nature of God, meaning who God is in God's attributes, powers, and manner of being — God's character. I call this the *theo-centric* concern. The second concern follows from the sense that one's life lacks appropriate relationship to God, fidelity to God, or clarity about God's claim on him or her — in other words, one's standing before God. I call this the *theo-relational* concern. The third concern, connected to the second, follows from the sense that one's life lacks a core foundation, basis, or grounding, and thus lacks an identifiable and affirming meaning or purpose. I call this the *vocational* concern. The fourth concern follows from what modern psychology has frequently identified as the root of anxiety — namely, one's fear of death. I call this the *mortal* concern.

I want to stress here that anxiety has to do with the soul, the whole person in relationship to God. As such, the disquiet of the soul is a profoundly *spiritual* condition whose care and improvement requires perspectives and practices grounded in the Christian faith. Before taking a closer look at these perspectives and practices, we need to look through a second type of lens that provides a different point of view on anxiety. This psychological lens, utilized in the next chapter, opens unto additional conceptual frameworks that may assist pastors in ministry with disquieted souls.

Chapter 4

WHY WE ARE ANXIOUS

Three Psychological Views

Another conceptual perspective that helps pastors understand more about anxiety and enhance their ministry with disquieted souls draws on psychological views on the condition. This chapter presents three ways to think psychologically about anxiety: the psychoanalytic perspective of Sigmund Freud, the interpersonal theory of Harry Stack Sullivan, and the cognitive perspective of Aaron T. Beck and Gary Emery. Each holds value for helping pastors think more deeply about ministry with disquieted souls.

Psychoanalysis: Sigmund Freud

Modern psychology and its concern for anxiety began with Sigmund Freud. Writing in the late nineteenth century, Freud placed anxiety at the center of human motivation and experience. Claiming that anxiety lies at the core of all psychological difficulty, he sought scientific explanations for its causes and cure. The precision with which he defined anxiety varied during his career. Sometimes he distinguished sharply between anxiety and related phenomena, like fear. At other times he seemed less concerned with those distinctions and used the terms *anxiety* and *fear* interchangeably. He tended to view anxiety as an unpleasant experience associated with the kinds of symptoms that have been mentioned previously, but something that we do not understand in the sense of knowing where it comes from or what it is all about. For example, Meryl feels uneasy much of the time, George lives with a constant sense of dread, and

Wayne routinely feels nervous for much of the day, but none of them really knows what is going on or why they feel this way. Sometimes we use the phrase "free floating anxiety" to get at this quality of ambiguity associated with anxiety. An experience of fear, on the other hand, includes some understanding of what is happening, because the fear can be attached to something, to some "object." For example, June is afraid of speaking in public, Roshanda fears living alone, and Maria is frightened by certain behaviors in others. These distinctions, which Freud maintained to varying degrees, get at anxiety's uncertain and "objectless" qualities and fear's more concrete ones. Freud revised his thinking on anxiety multiple times and offered two principal theories on the condition.

In the first theory, formulated in the late 1800s, he conceptualized anxiety primarily in physiological terms, drawing an analogy to what happens in machinery that works on hydraulic energy. Hydraulics makes use of energy that comes from pressure. Working with a material that cannot be compressed past a certain point, usually some kind of fluid, hydraulic systems use pumps to pressurize material and then move that material around in order to assert pressure in particular places and, subsequently, to discharge energy. Freud likened this process to what happens within us. He initially posited that a primary instinct or "drive" energizes both our internal and our external lives. That drive is sexual in nature. Subsequently, he identified another instinct: aggression. Each operates mostly beyond our awareness, on an unconscious level. These drives for sexual and aggressive gratification are like a kind of internal energy, called libido. Though present largely outside of our conscious awareness, we exchange (discharge) this energy consciously in our feelings, thoughts, and behaviors.

At times we do not welcome this energy and its manifestations, particularly when, after becoming aware of it, we deem its ways of being exchanged unacceptable. We experience psychological conflict over what we desire and what we consider permissible. For example, becoming aware of certain sexual or aggressive feelings, thoughts, or behaviors, we regard them as immoral or otherwise unacceptable. Consequently, we respond by seeking to push back on the instincts and their energy in order to prevent its discharge. Like a hydraulic pump moving its contents around an internal chamber, we steer this unwanted energy to another place. Specifically, we push it down into our unconscious in a phenomenon that Freud called *repression*.

92

This energy does not cease to exist, however, and eventually the pressure created by moving it around has to be discharged. A hydraulic pump that moves a given amount of fluid in order to transfer energy must release the pressure that builds on its walls in that process. Otherwise, the pump or the chambers it services will explode. In a similar way, unwanted sexual and aggressive drives and their energy require that we have means for relieving the pressure that comes with repressing them. Freud initially thought that this happens through anxiety. When a person cannot discharge his sexual or aggressive energy, he becomes anxious. The symptoms of that anxiety, like those discussed in Chapter 2, essentially become means for relieving the pressure associated with it. Dealing with the symptoms, painful though they may be, poses less of a threat and less pain than attending to the anxiety itself. In his early work, Freud thought of dreams as perhaps the most significant way that we unconsciously fend off anxiety, whether those dreams are interpreted in psychoanalysis or not. The dream becomes an acceptable — if disguised — way of desiring in the face of various inhibitions that we, or others, place on those desires. This more acceptable way of desiring serves to release excess anxiety.

Let me summarize the process in Freud's first theory on anxiety. We become aware of unwanted feelings or thoughts. We do not want to act on them because, for whatever reason, we deem it wrong to do so. We therefore push these unwanted feelings back to where they came from, into our unconscious lives. In other words, we repress them. Consequently, we experience anxiety. Essentially, the anxiety becomes the force that holds the unwanted feelings or thoughts in abeyance, tucked into the unconscious life, where they need not receive our attention.

Freud was content enough with this theory for thirty years, but he eventually saw a problem with it. If we feel anxious only after we repress our unwanted feelings or thoughts, why do we repress them in the first place? In other words, what prompts us to feel the need to repress? This concern made Freud wonder whether the process he proposed actually happens in reverse fashion: We first feel anxious, and because of this we repress our unwanted feelings and their associated thoughts. In 1925 he published a second, revised theory on anxiety.[1] Having reworked his

1. Sigmund Freud, *Inhibitions, Symptoms, and Anxiety*, ed. James Strachey, trans. Alex Strachey (New York: W. W. Norton, 1959).

thinking, he claimed that anxiety is more basic than repression and actually causes it. Furthermore, he moved from a primarily physiological orientation — which involved more or less abandoning his hydraulic theory — to embrace a more psychological view of the condition that accounted for the phenomenon of repression on the one hand, and the more complex nature of mental functioning on the other.

In his revised view, Freud concluded that anxiety occurs when we feel helpless in the face of some perceived danger. This feeling of helplessness begins in infancy and is largely operative then, but it continues throughout life. In infancy we first become anxious about a number of predictable matters. We feel anxious about losing the primary caregiver. Typically this has been the mother, whom Freud called the "love object." We also feel anxious about losing what the caregiver provides. At first we associate her with provisions of food, warmth, and other comforts. But before long, as we become aware of her love and affection and what those offer us, we also grow anxious over losing them. Eventually, the locus of our anxiety expands to include threats of bodily injury, such that we become anxious about physical harm. As we mature further, interacting and forming relationships with additional significant persons in our expanding social world, anxiety may be associated with the threat of losing the appreciation of those significant persons or, worse, the threat of being punished or forsaken by them.

Experiences of anxiety in childhood become the foundation for similar experiences throughout life, as previous experiences of anxiety serve as the basis for expectations of future ones. Anxiety thus has a future orientation, just as Kierkegaard suggested. It has to do with our anticipations. As we feel threatened by something in the present, or imagine it threatening us in the future, the feelings of helplessness that we have known in past occurrences of danger are reproduced. We anticipate experiencing the same kind of danger and helplessness that we have known before, and we expect not to have the resources to fend it off. Anxiety thus becomes a "signal for help" in the face of a new danger, one that we associate with a previous danger and one over which we sense a lack of power. Adding this quality of future orientation to his theory of anxiety allowed Freud to account for "such phenomena as apprehension, dread, or the sense of impending doom," which most anxious persons confirm experiencing and which Freud's first theory of anxiety could not account for.[2]

In his revised theory, Freud essentially maintained the distinction between anxiety and fear, the latter being tied to an identifiable object and the former having qualities of "indefiniteness and lack of an object." But in distinguishing between three kinds of anxiety (real, neurotic, and moral or social), he pointed to the close relationship between anxiety and fear. *Real anxiety* is essentially fear. It centers on something known, like a threat coming from an external object: a particular person, a snake, a hurricane, or a situation like asking one's boss for a raise. *Neurotic anxiety,* on the other hand, fixes on something unknown and in need of discovery. Freud claimed that psychoanalysis indicates that neurotic anxiety has to do with a threat tied to an internal instinctual demand: a desire for a sexual affair, vying for inappropriate control in a relationship, or lying to advance one's status in the community or workplace. The third type of anxiety, *moral or social anxiety,* has to do with one's conscience and the social expectations that inform it. We keep this anxiety "concealed" from awareness as much as possible. We do that by adhering to moral and social customs and expectations on the one hand, and by avoiding (repressing) or at least regulating through inhibitions whatever urges, thoughts, or behaviors we deem unacceptable or otherwise taboo on the other. These three types of anxiety, while distinct, are not mutually exclusive. They may actually dovetail with one another, so that an anxious person may have anxiety tied to any or all of these at the same time.

For our purposes, the primary thing to remember is that Freud believed that anxiety holds a central place in both our internal and our external lives. It stems from perceiving that we face a dangerous situation that threatens us and our well-being. Whether this threat is of a physical, emotional, relational, social, or economic nature, or whether it is tied to some other facet of our lives, we become anxious principally because we feel powerless to stand up to the threat and fend off its potential harm. Moreover, because early anxiety experiences shape our assumptions about future ones, psychologically speaking those early ex-

2. Barry E. Wolfe, *Understanding and Treating Anxiety Disorders: An Integrative Approach to Healing the Wounded Self* (Washington, D.C.: American Psychological Association, 2005), pp. 26-27.

periences become a kind of prototype for subsequent ones later in life. To treat anxiety, we seek to create a psychological space that allows a person to explore, identify, and work out the roots of his anxiety in safety, without any threats — such as disapproval and judgment — to his well-being. Deeper awareness of his own anxiety, including its causes and manifestations, becomes the means for keeping it in check. This includes understanding it, recognizing its presence and power, and working out ways to live with it to minimize its harmful effects. For Freud, psychoanalysis provides the best means for meeting these treatment goals.

Interpersonal Theory: Harry Stack Sullivan

Best known for his interpersonal theory of psychiatry, developed in the early to mid-twentieth century, Harry Stack Sullivan claimed anxiety as the most important factor for how one experiences the world and how one's personality develops. Though greatly influenced by Freud and indebted to him, the two men differed in their thinking and clinical approaches. Throughout his career Freud focused first and foremost on the individual person's inner world, particularly its instinctual impulses, wishes, and fantasies, and how that world influenced psychological and relational health. Sullivan did not discount the inner world or its impact, but he held that what goes on there plays a smaller part in a larger phenomenon. He contended that individuals and their inner world cannot be separated from their interpersonal engagement with others in the social world. Drawing particularly from social-psychological concepts, he claimed that, by and large, our personality forms *as* we engage interpersonally with others.

In early life, parents or primary caregivers play the most significant role in our lives and provide the most influential interactions.[3] As the individual develops, other significant persons enter the picture and make their own impact on the individual's psychological development.

---

3. Sullivan, as was true of almost every psychoanalytic thinker of the time, referred to the "mother" when talking about the most significant person in relationship to an infant. While upholding the unique qualities of motherhood, he would have accepted the alternate language of "primary caregiver," "maternal figure," and the "parent" who provides adequate care.

Sullivan thought that Freud placed too much emphasis on the individual emotional life as somehow self-contained and isolated, largely cut off from the effects of sociality. For Freud, what matters most is how one negotiates living with internal drives and their effects. Sullivan recognizes the importance of the drives, but he thinks that Freud fails to account for the central role that living in an "interpersonal field" plays in who we are, including our personality, how we experience the world, how we feel, and our overall emotional and psychological state.

Living with significant persons in an interpersonal field by itself does not guarantee psychological well-being. We all live and interact interpersonally to some degree from the earliest moments of life. Most important for Sullivan is the kind of *communication* that takes place between persons. Communication between infants and their parents in the early years remains most significant. But also significant is the interpersonal communication over the entire course of life. Managing innate urges from our internal life plays a role, just as Freud suggested, but Sullivan insists that interpersonal relationships and communication shape us more than anything else. In a real sense, these make us who we are and who we become.

Several assumptions guide Sullivan's work. He assumes first that the human personality forms by virtue of how it interacts (communicates) with significant others. By this he means how we relate to each other, making our needs known and responding to others in kind. In fact, he defines personality as "the relatively enduring pattern of recurrent interpersonal situations which characterize a human life."[4] Much of mental stress and disorder follows from inadequate communication between human beings, particularly in our early years but also throughout our life span. Sullivan's second assumption is that anxiety is what gets in the way. It interferes with communication. The more anxious we become, the less appropriately we communicate. Third, Sullivan assumes that individuals in relationship each contribute a portion to the shared interpersonal field. This means that interactions (communications) between two or more persons affect, and are affected by, each individual.[5] We

---

4. Harry Stack Sullivan, *The Interpersonal Theory of Psychiatry*, ed. Helen Swick Perry and Mary Ladd Gawel, Introduction by Mabel Blake Cohen, M.D. (New York: W. W. Norton, 1953), pp. 110-11.

5. Sullivan, *The Interpersonal Theory of Psychiatry*, pp. xi-xviii.

readily observe this type of interactive relationship between anxious persons and their close associates, in that the anxiety of the former tends to raise the same in the latter.

Two additional concepts central to Sullivan's thoughts on anxiety include "tensions" and "integrating tendencies."[6] Tensions describe the feelings associated with having needs. Sullivan believed that, from the earliest moments of life, human beings move between a condition of essential comfort on the one hand, and some kind of need (discomfort) on the other. A baby, for example, moves between feeling full and feeling hungry, being dry and being wet, being rested and being tired. A baby also alternates between feeling relatively pain-free and feeling irritated (teething is a good example), feeling connected and feeling disconnected (being held or being left alone), and being stimulated and being uninspired (as in the case of play).

Tensions arise when the baby experiences a need that requires attention. The need calls for some kind of response on the part of the parent. As long as the parent responds adequately, he or she supplies the need and reduces the tension associated with it. This reduction in tension provides satisfaction and returns the baby to a more or less comfortable state. In these cases, the baby and the caregiver are communicating well. Sullivan calls a person's needs and the associated tensions "integrating tendencies." Both natural and necessary, they serve to draw individuals together, to integrate them in reciprocally beneficial ways.

These integrating tendencies promote the kinds of interpersonal exchanges required for proper communication and satisfying lives. Although our needs change to some extent as we mature, basic human needs remain with us across our life span. These include the need for food, warmth, touch, sexual gratification, security, feeling loved and important, and engaging in meaningful relationships and creative endeavors. Throughout our lives, we meet these needs through interpersonal means. Engaging in an interpersonal dance, moving back and forth between needing from others and meeting others' needs, remains necessary for healthy personhood.

6. For helpful commentary on these concepts, see Stephen A. Mitchell and Margaret J. Black, *Freud and Beyond: A History of Modern Psychoanalytic Thought* (New York: Basic Books, 1995), pp. 66-67.

So how does anxiety come into play? Sullivan agrees with the general distinction between fear and anxiety, locating the former in some identifiable, concrete source and the latter in an indefinite one. His distinct claim is that anxiety does not arise within us per se, but rather that it comes upon us from outside, as a condition in our interpersonal field. Specifically, anxiety stems from a breakdown in communication between two persons and a corresponding failure to attend adequately to one or the other's experiences of tension. Anxiety begins in infancy as the child begins to pick up on his caregiver's "emotional disturbances."[7] By this Sullivan means anything that alters the caregiver's responsive interactions with the infant and prevents tending to his states of tension appropriately. If, for example, the mother feels sad, angry, bored, preoccupied, or negatively excited, she may not respond adequately to the infant's needs. Consequently, the infant "catches" the emotional disturbance and becomes anxious himself.

Sullivan uses the term *empathy* to describe how this phenomenon occurs. In a sense, the infant internalizes the mother's state as he empathizes with it. Sullivan quickly notes the difficulty in defining this term more specifically. He suggests, therefore, that we should focus less on *how* the infant takes in the disturbances and becomes anxious and focus more on the fact that this routinely happens.

The process of becoming anxious unfolds as follows.[8] The child senses in his caregiver that something is wrong. He then experiences some sort of tension that requires relief. Feeling uncomfortable, similar to when hungry, wet, or tired, he looks to the caregiver to help him feel comfortable again. However, while the caregiver can satisfy these physical needs, in this emotional situation the anxious caregiver cannot satisfy the infant's need for comfort. In fact, the more responsive she seeks to be in her offers of care, the closer she brings her anxiety to him. This closer proximity to the caregiver's anxiety tends to make the infant even more upset, which increases the caregiver's anxiety and its effects.

Whether this linkage is accurate or not, the child eventually associates the caregiver's anxiety with himself. He assumes that it somehow relates to him. Rather than primarily seeking satisfaction, as he does

---

7. Sullivan, *The Interpersonal Theory of Psychiatry*, pp. 8-10.
8. See Mitchell and Black, *Freud and Beyond*, pp. 68-69.

when hungry, wet, or tired, in the face of anxiety what he seeks foremost is security. This need for security leads to the formation of what Sullivan calls the "self-system," which may be thought of as "an organization of educative experience called into being by the necessity to avoid or to minimize incidents of anxiety."[9] The self-system regulates behavior. The child who senses the caregiver's anxiety increasingly acts in ways to curtail that anxiety, which has the effect of curbing his own corresponding feelings of insecurity. He seeks others' approval, which makes him feel secure and at ease, and he avoids disapproval, which tends to prompt anxiety. Over time, he becomes the person that significant figures in his life, and especially his parents, want and need him to be. Why? As he becomes what others want him to be, he gains their approval, relieves their anxiety, and thereby minimizes his own. Sullivan's claim is that anxiety, more than anything else, shapes the child's emerging self.

Sullivan stated explicitly that he offered no "last word" on anxiety. He expected that his theory would be expanded and enriched. While that has occurred, the core of his reflections remains useful, both for thinking about anxiety and for working to relieve it. For Sullivan, anxiety is not merely a personal condition, one generated in isolation from within, but rather a deeply interpersonal one that centers on how human beings in relationship express and attend to one another's deepest needs. The extent to which we "catch" anxiety in infancy has lasting effects, as the same dynamic process tends to reoccur throughout life. Specifically, we continue to feel anxious when we perceive anxiety in significant others, those who, like parents, provide things that satisfy us and keep us secure. Regardless of our age, the need for approval remains at the center of our interactions with significant others. When we sense their approval, we feel secure (non-anxious). When we sense their disapproval, we feel insecure (anxious). For that reason, anxiety shapes us throughout life.

So what can an anxious person do? How does a caregiver foster anxiety's relief? Similar to Freud, Sullivan placed great importance on helping anxious persons explore the causes of their anxiety, identifying when they first recall feeling that way, who was involved, and what exactly took place. Unlike Freud, however, who typically refrained from

---

9. Sullivan, *The Interpersonal Theory of Psychiatry*, p. 165.

asking questions of his patients and instead worked with their "free associations," Sullivan thought it essential to ask many exploratory questions in order to bring out as much detail as possible.[10] Furthermore, Sullivan focused not simply on understanding anxiety's roots and manifestations, but particularly on what he called "security operations." These include the various behaviors that anxious persons engage in to attempt to relieve their anxiety. Anxiety-reducing behaviors are regulated by the self-system, which has learned to order conduct in ways that meet others' expectations. Meeting their expectations minimizes their anxiety and, consequently, helps to prevent one's own. Sullivan thought that relieving anxiety requires altering these security operations because they reinforce the anxiety they presume to keep at bay. Only by altering them or removing them is the anxiety exposed long enough so that it can be worked with. By this I mean fully understanding it, recognizing its various manifestations, and ultimately finding the courage to "confront" it.

Confronting anxiety requires openness to reworking the self-system and its associated responses to others' expectations. Sullivan advocated that analysts nurture anxious persons interpersonally to help them feel secure. This nurture happens through close, intentional listening and a demonstrated respect for the person's experience. Sullivan called this therapeutic stance one of "respectful seriousness." One Sullivan commentator described its significance this way: "The client's experience of the psychotherapist's respect for, interest in, and knowledge of his or her problems in living provided a core security in which the client could elaborate and evaluate increasingly more anxiety-ridden interpersonal assumptions, confusions, and inadequacies as well as reveal and correct these difficulties in a here-and-now relationship."[11]

Respectful seriousness serves as the "necessary pre-condition" for interpersonal learning or, in the case of anxious persons, needed relearning. Sullivan was convinced that we learn to be anxious by virtue of interpersonal patterns that we encounter and adopt. In the case of anxiety, we adopt patterns based on false assumptions about others, ourselves, or both. Creating a safe space that results in a newfound core security al-

10. Mitchell and Black, *Freud and Beyond*, pp. 71-74.
11. F. Barton Evan III, *Harry Stack Sullivan: Interpersonal Theory and Psychotherapy* (London: Routledge, 1996), p. 166.

lows anxious persons to revisit these patterns and their associated qualities in a nonthreatening environment, outside the dangers of judgment, rejection, and abandonment by significant others. Among other things, this revisiting allows anxious persons to build their self-esteem, which anxiety inevitably compromises. This revisiting also provides a psychological space wherein new interpersonal patterns, which have less anxious qualities, may be considered, tested, and adopted.

A Cognitive Perspective: Aaron T. Beck and Gary Emery

Psychiatrist Aaron T. Beck has proposed a different way of thinking about and working with anxiety. Drawing from his work with depressed patients, in the late 1960s he asserted that emotional problems are closely related to how one thinks and believes. He had noticed that depressed persons tend to operate out of particular kinds of patterns in their thinking. These involve negative assumptions and beliefs about themselves, including their worth, their abilities, and their achievements. Beck viewed these negative patterns as erroneous, because they did not accurately reflect his patients' lives. He suggested that depressed persons need to become aware of their cognitive patterns, which he would also call "schemas" and "sets," and then need to learn how to discard them and replace them with new cognitive patterns. This latter process happens as one identifies and internalizes new ways of thinking that are less distorted and more positive in nature, so that one organizes and deals with one's experiences less anxiously. What Beck would eventually term "cognitive therapy" provides the opportunity for meeting these needs having to do with one's cognitive patterns.

Beck applied this concept of cognitive schemas and their effects on emotions to the problem of anxiety. He was quick to point out that, at a basic biological level, some measure of anxiety likely serves an adaptive purpose — namely, to sustain life. To a degree, then, anxiety's symptoms provide a protective function as they warn us about potential dangers that may harm us, which led Beck to suggest that "the cost of survival of the lineage may be a lifetime of discomfort."[12] Even so, Beck

12. Aaron T. Beck and Gary Emery, *Anxiety Disorders and Phobias: A Cognitive Perspective* (New York: Basic Books, 1985), p. 4.

recognized too that excessive or maladaptive anxiety brings with it a great deal of pain and poses many problems for daily living. He believed, therefore, that we need to find ways to minimize anxiety's severity and effects.

Beck concurs with Freud and Sullivan in recognizing the close relationship between anxiety and fear. However, Beck suggests a different way of understanding this relationship. Specifically, he describes anxiety as a "fear episode," claiming that fear involves an "appraisal" of a dangerous situation. The process of appraisal begins as something or someone threatening enters into our awareness. We then immediately evaluate just how much of a threat the person or situation poses, and consider what kinds of resources we have to fend it off. This process suggests that fear involves a cognitive process. We have to *think* about the danger (threatening stimulus) lurking in our midst. When we deem the threat to be sufficiently high, an assessment that involves the belief that we do not have the resources to fend off the threat, our fear gives rise to anxiety, which is the emotional process or "feeling state" that follows from being afraid. This means that thinking about what we deem as threatening (our fear) precedes feeling anxious about it. In more technical terms, fear's cognitive component gives rise to its affective one — namely, anxiety.

To give an example of how anxiety unfolds, Beck cites the experience of a forty-year-old man who goes snow-skiing and experiences physical symptoms that he attributes to a heart attack.[13] These include perspiring heavily, experiencing shortness of breath, feeling faint, and feeling cold and weak. The man has to be removed from the ski slope by stretcher and taken to the hospital, where doctors discover no physical problem and attribute his experience to an acute panic attack. Beck says that the reason this man had such a powerful anxiety episode has to do with the role that his thoughts and related imagery played in this experience. As it turns out, not only are his physical symptoms common among those exercising at higher altitudes than they typically do, but this very man had experienced these same physical sensations on previous ski trips without difficulty. What he felt physically in this latest episode was nothing new. The difference was that before leaving for this present trip, the man had a recurring thought about what would

13. Beck and Emery, *Anxiety Disorders and Phobias*, pp. 4-5.

happen if he had a heart attack on the slope: "It would be almost impossible for me to get emergency care." Accordingly, when the man went skiing and experienced the above-described physical sensations, his "cognitive set" informed his response to those sensations. He thought, "I must be having a heart attack. . . . This is what it's like to be dying." He also imagined himself lying in a hospital bed, surrounded by physicians, wearing an oxygen mask, and being administered intravenous drugs. Each time he invoked this image, and each time he thought about his experience in these terms, his symptoms increased.

Working with this man in therapy, Beck discovered something further. The man had become concerned about having a heart attack several weeks before the ski-slope incident, just after his brother, who was ten years older, died of a heart-related problem. Beck surmised that because the man had been *thinking* about his brother's death, and the possibility that the same thing could happen to him, he had in place a particular cognitive pattern. As a result, when he experienced his physical symptoms, he *thought* that his great fear had been realized. He thought that he was in fact having a heart attack, and then he *imagined* himself lying in the hospital and receiving care.

Beck concluded that our thoughts follow largely from the cognitive sets that we have in place and operate with, so that the content of these sets actually influences the kinds of thoughts that we have. Furthermore, the thoughts informed by our cognitive sets come automatically — that is, involuntarily — and they subsequently provoke the emotions or affective states associated with them. This means that the way we *think* about what we experience, including how we process information and consider matters associated with relationships and life events, actually determines how we *feel* about them. Using our previous example, the skier's cognitive set consisted of thoughts that were tied to fears about his brother's recent heart attack and death, and also fears about suffering a similar fate himself. Consequently, after he experienced the physical symptoms on the ski slope, a cognitive alarm sounded. He automatically thought that he was having a heart attack, that he might be stranded on the mountain, and that he would ultimately die. That prompted his acute anxiety, which worsened as he dwelled on his symptoms and fears, and as he imagined what it would be like to lie in a hospital bed, presumably hanging precariously onto life.

Ordering the fear and anxiety processes in this way leads Beck to make additional claims. One is that fear typically has a future orientation. Fear centers on a situation or circumstance that may occur at some point in the future, and we tend to become more fearful the closer in time we get to what frightens us. This differs from Freud's and Sullivan's views, which attribute a future orientation to anxiety and a more immediate orientation to fear. Beck also claims that distinguishing between realistic and unrealistic anxiety, or rational and irrational anxiety, as Freud and others have, proves both illogical and unhelpful. As Beck puts it, "It is illogical to qualify an emotion or feeling state with adjectives . . . that are usually applied to ideas or concepts." He agrees that we may describe the qualities of *fear* in this way, as fears can indeed be rational or irrational: "A fear is realistic if based on a sensible assumption, logic, and reasoning, and objective observation. It is unrealistic if based on fallacious assumptions and faulty reasoning and is contrary to observation." Not so with anxiety. Anxiety refers to an emotional (affective) response, not to a (cognitive) "process of evaluating reality."[14]

Another of Beck's central claims has to do with the common practice of confusing the symptom (anxiety) with the cause (fear). We tend to think of anxiety as "the problem," and we seek to alleviate it by addressing it directly. This poses difficulty because "the main problem . . . is not in the generation of anxiety but in the overactive cognitive patterns (schemas) relevant to danger that are continually structuring external and/or internal experiences as a sign of danger."[15] Since anxiety is the response to a problem (fear of perceived danger), as opposed to the cause of it, we should not focus our efforts on anxiety itself. Rather, we should focus on identifying, understanding, and striving to diminish or alleviate the fear that prompts the anxiety response, and also on working on the manner in which the anxious person appraises the fear that eventuates in anxiety.

A related claim centers on the distinction between emotions and behaviors. Beck maintains that conceptual clarity between these terms remains necessary, for while they often go hand in hand, they are not mutually dependent: "It is possible to activate one system without the

---

14. Beck and Emery, *Anxiety Disorders and Phobias*, p. 10.
15. Beck and Emery, *Anxiety Disorders and Phobias*, p. 15.

other."[16] One may behave anxiously and not feel anxious. Or one may feel anxious but find a way not to demonstrate that in one's behavior. Beck cites the example of an actor. He may exhibit behaviors consistent with anxiety, including shortness of breath, wringing of hands, pacing back and forth, and quick or stammered speech, but he may not *feel* anxious at all. Conversely, he may feel quite anxious and yet still be able to keep his feelings "inside" and out of others' awareness through his behaviors. Beck concludes that we do not have direct access to another person's emotions, but can only "infer" the emotion as we observe the behavior.[17]

The relationship between emotions and behaviors unfolds like this. When a person faces a situation that she deems dangerous, she becomes anxious. The anxiety then "feeds back into the cognitive system and, consequently, enhances the decision to prepare for defensive action."[18] This suggests that anxiety (how one feels emotionally) does not lead directly to any particular behavioral response. Rather, anxiety (what is felt) has to be *thought of* again (appraised) in the cognitive process, so that one may decide how to respond behaviorally. While making this distinction may seem picayune, Beck points it out because, again, he wants to make a case for anxiety as fundamentally a cognitive process, or thinking disorder.

Beck claims further that an experience of vulnerability lies at anxiety's core. I have alluded to this already, in the context of saying that anxiety stems from a perceived dangerous situation that we feel ill-prepared to fend off. Beck uses the term *vulnerability* to describe the base experience or condition that subsequently leads to a variety of responses, what he calls "dysfunctional cognitive processes." He defines vulnerability as "a person's perception of himself as subject to internal or external dangers over which his control is lacking or is insufficient to afford him a sense of safety."[19] This vulnerability prompts at least six related responses — dysfunctional cognitive processes — that tie into anxiety.

One response, *minimization,* involves underestimating our personal resources and their power to overcome the perceived danger. Using the

16. Beck and Emery, *Anxiety Disorders and Phobias,* p. 45.
17. Beck and Emery, *Anxiety Disorders and Phobias,* p. 45.
18. Beck and Emery, *Anxiety Disorders and Phobias,* p. 46.
19. Beck and Emery, *Anxiety Disorders and Phobias,* p. 68.

previous example, the man on the ski slope overlooked his overall good health, athleticism, and ability to exercise at high altitude, which had been confirmed on previous ski outings. Another response, closely related, is *selective abstraction*. This has to do with focusing intently on our weaknesses or perceived lack of resources. We can imagine that as the skier began to feel physical sensations that he associated with a heart condition, he focused on a medical concern that he had experienced before, even if it had nothing to do with his heart. Or he may have abstracted from his being the brother of a man who recently died of a heart condition, saying to himself, "It happened to him while he exercised, and we're siblings, so it must be happening to me." Another, closely related response to vulnerability is *magnification*. This involves amplifying our concern and its presumed effects. To say it another way, we make mountains out of molehills. The skier seems to have magnified his experience. Because he felt so vulnerable, he mistook what were relatively minor physical sensations as an indication of something more serious, and that led to exaggerating his symptoms. Another response, *catastrophizing*, involves the assumption that a worst-case scenario will follow. While on the slope, the skier interpreted what was happening to him in terms of what he most feared and thought the worst: "I'm going to die."

Other related responses include *selective recall* and *thinking in absolute terms*. Selective recall describes the tendency to draw on negative or threatening past experiences and to assume that these are indicative of a current experience, rather than considering more positive or affirming past experiences when interpreting a present situation. Thinking in absolute terms involves judging a situation as either all bad or all good: "Either I'm having a heart attack and dying, or nothing is wrong."

Beck recognizes how little influence positive or successful past experiences with fear or concern can have on present ones for a person with a dysfunctional cognitive set. He notes, "Even large successes in the past may have no permanent effect because the 'vulnerable' person believes that he can always slip in the future, and that the consequences of the slip will be far more drastic than any success could be. He apparently has greater access to negative memories of previous performances than to positive ones."[20]

20. Beck and Emery, *Anxiety Disorders and Phobias*, p. 68.

Beck recognizes too that the tendency to minimize successes and dwell on failures or deficiencies inevitably has a negative impact on a person's self-confidence, which Beck defines as "the individual's positive appraisal of his assets and resources in order to master problems and deal with threats." The "vulnerability" cognitive set replaces the "self-confidence" set. A lack of self-confidence eventuates in "self-doubt," which perpetuates a "stream of negative ideation" and thus fosters ongoing negative responses in the face of perceived dangers and difficulties.[21]

Another of Beck's principal claims that bears mentioning here has to do with what must happen to relieve anxiety, which derives from the kinds of cognitive dysfunctions just mentioned. Relieving anxiety requires learning how to think, to imagine, and thus to feel differently than one thinks, imagines, and feels when in the throes of an anxiety-producing experience. To those ends, Gary Emery applies Beck's principles of cognitive therapy to anxiety disorders, claiming that relieving anxiety requires "cognitive restructuring." At base this involves an educative process focusing on five matters: (1) enhancing self-awareness; (2) modifying negative imagery, which involves replacing it with more positive and presumably realistic imagery; (3) modifying the affective component tied to anxiety (how it feels), so that when one becomes anxious, one experiences one's anxiety differently — meaning less severely — than before; (4) modifying the behavioral component tied to anxiety, which tends to involve avoiding anxiety-producing situations, persons, and other matters; and (5) restructuring one's assumptions concerning three major life issues: acceptance, competence, and control.[22]

The most extensive discussion of my remaining considerations pertains to the first of these matters, enhancing self-awareness, and how this changes not only how and what we think but also how we feel. Enhancing self-awareness garners most of my attention for two important reasons. First, cognitive restructuring begins with and largely resides in this capacity. If anxiety is rooted in a thinking disorder, one relieves anxiety by learning to think differently; and in order to think differently, one must become as aware as possible of one's thoughts.

---

21. Beck and Emery, *Anxiety Disorders and Phobias,* pp. 68, 70.

22. Gary Emery devotes a chapter to each one of these facets of cognitive restructuring. See Beck and Emery, *Anxiety Disorders and Phobias,* Part II, pp. 167-322.

Second, typical pastors, by which I mean those without specialized or advanced training in counseling or therapy, may assist parishioners with enhancing their self-awareness in their standard ministry practice.

Enhancing Self-Awareness

Cognitive therapy with anxiety-related concerns usually begins with helping an anxious person become as aware of himself as possible, particularly his thought processes. While this may also occur outside of therapy, and should, the therapist plays a particularly important role in educating the client on several matters. Cognitive therapy as a whole grows out of an educational model. A focus of this model is how to enhance a client's ability first to identify his thoughts and then to "catch" them as early as possible in his cognitive process. Catching his thoughts involves examining them more closely and, when needed, altering them. Of particular concern are thoughts in his chain of automatic thinking that lead him to feel anxious.

For example, a person may get overly anxious when he hears a siren in the distance. Maybe this occurs while he is at work, or perhaps while he is visiting someone across town from his home. He thinks, "I hear a siren." But because he is an anxious person, it does not stop there. He begins a string of linked automatic thoughts, so that he also thinks the following: "That sounds like a fire truck. It must be on the way to a fire. It sounds awfully close to my neighborhood. It must be in my neighborhood. I bet I didn't turn the iron off before I left. That must have caught on fire. My house is on fire. The fire truck must be on its way to my house. My wife and children are there. They must be in danger. They're going to be harmed." This scenario illustrates a fairly typical pattern of automatic thinking associated with anxiety. An initial thought leads to a series of others, seemingly automatically. Again, these thoughts follow from the type of cognitive set with which a person operates.

A therapist utilizing a cognitive approach would seek to help this anxious man become aware of his thought processes, including his chain of thinking. Specifically, the therapist would seek to play a supportive and educative role in helping the man discover how he gets from "I hear a siren" to "My family is going to be harmed." The thera-

pist would focus particular attention on how this man can learn to recognize his automatic thinking immediately, early in the linking
thought chain. The primary therapeutic goal, which typically requires
a multiple-step process, would involve the following:

1. *Helping him become aware of his thought process as early in the chain as
   possible.* "I'm beginning an anxiety-producing way of thinking."
2. *Helping him learn to catch himself in this thought process.* "It's very, very
   unlikely that the fire truck is going to my house. I'm very good
   about making sure the iron is unplugged. There's probably nothing wrong."
3. *Helping him discover ways to stop the automatic thinking process.* "I actually remember turning the iron off, and, in any case, if my wife
   smelled something burning, she'd know how get herself and the
   kids outside quickly. They're fine."
4. *Helping him learn to substitute in his cognitive set certain positive, calming
   thoughts for the currently prevailing, more negative and anxiety-laden
   ones.* "The siren may not have been a fire truck's — it probably
   wasn't. If it was, then I know that comparatively few homes catch
   on fire, and in the cases of those that do, even fewer of those fires
   result in harm to people. Everything's very likely okay at my house.
   I hope that no one else's house is burning, and that no one else is
   in any danger."

For the client, learning to observe how he thinks, and also how his
thoughts link together in a patterned form that eventuates in an anxiety response, is a necessary first step for learning to react differently to
his thoughts when they arise and thus to stop the linking chain of automatic thinking.

The therapist may use a variety of techniques to encourage this enhanced self-awareness about thought processes.[23] One involves asking
a client about her fears and then writing down her responses so that
both she and the therapist may observe her thoughts, analyze them (including how different thoughts may easily link together), and then
work together to help her gain more cognitive and emotional distance
from them. Another exercise involves having the client complete a se-

---

23. See Beck and Emery, *Anxiety Disorders and Phobias*, pp. 190-209.

ries of sentences and then looking for particular patterns that emerge, including memory associations. Emery offers these examples: "Being rejected would mean . . ." and "Making a fool of myself would mean. . . ." Through enhanced self-awareness, the client may learn to place his thoughts and thinking processes "beyond" himself. He may externalize them, in a sense, so that he examines them more closely and, perhaps, differently. This process allows for appropriate emotional distancing in that the client's thoughts and related feelings do not have to pervade his inner life in the same way, or to the same degree, as before. Emotional distancing may serve to quiet the soul.

At the core of this approach that places so much emphasis on enhancing self-awareness is the view that anxious persons tend to operate from cognitive sets with "faulty ideas and logic." Emery provides fifteen questions that cognitive therapists may make use of, and teach clients to use as well, to examine and gauge their ideas and logic. I will not list them all, for some of them center on matters that take us well beyond the scope of what a typical pastor will have the time and know-how to provide. However, I will describe what Emery terms "three basic approaches" that, in making use of three broad questions, essentially capture the gist of the fifteen questions he offers. The three questions are these: (1) "What's the evidence?" (2) "What's another way of looking at the situation?" and (3) "So what if it happens?" Emery notes that some clients may respond more easily to one question or another, but that every client needs to develop an ability to make use of each one.[24]

The man who hears the siren and quickly assumes that his family is in harm's way would need to learn to ask himself first, "What's the evidence for assuming it's a fire truck, that it's responding to a fire as opposed to something else, and that it's heading toward my neighborhood?" He needs to ask these questions too: "What's the evidence that if a house is on fire in my neighborhood, it will be my house? Why should I think it's my house when I remember turning the iron off? And even if my house was on fire, why would I think that my wife and children would be harmed when my wife knows full well how to get out of the house if necessary?" These and other self-questions like them give this man a way to examine the logic of his initial (automatic) thinking. They also help him mitigate his tendency to engage in

24. Beck and Emery, *Anxiety Disorders and Phobias,* p. 201.

minimization, selective abstraction, magnification, catastrophizing, selective recall, and "absolute" thinking.

A second approach to examining and gauging ideas and logic would entail the man asking himself, "What's another way of looking at the situation?" or "What's a different, perhaps more likely scenario?" These questions seek to expand one's operative cognitive set, challenging it by means of considering possible scenarios (which include thoughts and images) that lie beyond it. The man in our example may be helped to expand his operative cognitive set as he considers the following: "It may be a fire truck on its way to something other than a house fire." "It may actually be a police car or an ambulance, and not a fire truck." "Even if it's any of those, it's much more likely than not that, first, nothing catastrophic has happened and, second, that my family is not involved." Of course, considering this latter response, "my family is likely not involved," does not suggest that we want to help ourselves feel better at another's expense — "As long as it's not my family, all is well." Nevertheless, most anxious persons feel better when they find ways of working through alternative scenarios that do not, in the end, pertain to what they fear most.

A third approach to restructuring thinking by examining and gauging ideas and logic involves pondering the question "So what if the scenario that I'm anxious about actually happens?" Here we entertain a worst-case scenario. We do so for two primary purposes: first, to foster "decatastrophizing" the envisioned course of events, which are so anxiety-laden; and second, to imagine, painful though that may be, how we would cope with a worst-case scenario if, in fact, it came to pass. The goal here really centers on helping one to face one's greatest fear — namely, that what one has such anxiety about will in fact happen. To the extent that we avoid our fears, they tend to grow more powerful. On the other hand, imagining what life would be like if what we fear were to come about, painful though that may be, paradoxically leads to reducing its power over us. In our example, the man would likely find it extremely difficult to imagine what it would be like if his worst fear — his family perishing in a house fire — came to pass. But cognitive therapy principles hold that doing so, for any amount of time, may help to lessen that scenario's grip on him. Other cases of anxiety, like those that involve public speaking, losing one's job, being rejected by another person, or perhaps being passed over for a promotion, may prove to be better situations for using this third approach. Different people with different anxiety-related concerns may call more for one of these approaches than the others. Nevertheless, according to Emery, it is most helpful if anxious persons make use of each of these approaches, and they should be encouraged to do so to the best of their abilities.

Emery claims further that an approach called "point/counterpoint" may provide the same benefits as the "So what if it happens" question.[25] This "point/counterpoint" approach involves the therapist and the client working collaboratively to refute the client's anxiety-laden thinking. The approach consists of the therapist offering up fearful ideas (point) that the client then refutes (counterpoint). When the client runs out of responses, the two change roles, and the therapist offers the counterpoints. This strategy tends to focus on four basic concerns: the feared event's likelihood or probability; its degree of awfulness or horror; the person's ability to prevent it from occurring; and the person's ability to accept and deal with the worst-case scenario.[26]

Although enhancing self-awareness and understanding its role in changing both how and what we feel will receive much of our focus, I want to comment briefly on the remaining four matters that cognitive therapy attends to in support of cognitive restructuring. This overall cognitive approach to anxiety and its relief will inform my claims about how various faith practices serve to quiet the soul. Faith practices do this as they restructure one's operative cognitive set and alter related imagery, feelings, behaviors, and assumptions.

Modifying Negative Imagery

Another component of this cognitive approach to changing how one thinks and feels focuses on imagery associated with anxiety. Although the roots of anxiety lie in one's thoughts, various stimuli inform one's thinking. How and what one sees, hears, touches, smells, or tastes may relate closely to an experience of anxiety. Recall the man who heard a siren. It was only after he heard something that he began to think anxious thoughts about his family's well-being.

Presumably, not only did this man think about his home being on

25. Beck and Emery, *Anxiety Disorders and Phobias,* p. 209.
26. Beck and Emery, *Anxiety Disorders and Phobias,* p. 209.

fire and his family being inside, but he also *visualized* it to some degree. He could "see" it happening. This would not be unusual. Many anxious persons report having visualized scenarios that cause them to feel anxious. They "see" themselves in a particular situation, relationship, or set of uneasy circumstances, and that leads them to respond as if what they see is actually taking place. As Emery points out, "Numerous clinical observations suggest that a person visualizing a scene may react as though it were actually occurring."[27] These fantasies can be quite powerful and distressing.

Anxiety thus has to do not only with what we think but also with what we *imagine*. The man who hears the siren begins a process in which his imagination runs wild, so much so that he reacts as though a fire truck has headed to his home and his family faces grave danger. Cognitive therapy seeks to help modify the *imagery* associated with fantasies in ways similar to those it uses to modify *thoughts* that lead to anxiety. Specifically, in cognitive therapy we attempt to modify the imagery associated with what anxious persons think and imagine, replacing unrealistic, harmful, and anxiety-laden images with more realistic, helpful, and calming ones.

A variety of strategies and techniques used in a therapeutic context lend themselves to helping facilitate this altering of imagery. Beck and Emery detail them in their book. I want to comment on three strategies that pastors may use, easily and regularly, in their ministry with disquieted souls: the "turn-off technique," "repetition," and "substituting contrasting imagery."

One way to modify imagery is to "turn it off." This involves training the anxious person to obstruct a fantasy currently unfolding by increasing "sensory input." Examples that Emery cites include blowing a whistle, ringing a cowbell, clapping one's hands, or giving one's attention to something constructive. A cognitive therapist will have a client use this strategy when he first becomes aware that he is awash in anxiety-laden images and fantasies. Essentially, "turning off" interrupts the imaginative process, including its associated chain of thinking, by interjecting something that jars the anxious person and his reality. The ability to interrupt the imaginative process gives him a sense of power and control over it. If the man who hears a siren catches himself progressing toward "My family is in grave danger," he may blow a whis-

---

27. Beck and Emery, *Anxiety Disorders and Phobias,* p. 210.

tle to jar his reality, "turning off" the cognitive chain and its associated images. Even a very brief jarring tends to have the effect of significantly altering the operative imagery.

Another technique for altering imagery entails articulating over and over again the fantasy with which the imagery is associated. This *repetition* may be done in the context of therapy, of course, but one may also do this exercise alone. If possible, this "self-talk" should involve speaking out loud, so that one may audibly hear oneself say what one is experiencing. This has the effect of raising awareness about both how and what one thinks. By virtue of repeatedly articulating the fantasy and becoming more fully aware of its content and contours, a person typically alters the particulars associated with the fantasy, including its anxiety-laden imagery. As a result, those particulars become more in synch with reality (and involve less anxiety) than fantasy (which involves more anxiety). This changing of the content of one's fantasy (its concurrent images) tends to result in changes in one's attitudes about the fantasy. The man who hears the siren would simply want to articulate his fantasy until he notices that he comes to regard the situation differently. In repeating the fantasy to himself, he may recognize that what he imagines will almost certainly *not* come to pass. Consequently, he may discover that he feels differently about that imagery: "This is so far-fetched that I should spend time thinking about other, more realistic matters."

A third technique for modifying imagery involves *substituting contrasting imagery* for that which leads to anxiety. This approach closely follows the one just mentioned. Specifically, as one becomes adept at calling attention to and describing the anxiety-laden fantasy, especially as it unfolds, one may begin to imagine contrasting things that enlist new fantasies that link with different and more calming or pleasant imagery. As this substituting practice is repeated over time, it has the effect of helping the one making use of it to visualize and thus "see" things differently than before. When the man hears the siren, he can stop his thought process and quickly substitute "My family is just fine, likely out at the park enjoying this lovely day" for "My family is in grave danger." Recall the image that Leticia learned to use for managing her own anxiety: "The one that works for me is actually the image of a crossing guard, like a school security guard, with a stop sign. So I can actually stop my thoughts before they get to where I can't stop them; and that works. . . ." More pleasant imagery helps to produce more pleasant thinking, which in turn helps one feel better and less anxious than before.

Modifying the Affective Component

Another helpful strategy for managing anxiety attends to changing the condition's "affective component," which means altering how one feels about being anxious. Because anxiety can be so distressing, both to anxious persons themselves and to others around them, those who experience anxiety with regularity tend to develop what are called "second-level" feelings associated with it. Those include feelings of fear, guilt, shame, frustration, and sadness or depression. When experiencing these second-level feelings, anxious persons not only feel uneasy about whatever makes them anxious (e.g., hearing a siren), but also tend to feel uneasy *because* they are anxious and are aware of how that affects them and others in painful ways. Anxious persons tend to exacerbate their anxiety as they take on additional feelings associated with it.

A principal way to change the way one feels about one's anxiety involves simply accepting it for what it is. As Emery points out, "Accepting the presence of anxiety is crucial," even though anxious persons tend to want to "avoid or fight anxiety symptoms."[28] Cognitive therapy encourages one to accept the fact that one will feel anxious, thereby lessening the second-level feelings that tend to go along with it. Acceptance frees one up psychologically to give greater focus to learning how to tolerate the anxiety better. This approach is "based on the rationale that once anxiety reaches a certain level, the client can no longer control the symptoms," and giving up the notion of control over anxiety, paradoxically, sets the stage for learning how better to control anxiety by living with it in a different way.[29] In a sense, this approach resembles "turning the other cheek" to anxiety and thereby diminishing its coercive power.

Søren Kierkegaard's sense of how anxiety, in spite of its pain, may actually be a kind of spiritual gift bears another mention. Anxiety's gift or benefit lies in its usefulness for the Christian life. Specifically, anxiety has the capacity to prompt faith, to help the anxious person make

28. Beck and Emery, *Anxiety Disorders and Phobias,* p. 232.
29. Beck and Emery, *Anxiety Disorders and Phobias,* pp. 232-33.

appropriate choices for a life that rests in Christ, who provides the means for relieving anxiety. One finds anxiety's gift in its ever-present reminder that one needs Christ. Thinking about anxiety as a gift, as something not only painful but also potentially useful, may help one to feel differently about it. Furthermore, considering anxiety's potential benefits may assuage some of the fear, guilt, shame, frustration, and sadness that so often accompanies it. In other words, changing how one feels about being anxious may serve to remove what Jürgen Moltmann describes as the "suffering in suffering" and what Emery terms one's "anxiety about anxiety."

Modifying the Behavioral Component

Along with thoughts and images, anxiety tends to involve particular behaviors that prolong and intensify the condition's effects. In order to change anxiety-laden thoughts and related beliefs, one must change how one behaves in relation to anxiety. Specifically, one must learn how to confront situations that produce anxiety in a different way. The kind of confrontation called for occurs more readily in the therapeutic setting. Nevertheless, the client must learn to engage in behaviors outside of therapy that emulate the therapeutic setting. One way to do this involves actually putting herself in situations that give rise to feeling anxious and subjecting herself to experiencing anxiety. As she directly confronts situations that cause discomfort, she increases her capacity to tolerate uneasiness. Typically, some variation on the notion of "desensitization" informs this therapeutic approach. Most behavioral modification approaches typically will not lend themselves to use by pastors, however, and should therefore be left in the hands of those who have training and experience in using them — namely, therapists.

One therapeutic approach does lend itself to use by pastors: the "as if" technique. It involves learning to act "as if" what causes one to feel anxious (whether a person or an event) does not, in fact, have that effect. As Emery puts it, "The anxious patient gives himself a suggestion ('What if') and then acts on it *as if* it were true."[30] A person who begins to feel anxious could, for example, behave "as if" he were calm, un-

30. See Beck and Emery, *Anxiety Disorders and Phobias,* pp. 281-82.

afraid, and secure instead of vulnerable. Over time, this approach works to diminish the power that anxiety-laden situations hold, while simultaneously serving to build an anxious person's confidence in his own power to control the anxiety when it appears.

There are three components to the "as if" technique. The first involves learning to develop images. This entails describing how one would like to behave if one were not in fact anxious. It may also involve watching persons who live less anxiously and seeking to emulate them. Both of these practices seek to foster the development of an "ideal image" that an anxious person may utilize to modify behaviors associated with his anxiety.

Emery provides the following illustration for how this worked with a client who got anxious about the prospect of meeting other people:

1. I focus on the other person. I look straight at the other person. My eyes stay fixed.
2. I hold my ground and let him move more toward me, rather than rushing to him.
3. I keep my body straight and project presence. I stay balanced rather than shift my weight from foot to foot.
4. I communicate openly. I keep my arms down rather than taking a defensive position.
5. I keep my head erect rather than nodding or looking away.
6. I speak confidently in a clear, direct way rather than qualify excessively, apologize, or overexplain.
7. I ask questions about the person and call him by name.
8. I'm friendly but quiet and sincere.
9. I'm dressed in a way that allows me to feel good about myself.
10. I'm really enjoying meeting the person.[31]

The client constructed this ideal image by watching others and observing how they acted when meeting people.

Two remaining components of the "as if" technique include the practice of using less anxiety-laden imagery to act *as if* anxiety has diminished, and also incorporating that imagery into role-playing. Cognitive therapy will often involve the client's keeping a diary of how us-

31. Beck and Emery, *Anxiety Disorders and Phobias,* pp. 282-83.

ing imagery through role-playing affects the frequency, degree, and duration of anxiety experiences.

Restructuring Assumptions concerning Acceptance, Competence, and Control

Another component of cognitive restructuring attends to the anxious person's assumptions that are part of her cognitive set. Of particular interest are assumptions that have to do with what Beck and Emery call "three major issues": needing to be accepted by others, needing to think that one is competent, and needing to remain in control of one's life. Beck and Emery claim that we typically can understand and work better with all sorts of "vague fears" that the anxious person experiences when we examine them with respect to these three major issues.

Thinking, acting, and feeling in relationship to these major issues becomes "habitualized, fixed, and largely automatic" for the anxious person, so that, in the case of the question of self-competence, for example, she has thought about it, spoken about it, and acted on it thousands of times. In fact, by virtue of having been "overpracticed" and "overlearned," her major concern "has developed a life of its own."[32] Consequently, her "anxiety-producing assumptions" are set in motion when she encounters some stressor or series of stressors that touch on one or more of her major issues.

Beck and Emery illustrate how the assumptions one holds about acceptance, competence, and control may inform an experience of anxiety by comparing three persons who presented in therapy with a fear of developing a terminal illness.[33] The first person's major concern centered on acceptance, particularly her belief that if she became ill, then her family and friends would reject her, and she would be left to die alone. She believed that if she became ill, she would lose the acceptance that she so prized. The second person was primarily concerned about his competence, believing that if he developed a terminal illness, he would show himself to be incompetent by losing the "contest" for good health with his peers. Presumably, this person derived self-esteem, and

32. Beck and Emery, *Anxiety Disorders and Phobias*, p. 293.
33. Beck and Emery, *Anxiety Disorders and Phobias*, p. 288.

perhaps a central part of his identity, through demonstrating — often in competition with others — that he was in fact strong, able, and fit. The third person's principal concern had to do with his ability to control all the facets of his life, including his physical health. He drew self-esteem and self-understanding from this ability, and an illness would mean that he had lost control.

As is typically true with anxious persons, these types of assumptions follow from an acute sense of vulnerability. In each of the scenarios presented, the anxious person's unease was closely related to the sense that something deeply valued was threatened or in danger of being lost. Moreover, according to Beck and Emery, the anxious person's assumptions — whether they have to do with health, religion, relationships, accomplishments, or some other "major issue" or concern — tend to be "framed in extreme, all-or-nothing terms."[34]

The following lists contain examples of various assumptions that may inform the three major issues:[35]

Acceptance

1. I have to be cared for by someone who loves me.
2. I need to be understood.
3. I can't be left alone.
4. I'm nothing unless I'm loved.
5. To be rejected is the worst thing in the world.
6. I can't get others angry at me.
7. I have to please others.
8. I can't stand being separated from others.
9. Criticism means personal rejection.
10. I can't be alone.

Competence

1. I am what I accomplish.
2. I have to be somebody.
3. Success is everything.
4. There are only winners and losers in life.
5. If I'm not on top, I'm a flop.

---

34. Beck and Emery, *Anxiety Disorders and Phobias*, p. 289.
35. Beck and Emery, *Anxiety Disorders and Phobias*, pp. 289-90.

6. If I let up, I'll fail.
7. I have to be the best at whatever I do.
8. Others' successes take away from mine.
9. If I make a mistake, I'll fail.
10. Failure is the end of the world.

Control
1. I have to be my own boss.
2. I'm the only one who can solve my problems.
3. I can't tolerate others telling me what to do.
4. I can't ask for help.
5. Others are always trying to control me.
6. I have to be perfect to have control.
7. I'm either completely in control or completely out of control.
8. I can't tolerate being out of control.
9. Rules and regulations imprison me.
10. If I let someone get too close, that person will control me.

A person believes that his assumptions serve to insure that what he wants to happen to him will happen, and what he does not want to happen to him will not. Somewhat paradoxically, the anxious person assumes the kinds of things noted in the lists above in order to keep his anxiety at bay. He thinks that living in light of these assumptions will keep what he dreads from coming to pass. However, these assumptions actually inform an anxiety-laden cognitive set. Rather than helping him feel less anxious, these assumptions become the impetus for setting himself up for anxiety. For example, a man who "believes he needs love is afraid that he cannot exist without it and anticipates that with love will come eternal happiness."[36] Similarly, a woman who thinks she needs to remain perfect in order to stay in control lives in fear of not being perfect and losing control, so that she feels anxious about her imperfection. An individual's assumptions about any of these three major issues have been formulated in relationship to his personal and familial experiences, and typically have been reinforced in his thoughts, behaviors, and feelings for a long period of time.[37]

36. Beck and Emery, *Anxiety Disorders and Phobias*, p. 290.
37. Beck and Emery, *Anxiety Disorders and Phobias*, p. 290.

How then does a therapist work with someone to change her assumptions concerning acceptance, competence, and control? Each of the previously discussed strategies and techniques for cognitive restructuring may have a place in helping to change those assumptions. The client and therapist may work together on enhancing self-awareness and on modifying negative imagery, the affective component (how it feels), and the behavioral component. However, the therapist initially pays particular attention to enhancing the client's self-awareness, especially as it relates to identifying a core belief associated with the assumptions. Each set of assumptions derives from a core belief.[38] In the case of the person concerned about acceptance, the core belief is that "he may be flawed in some way and thus be unacceptable to others." For the person for whom competence is the major issue, the core belief is that "he does not measure up" and that "he is inferior." Likewise, for the person whose major issue is staying in control, the core belief centers on "the possibility of being dominated by others or by events outside of his control," resulting in a belief that he cannot "tolerate ambiguity because he cannot control the outcome."[39]

Cognitive therapy with the anxious person involves challenging these assumptions and presenting her with alternative ones to consider and internalize, so that the new assumptions become part of her operative cognitive set. This cognitive restructuring can and does happen through a variety of approaches, some of which have already been detailed. Whatever approach the anxious person takes, it remains essential for her to enhance self-awareness about her assumptions, and also to pay explicit attention to how she might "reformulate" or "restructure" those assumptions so that they prompt a different thinking, behaving, and feeling process — namely, a less anxious one.

Conclusion

I endorse Beck's view that anxiety follows largely from misguided thinking. Anxious persons have learned to think in ways that lead to becoming anxious. In order to feel less anxious, they need to learn to

---

38. See Beck and Emery, *Anxiety Disorders and Phobias,* pp. 302-10.
39. Beck and Emery, *Anxiety Disorders and Phobias,* p. 308.

think differently. I do not suggest that anxiety is merely, or exclusively, a thinking disorder. Both psychoanalytic and interpersonal dynamics also play a significant role in many cases of anxiety, just as Freud and Sullivan suggest. No single theory on anxiety, including its causes and cures, may be sufficient by itself. People may be anxious for a variety of reasons and may require different means for explaining and treating it.

Anxiety may also be tied to physiological factors, including brain chemistry and hormone levels. As is true with depression, the physiological component may be the initiating factor or the consequential one, such that, while brain chemistry may lead one to feel anxious, feeling anxious may also alter brain chemistry. Furthermore, anxiety may link to interpersonal struggles or failures, particularly in childhood but also throughout life. It may also relate primarily to spiritual or religious questions, concerns, and difficulties, the primary focus of this book. Even so, I want to stress anxiety's *cognitive* component, including how thinking impacts behaviors and emotions, and how relearning both what and how one thinks holds power for quieting the soul. Beck's approach proves especially helpful in that regard.

Considering the case of the man whose anxiety centered on his home catching fire, one could conclude that Beck really is more concerned with fear of tangible, objectified threats — what may *happen to us* — than he is with anxiety, which centers on less tangible, nonobjectified threats having more to do with *who we are*. If so, one might conclude further that a cognitive approach to understanding and alleviating anxiety, which focuses so intently on *thinking*, will prove less effective than an interpersonal or psychoanalytic approach, which looks first at how our relationships, and particularly those in early childhood, shape how secure we feel and thus how vulnerably we experience life.

However, Beck recognizes that a feeling of vulnerability lies at anxiety's core. This recognition suggests that in his consideration of anxiety disorders and how to assuage them, he has more in mind than tangible, objectified fears on the one hand, and thought processes on the other. Beck trained as a neuroscientist. He operates from a perspective informed by his field's norms, values, and goals. Understandably, he attributes great importance to cognitive functioning for understanding and treating anxiety.

At the same time, Beck's approach leaves room for broader existential concerns, including spiritual ones. I suggest that many persons struggling with a disquieted soul will be most concerned with their assumptions about God, their standing before God, *and* the difference these make in how their personal life story takes shape. While these concerns surely involve thinking, they actually touch us at the core of who we are, in our core self, in Beck's terms.

I believe that many anxious persons who live in relationship to faith communities and call upon pastors for assistance need help with their core self. They especially need help with their self's (their soul's) relationship to God. In the next chapter I detail more fully how feelings of vulnerability and disconnection lie at the core of the disquieted soul. In subsequent chapters I describe how faith practices may help us learn to think differently about God, ourselves, and the relationship we share, and thus how these practices may foster a greater sense of connectedness among anxious persons, assuage their sense of vulnerability, and quiet the disquieted soul.

Chapter 5

CONNECTEDNESS

What the Disquieted Soul Needs and Desires

In a recent and popular self-help book, psychiatrist Edward M. Hallowell states as his primary concern helping people "put aside irrational worry — worry that makes no sense, but hurts you and haunts you every day." He wisely recognizes worry's power and potential for harm, noting that it invites "brain burn," an "infinite web of 'what-ifs,'" an "intruder that can't be forgotten," and even an "ominous core of life."[1] Even so, he remains hopeful. His hope stems from a belief that worry and its effects can be diminished. Through educating worriers on how this can be done, he seeks to help them become more hopeful themselves.

Connectedness Matters

According to Hallowell, the single most important thing one can do to ease worry and minimize the potential for it is to strengthen one's ties of connectedness. By *connectedness* he means first and foremost being a part of something larger than oneself. This may involve social ties, but also close associations with the following: family, one's history and tradition, information and ideas, institutions and organizations, and the realms of the transcendent, spiritual, or religious.[2] Establishing and maintaining

---

1. Edward M. Hallowell, *Worry: Hope and Help for a Common Condition* (New York: Random House, 2002), p. 275.
2. Hallowell, *Worry*, pp. 267-74.

these kinds of close associations, these connections, serves not only to prevent excessive worry but also to alleviate it when it strikes.

In using the term *connectedness,* Hallowell means to lift up the significance of living more intentionally in relationship with others. Of course, relationships matter for many reasons. In different though complementary ways, both psychological and theological understandings of personhood underscore the view that human living and thriving require particular kinds of relationships. Theologically speaking, human beings are inherently relational creatures. We have been created to live in a particular kind of connectedness, to other people and to God, in community. Indeed, the second creation account in Genesis reveals the divine intentionality of the first human-human relationship: "The Lord God said, 'It is not good that the man should be alone; I will make him a helper as his partner'" (Gen. 2:18). Moreover, as Luke puts it when describing the human-God relationship, God is the one in whom "we live and move and have our being" (Acts 17:28). Luke makes this claim, and we embrace it as we live and tell the Christian story, because God has first claimed us for relationship. This special kind of relationship, one based on a covenant, is depicted in the Genesis narrative recalling God's declaration to Abram: "I will establish my covenant between me and you, and your offspring after you throughout their generations, for an everlasting covenant, to be God to you and to your offspring after you. And I will give to you, and to your offspring after you, the land where you are now an alien, all the land of Canaan, for a perpetual holding; and I will be their God" (Gen. 17:7-8).

In Hallowell's language, our faith holds that human beings have been created for connectedness, with one another and with God. In the case of connectedness among Christians, Bonhoeffer maintains that nothing offers more in the way of happiness and support than being with other believers in community: "The physical presence of other Christians is a source of incomparable joy and strength to the believer."[3] If for no other reasons than these two, human connectedness remains an end in itself. This suggests that we should never think of connectedness merely as a means for meeting some greater aim, including one characterized by less worry.

---

3. Dietrich Bonhoeffer, *Life Together,* translated and introduced by John W. Doberstein (New York: Harper & Row, 1954), p. 19.

Hallowell makes the additional point, however, that connectedness, whether to persons or to impersonal things like information, ideas, institutions, and traditions, serves as grounds for reassurance. He describes this reassurance in terms of "a voice that says everything will be OK."[4] Connectedness provides for our being told that things will work out in the end. Being connected offers a way for us to hear again and again that whatever we struggle with presently will not have the final say. The connections we form and maintain in our relationships can assure us that just as others have journeyed through the precarious waters on which we now sail to arrive at their destination safely and intact, so too shall we. Persons who worry tend to need precisely this kind of reassurance. Some may need it frequently.

At times the reassurance we want and need comes principally from within us. We look inside ourselves to find confidence in the midst of uncertainty, courage amid trepidation, and hope in the throes of despair. Various kinds of psychotherapies seek to foster an ability to muster these kinds of internal responses. This happens as they teach one how to gain greater awareness of one's thoughts, perceptions, motivations, and feelings, and subsequently, how to take steps to alter the negative ones, let go of them, or minimize their harmful effects by otherwise keeping them in check.

At other times the reassurance we want and need lies beyond us. It may come from parents or other significant figures in our lives, those whose care and concern buoy our confidence, courage, and hope. Reassurance also may come from ideals or valued commitments that we espouse and live out, whether alone or in solidarity with others. An example: When a group of people working for peace perseveres in the midst of violence and grave threats because they believe deeply in what they are working for, individually and collectively, and they remind one another of their shared devotion and goals.

For some persons, and presumably those that pastors minister with often, the most significant and lasting reassurance comes ultimately from God. These persons turn to God, or want to turn to God, to hear in some form or fashion that "everything is going to be OK." Leticia, whom we met earlier, says as much about her own experience: "Part of it is that I don't necessarily trust God anymore; and so if I

---

4. Hallowell, *Worry*, p. 267.

could trust God, I think I wouldn't have anxiety because God would be taking care of me. So I think faith is a huge part of my anxiety." In ministry with people like Leticia, pastors observe frequently that the desire and need for "a word from God" has brought them to the church, to talk with the pastor, or both. By seeking out or agreeing to a relationship with the pastor, and also by virtue of their sheer presence in the faith community, such persons, whether they are aware of it or not, tend to be searching for connectedness. They come to church looking for meaning, for values to live by that have more promise than the ones they currently embrace; and they come to church for opportunities to associate with others looking for the same. Indeed, I have yet to meet a person in church who is not seeking in some form or fashion a deeper connection with God.

This suggests that people unite with churches, whether formally or informally, because they want to associate with, become part of, and usually contribute to something larger than they are. Usually these people are convinced that the "something larger" relates ultimately to God and God's provision. Related to this, in my experience (which I think is typical) most people come to church and seek out pastors because they long for ways to gain confidence, courage, and hope amid life's struggles. They need to find assurance that they themselves, those whom they love, and what they value truly matters, especially to God. They want to find support and sustenance while going through a divorce, facing an illness, struggling financially, or parenting an addicted teenager. They seek, sometimes desperately, to find a way to look forward to a time that will be better than the current one. Because they feel so vulnerable and threatened, whether physically, emotionally, relationally, economically, spiritually, or otherwise, they come to church or to the pastor in need of a way to fend off what threatens them. They hope to find security amid insecurity. They want to be assured *by God* that everything will be OK.

One might suggest that those coming to church principally out of a need for reassurance, as opposed to coming for "higher" religious purposes, like glorifying God and God's claim on them, merely reflects the overly therapeutic, anthropocentric, individualistic, and entitled culture that North Americans now inhabit, Christians included. To put it another way, one might wonder if viewing the faith community, its practices, and its pastors primarily as *resources,* whether for reassuring disquieted souls or those struggling otherwise, actually misses the point of the Christian story and living into it through the life of faith — the point being that the church is supposed to be more about God and communion with God than it is about us and our needs!

But this kind of perspective itself misses the point of Jesus' life and ministry. I would support pastors resisting and trying to counter the "triumph of the therapeutic" and its close associates of selfishness and entitlement, both in and out of the church. Furthermore, we must never view the Christian faith as a resource for some greater good than glorifying and communing with God. However, neither should we assume that human needs or God's desire and ability to provide for those needs may be divorced from such "higher" religious purposes as glorifying and communing with God. Deborah van Deusen Hunsinger makes this point with respect to prayer and the Christian life, a life that necessitates intentional and deeply rooted connectedness:

> The New Testament urges us to bear one another's burdens (Gal. 6:2), to confess our sins and pray for one another (James 5:16), to encourage one another (1 Thess. 5:11), and to care for one another (1 Cor. 12:25). Throughout the history of the church, Christians have undertaken ministries of intercessory prayer, visitation of the sick, and small groups that share the joys and hardships of the members' common life in Christ. . . . When individuals are upheld by one another in Christ, nurtured by the Word of God, and knit spiritually into a common body, they are blessed with vitality as they reach out to a world in need.[5]

In the living out of the Christian story, the faith community is precisely where disquieted souls and anyone else needs to turn for reassurance in the midst of what currently plagues them. In fact, we do a disservice to God and the Christian story when we draw such sharp distinctions between "higher" and "lower" religious motives, ones that tend to correlate with the equally misguided and problematic distinction between the sacred and secular realms. Jesus' tireless concern for human beings and their well-being, not only with respect to their

---

5. Deborah van Deusen Hunsinger, *Pray without Ceasing: Revitalizing Pastoral Care* (Grand Rapids: William B. Eerdmans, 2006), p. ix.

standing before God but also with respect to their physical, emotional, relational, economic, and spiritual needs, lies at the heart of the Christian story. Moreover, Jesus' attention to these wide-ranging needs derives from the human being's intrinsic — indeed, inseparable — connection to God and others. This connectedness holds the "highest" sacred value and informs the very relationships for which God has created us.

Christian faith and its practices foster deep connectedness, with God and with other persons in community. In so doing, they also impart what we could describe as spiritual fruit to those who engage them — namely, reassurance that increases one's sense of security. I will elaborate on how this happens in the next two chapters. Let me say here that the power of faith practices lies in their ability to shape how those who engage them see the world, how they think and feel about life and what it entails, and also how they live, with others and with God. In shaping their capacities for all of these matters in ways that deepen confidence, courage, and hope amid life's uncertainties, faith practices foster the sense that "everything is going to be OK."

Hallowell's claim — namely, that finding reassurance through deep connections provides the best means of relief for those who worry — has something to offer disquieted souls. I have already cautioned against assuming that worry and anxiety are the same. I do so again here. Nevertheless, Hallowell's observation concerning worry and its relief certainly applies to anxiety. Like those who worry, anxious persons feel vulnerable. They feel at risk because they believe that they are unable to fend off whatever they deem threatening, whether to themselves or to others about whom they care. Also, like those who worry, anxious persons tend to feel disconnected, even isolated, in their daily living. Often this disconnection follows from their realization that what they feel and how they act are not rational or normal, and from their subsequent efforts to wall off themselves and their condition from those around them. Many anxious persons feel embarrassed or ashamed about their condition. The result, as José put it earlier when describing his experience, is that many anxious persons became experts at concealing their anxiety.

Concealing anxiety usually involves withdrawing from relationships, ceasing to participate in various aspects of public life, and other kinds of isolating behaviors. If anxious persons do not isolate themselves, they may find others isolating them because their behaviors are puzzling and unpredictable if not altogether off-putting. In any event, because they feel so vulnerable, a condition that isolation further aggravates, anxious persons, like those who worry, need reassurance that everything will be OK. Anxious persons want to find a way to believe that who they are will survive intact, no matter what they may be experiencing at present and no matter what its "rational" basis. They need not only to believe but also to find ways to remind themselves of their belief and to make it increasingly part of their operative cognitive set. Feeling isolated and vulnerable, anxious persons need a way to live with deeper connections to others, God, and themselves. With these connections come more confidence, courage, and hope.

Keeping these needs for connection and reassurance in mind, and also thinking about ways that pastors and faith communities may foster and support these needs, in the rest of this chapter I focus on two matters. The first is the disquieted soul's vulnerability and disconnection and the relationship between the two. Paying particular attention to the disquieted soul's spiritual roots and manifestations, I suggest four concerns that tend to inform the soul's disquiet, particularly among those who find their way to faith communities. The second matter I will focus on is Paul W. Pruyser's "guidelines for pastoral diagnosis"[6] and how these may assist the pastor with two necessary goals. The first involves interpreting and discussing parishioners' experiences with a disquieted soul in spiritual terms. The second entails helping pastors think about parishioners' experiences while also helping parishioners think about their own experiences, using a different type of cognitive set than that which prompts anxiety.

The Disquieted Soul as Spiritual Dis-ease

I have already endorsed the value of focusing on anxiety's cognitive features. As Aaron Beck and Gary Emery suggest, it is primarily disordered thinking and thought processes that prompt the kind of emotional unease that characterizes anxiety, whatever its forms and

6. Paul W. Pruyser, *The Minister as Diagnostician: Personal Problems in Pastoral Perspective* (Philadelphia: Westminster Press, 1976), pp. 60-79.

expressions. Anxious persons feel the way they do chiefly because of a distorted sense of reality, one that includes a perceived threat to their core self — their soul — and involves who they are and what they hold most dear. This sense of threat eventuates in a pervasive kind of vulnerability that leads to feeling isolated from others and to a loss of vital connections. Both this vulnerability and this isolation follow from flawed ways of organizing their experience. Anxious persons operate with a faulty cognitive set. It orders and frames how they perceive various relationships and life events — namely, in anxiety-laden ways.

Charles, whom we met earlier, provides a good example. His cognitive set contains the belief that he constantly has to measure up to what others value and expect of him, rather than to what he values and expects of himself. His cognitive set also contains the belief that he often falls short of meeting others' expectations. These beliefs shape how Charles thinks, his interactions with others, and his feelings about others and himself. In other words, his cognitive set shapes his experience of life, which is an anxious one. Similarly, Leticia's loss of faith and trust in God, which followed her miscarriage, informs a cognitive set that arguably increases her feelings of vulnerability and a corresponding sense that she and her other children live constantly in harm's way. This sense of vulnerability and fear continues to shape how she thinks, acts, and feels, whether with respect to natural disasters, the possibility of fire in the home or at a hotel when the family vacations, or some other calamity. José and Karla (whom we met earlier) also operate with identifiable cognitive sets. These have an effect on how they see the world and their place in it, shape how they live out their lives, and certainly inform their anxiety. By finding a way to adopt a different cognitive set, such that a new frame of reference or way of seeing things would mold and organize their experience in a different and more peaceful way, they could in fact learn to think differently, feel differently, and thus live less anxiously.

Cognitive therapy seeks to foster precisely this kind of relearning how to think, which leads to establishing new cognitive sets that help persons to see life differently and thus to feel different than before. Cognitive therapy teaches persons how to apply techniques to identify, understand, and modify their thoughts on their own. It further requires of them a disciplined monitoring of their thought processes and corresponding emotions. It likewise fosters a deepening capacity for self-reflection and analysis.[7] Each of these components of cognitive therapy serves to alter inappropriate ways of thinking by replacing faulty, unrealistic cognitive sets with new, more realistic ones. For our purposes, the idea at work here and the point to underscore is that people can learn to think differently about what informs their disquieted souls, and in doing so they may also learn to feel and act in different, presumably less painful ways.

In the case of many disquieted souls, particularly those that find their way to churches, distortions in their *thinking about* God lie at the heart of their condition. A flawed yet operative cognitive set informs how they think about and understand several matters pertaining to God, which leads to their feeling vulnerable, disconnected, and anxious. These matters having to do with God include (1) who God is, particularly God's attributes and powers; (2) who they are in their place or standing before God, and especially how they measure up or fail to measure up to God's desires for them; (3) how their relationship to God plays out in daily life, including what they value, reject, and devote their life to; and (4) how they approach their life's end, particularly with respect to accepting or dreading death's eventuality. In other words, the way they think of God and about themselves in relationship to God, and subsequently, the way they live their lives and approach their deaths — these things *make* them feel anxious and therefore need to change. I have proposed thinking of these matters in terms of four related concerns, which I call *theo-centric, theo-relational, vocational,* and *mortal.* These concerns surely merge with one another, such that we shouldn't think of them as sharply distinct and unrelated. Nevertheless, keeping each of these four concerns in mind provides the pastor with a helpful way to ponder what she observes in or hears from those in her care.

Theo-centric Concerns

Theo-centric concerns pertain to God's nature and character. This concern pertains especially to *who God is* for the anxious person and

---

7. Allan Hugh Cole Jr., "Cognitive Therapy," in *The New Dictionary of Pastoral Studies,* ed. Wesley Carr (Grand Rapids: William B. Eerdmans, 2002), pp. 57-58.

thus how she views God acting or behaving in the world. It does not take long in pastoral ministry to discover that people hold and live with various understandings of God. Some of these understandings may line up well with conventional Christianity; others may not. Nevertheless, a person's understandings of God, which tend to begin forming in childhood and may be reworked throughout life, powerfully influence his views on a variety of things that eventually have practical implications. These views touch on matters like what God can and cannot do, what God will and will not do, and what God should and should not do. In a word, this concern has to do with God's *nature*.

How a person views God and understands God's nature informs how she ponders and responds to questions like these:

- Is God more apt to be gracious and forgiving, or judgmental and punishing? How do I know?
- Can God really forgive people's worst sins? What is the evidence for that?
- Does God still care about human problems? How can I be sure?
- Does God will that we struggle and suffer? What does the Bible say about this?
- Would God test people by bringing about adversity? How do I know?
- Does God allow bad things to happen to good people? If so, why?

A person's understanding of God's character may also impact his belief about God's presence in everyday life, and especially his own life. This may include a belief about God seeing and knowing everything and also having a hand in all matters, whether vital or trivial. The person may ask questions like these:

- How does God feel about what's going on in my life, with my family members, and in my neighborhood, country, and the world?
- Does God notice how difficult life is for so many people, including me?
- Does God have anything to offer to relieve human struggles, including my own emotional pain?
- Will God respond if I pray and ask for God's help?

Similarly, a person's understandings of God's nature and character may shape what she believes God will provide if and when God responds. This belief about God's responsiveness affects when and how she may reach out for God's provision in times of need. She may ponder or inquire about God's provision in these ways:

- How could God help me or those I love?
- What might God be able to do that my psychiatrist, my doctor, or my therapist has not?
- How do I get God to hear me and to respond to me in my time of need?

As any pastor knows, these kinds of questions arising out of views of God's nature and character routinely present themselves in pastoral ministry. People frequently come to pastors with some kind of problem, dilemma, or struggle. In doing so, they tend to seek not merely ways to alleviate the pain that one or more matters cause them and perhaps others — though that surely may be something they are after, and understandably so. They also typically need to explore, understand, and perhaps even be told by one whom they perceive knows and represents God something about God's nature and character. The perceptive pastor will see that these persons want to be assured that God is with them and that God remains a trustworthy companion on their life's journey. They want to be assured not only of God's presence but also of God's availability and concern. It is not enough for a person to hear "God is with you and shares your pain." While that may provide some measure of relief in the sense that it offers a degree of felt solidarity and shared meaning in suffering that otherwise would be absent, those who struggle want to know if God has enough concern for them to help them through their difficulties in identifiable, even concrete ways. Not only do people need assurance from pastors about God's concern for them; they need to learn how to assure themselves of the same.

Pastors should remain aware of this common need to know who God is and what God may offer because of who God is. The extent to which this need is met has a lot to say about one's soul and its state of quiet. Disquieted souls often experience a good deal of unease — dis-ease — over who God is and what this means for their own lives, needs, and struggles.

Theo-relational Concerns

If theo-centric concerns pertain to who God is, theo-relational concerns center on who we are in relationship to God precisely because of who God is. We must not separate our understanding of God's nature from our own nature. John Calvin follows Augustine in noting this, going so far as to say that without knowing who we are, we can never know who God is, and without knowing who God is, we shall never know who we are.[8] Knowledge of God and knowledge of oneself remain inseparable. Classical Christianity, in its belief that human beings have been created in God's image, affirms what Calvin claims.

For persons of faith, including those who may be struggling profoundly with faith questions, who we are in relationship to God matters a great deal. It matters because this relationship serves as the basis and model of all others. But it also informs our perception of how God views us, including whether God loves us, is happy with us, accepting of us, and more or less validating of who we are. We have a concern for what God desires and expects of us and the extent to which we fulfill those desires and expectations. Whatever our shortcomings, we want and need to believe that God still loves us, claims us, and keeps us close. We need assurance, and from time to time we need reassurance, that God never abandons us. Whatever we do or fail to do, however we measure up or fail to do so with respect to God's desires and expectations, we need to live with a measure of confidence that God remains true to God's promises. These promises declare that God abides with those whom God loves. Remembering these promises, we look to our relationship to God for assurance, and reassurance, that "everything is going to be OK."

Theo-relational concerns turn on what we might call our *personal relationship* to God. This includes what God thinks of us and the stance that God takes in relationship to us because of God's nature and character. Pastors routinely meet those who find the matter of what God thinks of them weighing heavily on their minds. In fact, pastors regularly meet persons who feel quite alienated from God and believe that they have fallen out of favor with God — maybe forever.

---

8. John Calvin, *Institutes of the Christian Religion*, ed. John T. McNeill, trans. Ford Lewis Battles (Philadelphia: Westminster Press, 1960), pp. 35-39.

These persons often make their concerns evident with questions or statements like the following:

- What does God want from me?
- In light of the life I have lived, what can I ask of God and expect from God?
- I'm afraid that lightning will strike the church if I show up there!
- How can God forgive me for what I have done?
- What might God say about what is happening in my life?
- I'd like to live a better life.
- How can I become closer to God and really feel that closeness?
- How can my faith in God help me become a better person?
- How can I be more true to God?
- How can I live more like Jesus lived?

Pastors frequently hear these kinds of questions and statements from persons who feel a sense of dis-ease, of dread, and who worry or at least are very concerned about some matter that relates to their standing before God. In fact, when it comes to personal or familial problems, my experience has been that individuals who seek me out for help tend to be pained, in some form or fashion, precisely by a theo-relational concern. To put it in terms that my maternal grandfather would have appreciated, they realize that something is wrong between them and God, and they come to the pastor to find out how to make it right. If any of us struggles from time to time with getting right with God, disquieted souls tend to struggle with that more frequently and more intensely.

Vocational Concerns

Vocational concerns often flow from theo-centric and theo-relational concerns. Vocational concerns involve explicit attention to who God has created and called one to *be* and what God calls one to *do* with one's life. More often than not, vocational concerns get expressed in struggles and questions pertaining to one's values, meaning, purpose, and identity, which may or may not center on one's job, career, or other chosen life tasks.

Pastors routinely listen to persons pondering vocational concerns who ask questions like these:

- What is life really all about?
- Who am I? What is *my* life all about?
- Why am I here? What is my purpose in life?
- What is really important to me?
- Is what I value valued by God?
- How might my life reflect what's important to me and to God?
- What kind of contribution can I make to other people's lives, to the world, and to the greater good?
- Is there more to life than I now experience and strive to achieve?

Most of us will struggle with these questions from time to time, whether we would call ourselves anxious or not. These concerns come to the fore predictably in particular circumstances — those involving expected developmental or life-cycle experiences. Such experiences include that of the young adult preparing to continue his education or enter the workforce full-time, that of a middle-aged adult pondering a career change, and also those involving significant life changes like the birth of a child, the last child's leaving home, caring for aging parents, and the death of a sibling or a parent. Other circumstances that give rise to vocational questions include situational crises, like the untimely death of a child or a loved one, an inability to get pregnant or a miscarriage, the loss of a job or financial security, a natural disaster or some other large-scale calamity, and a chronic or terminal illness. These kinds of experiences are profoundly unsettling. In various ways they call into question the things that we believe in, the values that we champion, the goals and objectives that we pursue. Situational crises often prompt us to take a long, hard look at who we really are and what we're all about. At their core, they have to do with our identity and how that gets lived out, with who we think we are and who God wants us to be or to become in our lives. Consequently, vocational concerns remain closely tied to theo-relational concerns.

I was serving as a pastor of a congregation in suburban New York City on September 11, 2001. The events of that day changed many lives in ways that we still try to sift through and understand. A notable change that took place among many of my parishioners centered on what I am calling the vocational concern. I lost track of how many pastoral conversations I had in the weeks and months following 9/11, conversations with individuals and couples who needed to re-evaluate who they were, what they deemed most significant, and what they were giving their lives to in their daily pursuits. Some wondered if they were in the right career, and pondered whether some kind of "service field" was more suitable for them. Others questioned if they had too long prioritized making money and climbing the corporate ladder, so that living through material accoutrements became their primary objective and motivator. I recall one man's perspective: "So much of my working life has been focused on what I could get, for my company and for myself, and now I think it's time I started thinking more about how to give back." Some people realized that they spent, on average, three or more hours a day commuting to and from a job that paid well but offered little enjoyment. This realization led them to consider whether they should find something closer to home, if not a different job altogether. Some people I spoke with were unsure about the wisdom of bringing children into a post-9/11 world, and whether or not they should delay or drop their plans for starting a family. Others reflected on whether giving more time, money, and energy to congregational life in order to "give back" and "take part in something more meaningful" would become their new practice and way of life. Many of these people wrestled with matters having to do with God's claim on them and their lives.

One may raise the question here of whether the vocational concerns I cite are not a luxury that only relatively privileged persons enjoy. We may wonder if those whose vocational interests and pursuits center, without choice, on simply putting food on the table, a roof over a family's head, clothes on children's backs, medicines in loved ones' bodies, and fractured relationships back together really have an opportunity to indulge in these kinds of ponderings and concerns. Would non-privileged persons even think of their lives in this manner? Are these questions reflective of bourgeois Christianity and culture at their worst?

I do not want to dismiss the value in raising such questions. Most of us in the Northern Hemisphere enjoy great privilege by global standards. Nevertheless, my experience has been that the vocational concern transcends privilege, whether socio-economic, educational, physical, or relational in kind. The persons I have spoken with about these matters lived on different rungs of the socio-economic ladder. They included wealthy, educated professionals, poor, comparatively less educated laborers, and many who fell somewhere in between. Not only that, but they were different ages and genders and came from different racial and ethnic backgrounds; some lived with significant disabilities and other health-related problems. I have found that this vocational concern is not only common, but tends to be shared among a diverse group of people. The particular content of questions surrounding vocational matters varies with respect to who is asking them. But the need to ask them seems widespread.

If these vocational concerns matter to most people, anxious persons tend to take them more seriously and feel them more immediately than others. One reason for this has to do with what Kierkegaard identified as endemic to anxiety — namely, a constant, restless gaze into the future that inevitably relates to one's freedom and ability to choose. Anxious persons often struggle deeply with making choices. Sometimes this struggle includes even the most basic choices about mundane things. When anxious persons do choose, often they lack confidence about what they have chosen. "How do I know I've done right?" they ask themselves. "What have I given up by going in this direction and not that one? Maybe I should have opted for something else." And sooner or later they may feel that they should have gone with another option.

If anxious persons dread having to choose, their dread tends to be more profound when choosing has to do with God. Their dread does not stem from a lack of desire for God; they desire God deeply. Rather, their dread follows from their awareness that in opting for something, anything, even something having to do with God, they forego other things that also may have to do with God. Once they do choose, anxious persons find it very difficult to remain confident in what they have chosen and are doing. Soon after making choices that have to do with God, they begin hearing that inner voice: "Have I done the right thing?" "Did I choose correctly?" "Is God pleased with my choice?" These dilemmas may very well seem odd. They may be quite difficult to comprehend by those whose souls live more quietly. For disquieted souls, however, these kinds of struggles result in painful, life-complicating, and sometimes debilitating scars with which they (and usually those close to them) live.

Anxious persons take matters pertaining to God with particular seriousness and immediacy because of the disquieted soul's more intense sense of vulnerability and disconnection, both from God and from others. When we are convinced, more or less, that our lives have meaning, that they unfold in synch with God's purpose and claim, and that what we value and strive for are extensions of what God prizes and would have for the world, we find ourselves, in our core selves or souls, feeling more secure, empowered, and protected from life's perils. Conversely, when we lack confidence about these matters, we feel vulnerable and uneasy. I am not suggesting that being right with God protects us from all pain, suffering, and calamity. Nor do I suggest that believing that it does serves a helpful purpose. This kind of thinking about God fits with what Frederick W. Schmidt Jr. calls "magical assumptions" about God, with the image of God as a cosmic Coke machine: we simply put in our money and get out whatever we want.[9] Both the Scriptures and history confirm that a faithful life lived in concert with God's calling may very well be as subject to profound struggle as any other. We have no better examples of this than the experiences of Job and Jesus.

Nevertheless, confidence in our standing before God matters. Our belief that who we are at least approximates who God has created and called us to be, along with the ongoing divine presence that God promises and a faithful life invites, prepares us to meet life's difficulties and to persevere in their midst with a kind of confidence, courage, and hope that otherwise would be lacking. In Moltmann's words, without confidence in God's promise to remain present in our lives, and particularly in the midst of suffering, we experience "suffering in suffering" and "wounds in wounds."[10] Furthermore, being right with God, such that we live out of our vocation as God's people in faithful ways, leads to feeling more connected in our souls to others. This includes connection to other persons, with whom we live out our own vocation and also share in the living out of theirs, and also connection to God, whom Luke described as being the one in whom "we live and move and have our being" (Acts 17:28, NRSV). As Edward Hallowell rightly observes, being connected, especially to something larger than oneself, serves to prevent and ease anxiety for the disquieted soul, particularly when the connection one finds, maintains, and values most centers on God.

9. Frederick W. Schmidt Jr., *When Suffering Persists* (Harrisburg, Pa.: Morehouse, 2001).

10. Jürgen Moltmann, *The Crucified God* (Minneapolis: Fortress Press, 1993), p. 46.

Mortal Concerns

Mortal concerns have to do with three principal matters: (1) life after death; (2) how much of life is yet to be lived before death; and (3) whether life has been meaningful, faithful, and true. As a result, mortal concerns relate closely to the other three concerns already mentioned. Pastors commonly meet people who find that mortality — their own and perhaps that of family members or loved ones — weighs heavily on their minds. Death terrifies many people, so much so that, in North America at least, people tend to keep death at arm's length, if they do not deny it altogether.

Three decades ago, cultural anthropologist Ernest Becker observed just how terrified people are of death and the great efforts we make to avoid it. In fact, avoiding death and living fearfully in the midst of its eventuality become primary forces that influence how we live our lives. In introducing his book's subject matter, Becker says that this phenomenon is "one of the great discoveries of modern thought: that of all things that move man, one of the principal ones is his terror of death."[11] If many people greatly fear death, some of them come to church looking for a way to assuage their fear. Indeed, I would go so far as to say that most people who come to church have given some thought to their mortality and that, in most cases, their unease with death has prompted their coming to — and staying in — church.

I make this claim too from my own experience, personally and pastorally. As a pastor, I met regularly with people feeling troubled about human mortality, whether their own or that of a loved one, and listened to the pain and anxiety that their fears about death caused them and those around them. I have known a similar kind of pain and anxiety myself, which began in my late teens and lasted for several years beyond. Like José, I lived with a significant fear of death and disease. But moving beyond my own experiences, I make the claim for the central role that the mortal concern plays in people's lives because many insightful thinkers, from a variety of perspectives, have pointed to the widespread fear of death and its influence on human beings. Noting the power that human mortality holds over life, Kierkegaard, James, Freud, and Tillich, among others, have suggested that this fear of life's

11. Ernest Becker, *The Denial of Death* (New York: Free Press, 1973/1997), p. 11.

end, whether we call it mortality, death, or non-being, is *the* principal driving force in our lives, particularly our religious lives. Death is always lurking. We cannot escape it, try as we may — and do. People who do not live with anxiety otherwise may feel quite anxious when thinking about death. Recalling James's words, this relates to the fact that "back of everything is the great spectre of universal death, the all-encompassing blackness." In the midst of that "great spectre," many people seek a way to live their lives and especially their *religious* lives with more confidence, courage, and hope.

For disquieted souls, anxiety often centers on a *profound* fear of death. As a result, anxiety commonly manifests itself in the form of heightened, even obsessive concern for physical health, if not in hypochondria. José's statement about his experience represents well what many disquieted souls feel: "I have a big fear of death and of disease. It's an unnatural fear. I know that logically, but the anxiety feeds off of that, or the anxiety creates that and then I can't get it out of my head." I have known people who developed eating disorders because of anxiety about their health and what they put into their bodies. I am aware of persons who couldn't bring themselves to exercise, which has proven health benefits, because they were afraid that they might have a heart attack. Even after medical experts assured them that this would not happen, they couldn't believe that they were in good physical health and act accordingly. I have also spoken with persons who worried excessively about environmental hazards, like drinking contaminated water, coming into contact with germs on doorknobs and toilets and chemicals on lawns and in public places, and eating beef that might be linked to mad cow disease or other forms of illness.

I recognize that none of these concerns should be dismissed. We should all be paying attention to our environment, including the food we eat, the water we drink, the air we breathe, and the materials with which we come into contact in daily living. Likewise, we should all strive for physically healthy bodies through a balance of proper diet, exercise, rest, and relationships. However, for disquieted souls whose anxiety stems largely from a fear of getting sick and ultimately dying, a concern for these matters often serves as *the* central and organizing force in their lives. They plan their days and their lives, often in great detail, in light of what they most fear: dying and what may come next.

Anxious persons wind up missing out on much of what life has to offer because they're so focused on that life ending.

Disquieted souls may reveal their concern about death when they ask the pastor about matters having to do with theo-centric, theo-relational, and vocational concerns. Disquieted souls who feel anxious about death and dying typically have some sort of anxiety that relates to God, specifically unease about what comes after death and whether and how God plays a role in that. My experience as a pastor convinces me that, in many cases, one's anxiousness over God's nature or character (theo-centric concerns), one's standing before God (theo-relational concerns), or one's faithfulness to God's purposes and claim on one's life (vocational concerns) actually informs one's dreading death (mortal concerns) so profoundly. Each of these concerns about God often overlaps and interweaves with the others.

Most people ponder these questions from time to time, particularly people in churches. But if most persons think occasionally about matters having to do with life, death, and life after death, anxious persons think about them quite often and become preoccupied by them. Their preoccupation becomes evident when they talk with pastors and raise questions and issues like these:

- What do you think happens to us when we die?
- What does the Bible say about the afterlife?
- How do I know that I'll be OK when I die?
- I worry about my soul. I think I need to change my ways.
- Will I see my loved one(s) again?
- Does one's soul immediately go to heaven when one dies?
- Why do we have to die? Couldn't God have made us so that we could live longer? Forever?
- I'm afraid to get sick and die.

These kinds of questions and concerns invite theological reflection and discernment on the pastor's part. They call for the pastor to have a working "theology of death" that informs her listening to persons struggling with these mortal concerns and her addressing them in pastoral care. The pastor also does well, as a matter of practice, to listen with an ear attuned to people's mortal concerns, just as she listens astutely to the questions and struggles generated by the other three kinds of concerns: theo-centric, theo-relational, and vocational. This attunement facilitates clarity in the pastor's understanding of what the care seeker experiences, wants, and needs, even as the pastor draws on the Christian faith and its wisdom in her role as caregiver.

Moreover, pastors should not attend to these concerns exclusively in one-on-one pastoral conversations. Indeed, pastors should attend to all four of these concerns, which lie at the heart of human experience and the Christian faith, in their preaching, teaching, worshiping, care and counseling, mission and outreach, and broader community life. The point is that pastors must cultivate a deep awareness of these four concerns that pertain to God and our relationship to God, and an understanding of how these concerns get expressed in the context of church life and pastoral relationships. With regard to persons in the faith community who seem overly eager to please, demonstrate perfectionist qualities, have difficulty getting along with others, seem to isolate themselves or behave erratically, evidence a preoccupation with death and the life to come, or exhibit any of anxiety's other manifestations, it just may be the case that feeling vulnerable and threatened lies at the heart of their experience. What drives their struggles and behaviors may be their disquieted souls. If so, perhaps what these persons seek foremost, from the church and from the pastor, is assistance with gaining more confidence in the midst of uncertainty, courage amid trepidation, and hope in the throes of despair. It could be that these persons want most to hear from one who has been charged with representing God and dares to speak on God's behalf with "a voice that says everything will be OK." How pastors listen to anxious persons, speak to them, and assist them with learning how to think, feel, act, listen, and speak for themselves in new ways, will impact the condition of these care seekers' souls.

Gauging the Soul's Condition and Needs: Paul Pruyser on "Pastoral Diagnosis"

Paul Pruyser's "guidelines for pastoral diagnosis"[12] may assist a pastor with caring for disquieted souls. These guidelines help the pastor listen

12. Pruyser, *The Minister as Diagnostician*, pp. 60-79.

to, understand, and discuss a person's experiences in spiritual terms. More specifically, these guidelines assist the pastor with considering what she hears the other person say, and not say, with respect to theo-centric, theo-relational, vocational, and mortal concerns.

Pastoral care involves listening closely to another person's story. Good listening facilitates helping the person make sense of that story and, in some cases, learn how to begin crafting a different personal story by "editing out" the current story's problematic features. As Donald Capps suggests, good listening requires that caregivers first create an environment conducive to effective listening. Creating this environment requires the caregiver's *intentionality,* or purposefulness, and *attentionality,* or maintained focus.[13] As the pastor listens to another's personal story, Pruyser's guidelines allow for shared interpretation and discussion of that story — including its problems, concerns, and needs — in relation to God, the things of God, and the person's faith journey. When a pastor hears in a person's story evidence of thoughts, feelings, relationships, or behaviors that point to living with anxiety, these guidelines help the pastor and care seeker think and talk together about the experience of anxiety in terms of how the individual's personal story is lived amid the Christian story.

Pruyser's way of thinking also may help anxious care seekers themselves with learning how to think differently about their experiences, and thus with crafting alternative, less anxious life stories. As they share their stories, they may learn to recognize and understand their disquieted souls as a spiritual condition, one tied deeply to how they think about God, the things of God, and Christian faith. When they learn to recognize and understand how the way they think about these spiritual matters informs their anxiety, they may learn to identify, embrace, and operate with an alternative way of thinking — with a new type of cognitive set — that differs from the one prompting anxiety. As they learn to think differently, they may learn to feel and act less anxious.

In presenting his guidelines, Pruyser contends that pastoral care-givers must be able to "diagnose" the situations that care seekers face from the perspective of faith. This ability makes pastoral caring distinct from other kinds of caring. Moreover, this pastoral approach em-

---

13. Donald Capps, *Giving Counsel: A Minister's Guidebook* (St. Louis: Chalice Press, 2001), p. 14.

ploys a point of view that people coming to pastors for help tend to embrace and expect pastors to utilize — what Pruyser calls "a pastoral perspective." They want talk about God to be central to gaining an understanding of their problem or concern. They also want the help that pastors or larger faith communities offer to be based in shared religious or spiritual commitments. When care seekers find that such care is not forthcoming, they tend to experience an additional layer of pain and frustration. These feelings usually arise because they feel they haven't been heard in the way that they wanted and expected. Pruyser thus urges pastors to become more proficient at "diagnosing" people's problems in spiritual or theological terms.[14]

Diagnosis has become a controversial term. It often conjures up negative, sterile images tied to a medical model for describing human beings and their condition. The term tends to be associated with illness and pathology, whether mental or physical, and that association may provide reason enough for concern when one considers using the term. However, Pruyser points out that it really means "distinguishing one condition from another," "grasping things as they really are," "and by derivation, resolving or deciding" "so as to do the right thing."[15] He notes too that, historically, Dominican thought as well as the diverse theologies of Jonathan Edwards and Søren Kierkegaard have appealed to the language of diagnosis. For Pruyser, the term remains perfectly appropriate. However, Pruyser also uses the term *assessment* to describe what he means by *diagnosis*. Because of the controversy surrounding this term, I will speak in terms of "pastoral assessment" or "gauging" the soul's condition and needs.

So what does Pruyser, the clinical psychologist, have to say about pastoral assessment? He holds that ministers do well to keep seven "diagnostic concepts" or "variables" in mind as they consider what those seeking care may struggle with and need. These concepts should be viewed as ordering principles that inform an interpretive framework for beginning to map the presenting problem from a pastoral perspective. These seven concepts spring from Pruyser's interest in a person's religious views, belief system, and value orientation. The concepts may

14. Pruyser uses the terms *spiritual* and *theological* interchangeably when speaking of "a pastoral perspective."

15. Pruyser, *The Minister as Diagnostician*, p. 30.

(and likely will) be joined with an appeal to other concepts provided by different perspectives, like psychotherapy and psychiatry. Nevertheless, Pruyser holds that a pastoral perspective, which these seven concepts inform, not only makes the pastor's work distinct but comes closest to meeting a care seeker's foremost hopes and needs.

A Person's Awareness of the Holy

One organizing concept for the pastoral perspective is a person's awareness of the holy. This principle's concern centers on what a person reveres or finds sacred in life. In assessing how this concept may be working in the care seeker's personal story, the pastor listens for how that story touches upon (or fails to touch upon) such matters as the following:

- the person's attentiveness to the sacred in life and capacity for viewing life through some sort of sacred lens
- the person's appreciation for the transcendent and tendency to order her life with an appeal to spiritual or divine realms
- the person's life evidencing values that arise from sacred, spiritual, or religious commitments
- the person's tendency to view herself as a dependent creature, living as part of a larger web of life, as opposed to being "self-inflated" and self-absorbed

Accordingly, the pastor may consider the following while listening to the care seeker's story:

- To what extent does the transcendent matter to this person?
- How is this evidenced?
- Could the person's sense of the sacred in life be squelched in a way that indicates a painful history with things sacred?
- What specifically prompted that pain, and how has it impacted the person since?

Here are some specific questions and responses that a pastor may offer in a pastoral conversation to explore and assess a person's awareness of the holy:

- I can sense that you're struggling. What or who do you think could be helpful?
- How have you thought about solving this problem?
- Who might help you the most with this need?
- I'm wondering where God is in what you're experiencing.
- Tell me about your sense of God's hand in your life.
- What do you value and why?

While the way in which a person answers these questions may spark further conversation and reflection, the primary interest here centers on discerning whether the care seeker is used to "flying solo" in life and being his own sole resource for understanding and solving a problem, or whether he views God and others as grounds of support and care. Knowing this may provide entree into how the care seeker's sense of the holy, sacred, and transcendent in life figures into his struggles, and also whether his sense of life's sacredness may provide a source of help.

Considering a care seeker's awareness of the holy is a good place to begin in pastoral assessment, as the qualities and degree of that awareness will likely have much to say about the other organizing principles for assessment. Knowing more about a care seeker's sense of the sacred in life provides the pastor with a cue to listen to questions and statements with an ear attuned precisely to theo-centric, theo-relational, vocational, and mortal concerns. Furthermore, as a care seeker gains awareness and understanding of the holy, including its presence in her life, she has more of a basis for rethinking how matters related to it may inform her anxiety. Here too self-awareness plays a key role in the caring process, with pastors aiming to help cultivate that awareness.

A Person's View of Providence

A second organizing concept is a person's view of providence. This concept of providence centers on the response to this question: "What is the Divine Purpose in its intention *toward myself?*"[16] As Pruyser notes,

16. Pruyser quotes psychologist Ernest Jones here, noting, "What one really wants to know about the Divine Purpose is its intention *toward oneself.*" See Pruyser, *The Minister as Diagnostician*, p. 64.

the term *providence* can mean numerous things, from a strict doctrinal claim to a more existential concern about human freedom and its limits. The term may to "belief in cosmic benevolence" or "a desire for guidance from on high," or it may "refer to a need for nurture: 'Tell me, Pastor, where can I find solace? What must I do? What have I left undone? What should I try to change in myself?'"[17] Making use of *providence* as an organizing concept helps the pastor and the care seeker think more deeply about what or who has final say in life and is in charge of the world. Closely related to one's sense of the sacred, one's view of providence affects one's capacity for trust. Without a sense of providence, by which I mean God's interest and influence that includes God's benevolence, we have little capacity for trust or hope that ultimately "everything will be OK."

The psychoanalyst Erik H. Erikson pointed out the inseparable relationship between trust and hope. He noted that one's capacity for faith and hope springs from the capacity to trust, and that this capacity begins to develop in the earliest moments of life.[18] With respect to one's relationship to God, or one's spiritual life, confidently placing one's trust, faith, and hope in the promises of God set forth in the Christian story lies at the heart of living well, particularly amid various theo-centric, theo-relational, vocational, and mortal concerns. Consequently, one's capacity for trust and hope deeply impact the state of one's soul.

For the purposes of pastoral care, the pastor would want to explore whether providence, in whatever kind of language the care seeker might express it, orients him in his world. The pastor embarks on this exploration by listening to the care seeker's story with an interest in how it relates to such matters as these:

- the person's sense that God remains faithfully involved in his life
- the person's belief that God has a deep interest in and concern for what happens to him
- the person's trust that God will be present and a source of support when he is seeking to solve his problems, alleviate his suffering, or quiet his soul

17. Pruyser, *The Minister as Diagnostician*, p. 65.
18. See, for example, Erik H. Erikson, *Identity and the Life Cycle* (New York: W. W. Norton, 1959/1980).

- the person's sense that the pastor represents God's presence and benevolence, and hence that she herself (the pastor) may be trusted

With respect to the last point, if the care seeker views the pastor as an instrument of God (and many persons seeking care from pastors not only do so but need to do so), then the care seeker's capacity for trust in God may have an impact on his capacity for trusting the pastor, and thus for entering into a meaningful relationship with her.

The focus should not be on precise doctrinal understandings of God's providence. The point here is not whether one follows Augustine or Aquinas, Calvin or Barth, Luther or Wesley in this regard. Rather, the point is to create a relational space wherein the care seeker has a sense that, in some way, a benevolent God shares in his experience and remains present, concerned, and desirous of fulfilling God's promise to care and to provide. Here are some specific ways that a pastor might respond to the care seeker's story when exploring his view of providence:

- Things seem really difficult for you right now. I wonder how you're coping.
- I can only imagine how painful this must be for you. Tell me, how to do you find strength each day?
- What or who has sustained you thus far?
- It seems like you feel all alone . . . [Pausing here to see how the person will respond to this open-ended statement — whether he will confirm it, deny it, or elaborate on it — would be appropriate.]
- How do you see this working out?

Like gaining a sense of a person's awareness of the holy, paying attention to his view of providence serves to assist both the pastor and the care seeker with exploring his capacity to look beyond himself for support in his journey, and especially to trust in God's interest and concern for his well-being. In trusting, the care seeker may also hope for a future in which his difficulties are overcome — with God's help.

In calling pastors "agents of hope," Donald Capps highlights a distinct reason that people turn to pastors for help: they seek more hope-filled lives. As Capps puts it, "When persons who are experiencing problems and difficulties seek assistance from a pastor, they are, in this very act, seeking hope. They may not have much confidence that the pastor can help them, but their act of reaching out, however hesitant or uncertain it may be, is an indication of their desire to hope, to find grounds for hoping rather than despairing. [Furthermore,] when the pastor initiates contact with a person who is in difficulty, the pastor, through this very gesture, offers hope."[19] In light of Capps's observation, the pastor does well to consider how she may be an instrument of a kind of hope that springs from her own belief in Paul's assurance of God's providential gift: "He who rescued us from so deadly a peril will continue to rescue us; on him we have set our hope that he will rescue us again" (2 Cor. 1:10).

A Person's Measure of Faith

A third organizing principle, related to the previous two, has to do with a person's measure of faith. Here the issue is not so much the content of one's faith, though that eventually comes into play, but simply that a person *has* faith or, at least, has the capacity for faith. By "faith" Pruyser means a person's belief in, or potential to believe in, something or someone that warrants abiding trust and commitment. When focusing on assessing a person's situation, problem, or concern, a pastor attends to the role that the care seeker's faith (or its absence) plays in his life. Consequently, the pastor will consider matters like the following when listening to a care seeker share his story:

- the person's deep belief in someone or something that serves as a basis for ultimate meaning, value, and hope
- the extent to which the person's faith functions as a life compass that provides direction and orders the way life is lived
- the degree to which a person's faith provides assurance that he will not ultimately be lost in his life journey
- a person's ability to make commitments, to others and to himself, in light of his basis for meaning, value, and hope

Related to qualities of trust and hope, which come with holding a place for providence, faith involves a welcoming posture toward life. Faith, as

19. Donald Capps, *Agents of Hope: A Pastoral Psychology* (Minneapolis: Fortress Press, 1995), p. 8.

Pruyser puts it, has to do with one's "affirming or negating stance in life, his enthusiasm or lukewarmness." As Pruyser notes, here the pastoral concern centers on utilizing this concept for assessing whether the care seeker is "typically a hearty yea-sayer to ideals and the general pattern of reality and life" or tends "to be a critical, cautious nay-sayer, full of ifs, buts, and howevers." In other words, does a person "embrace life and experience" in spite of difficulties, or does he "shy away from them?"[20]

When Pruyser speaks of faith in terms of one's disposition for engaging life and its experiences, he means one's ability to commit to something meaningful, and a related openness to the world and others. When commenting on one's measure of faith and how the pastor might explore it in pastoral conversation, Pruyser suggests the following types of questions:[21]

- Does it open up the world for him, or does it draw narrow boundaries, making a little niche for an area of safety?
- Does it enlarge the person himself, activating all his talents and stimulating his curiosity, widening the scope of his engagement, or does it put him into a straitjacket, stifling him and constricting his abilities?

Pastors do well to explore this measure of faith because the care seeker's faith serves as a personal strength that may be utilized in pastoral care for personal transformation. An ability to commit to someone or something, to engage in life and relationships with others, and to cultivate a willingness to look at life openly and partake of it provides a sound basis for working on life problems and concerns. Having faith, or at least a capacity for faith, means that the care seeker may find encouragement in a time of distress, particularly encouragement that comes from trust and hope in what or whom he has committed to in life. If the soul's disquiet is involved, a capacity for faith allows the pastor and the care seeker to explore together the content of faith, and especially how that faith may be contributing to anxiety. By reworking his faith so that he learns to embrace his faith story differently, the care

---

20. Pruyser, *The Minister as Diagnostician*, pp. 67-68.
21. Pruyser, *The Minister as Diagnostician*, pp. 68-69.

seeker may find his anxious soul soothed. On the other hand, the absence of faith makes pastoral care more challenging.

The pastor will thus want to look for the presence or absence of faith with the following kinds of comments and questions:

- What keeps you going?
- Where do you find peace and hope?
- I wonder how you see this situation turning around.
- How can this get better?
- What or who may be helpful to you?
- Tell me about your faith.
- Where is God in all of this for you?

The hope is that conversation about these concerns prompts a response from the care seeker that offers some indication of his more open outlook on life, a corresponding belief that things will indeed turn around and "be OK," and especially his commitment to trusting in God's provision and care. The pastor will want to gauge whether the care seeker *has* faith or a capacity for it that leads (or could lead) to a confident hope that, despite current difficulties and pain, life can and will get better.

I want to emphasize Pruyser's observation that the pastor does well to distinguish between different kinds of faith. A more positive faith serves to expand the care seeker's view of the world and his perspective on life's possibilities. A less positive faith limits this perspective and functions more like a security blanket of naïveté. A positive faith, which is motivated by joy, informs what a person believes he *may* experience, do, and expect in life. That type of faith liberates and empowers. The alternative tends to be motivated by fear and informs what a person believes he *may not* experience, do, and expect in life. This negative kind of faith imprisons and oppresses. Consequently, it hinders pastoral care. When pastoral conversation indicates that a care seeker lacks a measure of faith in the positive sense, the pastor's goal may be to help him adopt a more open posture or stance with respect to his faith.[22] This posture would include receptivity to hopefulness.

---

22. Pruyser, *The Minister as Diagnostician*, p. 69.

A Person's Perception of Grace or Gratefulness

A fourth organizing principle is one's understanding of grace, which includes a capacity for gratefulness. Pruyser keeps the focus here on two central concerns. The first has to do with a person's capacity to receive and offer forgiveness. Noting that the Latin cognate *gratia* makes up such related terms as *grace, graciousness, gratitude,* and *gratefulness,* Pruyser points out that all of these "have something to do with kindness, generousness, gifts, the beauty of giving and receiving, or 'getting something for nothing.'" He also recognizes that pastors will often meet persons whose perception of grace is "of dynamic importance."[23] If the care seeker has the capacity for extending forgiveness, whether to others or to herself, she will likely indicate that in a pastoral conversation. This capacity may become evident through statements and questions like these:

- I need to ask for forgiveness.
- I'm having difficulty forgiving her. As much as I'd like to be able to, I can't seem to do it.
- Nobody's perfect! We need to recognize our mistakes, apologize for them, and move on.
- How can we get past what has happened?
- Let's find a way to put this behind us and let bygones be bygones.

These responses and others like them indicate the extent to which the care seeker operates with a sense of what grace involves, with an appreciation for its place in life, and also whether she lives oriented toward such grace in her daily life. Consequently, the pastor and the care seeker may discover a basis for further engagement of what we might term "grace matters," wherein more in-depth reflection, conversation, and perhaps prayer may inform attempts to work with the care seeker's perception of grace or gratefulness and, if necessary, to enhance it. Additionally, focusing on a person's perception of grace or gratefulness may provide further insight into her ability and willingness to recognize the need for confession and forgiveness, whether her own or that of others. That ability and willingness is also a personal strength that can and should be utilized in pastoral care.

23. Pruyser, *The Minister as Diagnostician,* p. 69.

Of course, a person may indicate that grace is not part of her "life lexicon." She may indicate that she lives with a pattern marked more by holding grudges than by a penchant for letting bygones be bygones, and may evidence that by saying things like this:

- I just want to get even with her.
- That's simply unforgivable — the unpardonable sin!
- Nothing he says will ever change how I feel.
- I'm through with her. I'll never speak to her again.
- He's burned a bridge, and it can never be rebuilt.

Statements like these may simply indicate profound anger. If so, it's important to remember that while such anger may keep forgiveness at bay for the moment, it may not do so forever. In some cases, one may very well need to allow oneself to be angry before one can forgive. Consequently, these kinds of responses in and of themselves do not necessarily indicate that grace or forgiveness lies beyond the realm of possibility. However, such responses could indicate that grace is in some ways foreign to this person, whether in the realm of receiving it or offering it to others. Thus it will be important for the pastor to make this assessment part of the pastoral care offered.

Another of Pruyser's concerns about a care seeker's stance toward grace or gratefulness centers on whether it prevents her from recognizing the magnitude of her current situation. This may evidence itself in her minimizing life's difficulties and their harmful effects. For example, if she has suffered a tragic loss or a trauma of some sort, she may downplay that with the language of grace: "God doesn't give us more than we can handle, you know." "I remind myself that lots of people experience much worse in life than I have." "All things considered, God has been good to me." These types of responses *may* be a sign of strength in coping, because they may contain some element of truth for some people. However, more often than not, such responses follow from a reluctance to identify and own the pain of life, and usually for fear that doing so would slight God and God's providential care. Thus, responses like these may indicate a fear of getting angry, especially at God, and also a more pervasive immaturity of faith that would be important to address.

A Person's Capacity for Repentance

A fifth organizing principle, relating closely to the one just discussed, has to do with the person's capacity for repentance. Pruyser describes this capacity as "referring to a process of change, most often self-initiated from a condition of felt displeasure or anguish, aimed at a state of greater well being." This process of change may take on different forms, depending on the context in which we consider repentance or "repenting." Morally speaking, as Pruyser notes, this change has to do with "correction," or moving from "crookedness" to "rectitude," while in theological terms it has to do with "change from sinfulness to saintliness or from damnation to salvation."[24] In either case, this concept essentially has to do with one's facility for agency — one's capacity to consider and understand the role that one will have to play in bringing one's life in line with more of what one wants and needs. This agency includes not only pursuing life's goals and desires, but also solving life's problems and concerns. As Pruyser puts it, "The self is an agent in fair and bad times."[25]

Closely related to the capacity for grace, and especially for confession, the capacity for repentance gets at the "so what" that follows confession. Particularly important is the role one must play oneself, *as agent*, for living more fully into one's understanding of a grace-filled life. A pastor may learn more about the care seeker's capacity for repentance by listening to his story with a particular interest in whether and how it gives evidence of the following (the third thing being the most important):

- the person's facility with identifying not merely the shortcomings of others but also his own shortcomings
- the extent to which the person recognizes the role that he plays in a conflict or strained relationships with other persons
- after the person identifies his own shortcomings, the degree to which he seems able and willing to "repent" — that is, to turn from old ways of thinking, feeling, or relating to face new ways of doing so

24. Pruyser, *The Minister as Diagnostician*, p. 71.
25. Pruyser, *The Minister as Diagnostician*, p. 71.

How the care seeker demonstrates capacity with these matters provides valuable insight into his capacity for change, which finally depends in part on his own volition (choice) and agency (acting) in life. Of course, for the Christian person, one turns from "sin" and turns toward God in Jesus Christ, whose life and relationships, with other persons and ultimately with God, become models for imitation. Consequently, the pastor working with repentance as an organizing principle will draw on the wisdom of the Christian story when thinking about, and helping the care seeker think about, what repenting might involve.

Let me offer a cautionary word here. There will be some who operate with a hyperactive inclination toward repentance, and thus who assume responsibility and blame unnecessarily or inappropriately. Pastors routinely encounter persons who are much too quick to say "I'm sorry," "It's my fault," "I didn't do it correctly," "That's my responsibility," or something similar, which reflects their sense that they need to repent of what they have done or failed to do. This "hyper-repentance" may indicate an overactive conscience, what Pruyser calls a "hypertrophy of conscience" that "sees sin everywhere and lives blind to grace."[26] In my experience as a pastor, the church often attracts such persons. Many who come to church struggle with feelings of guilt and shame that frequently seem to evidence their inability to forgive themselves and let go of the need to keep asking for forgiveness, which repenting provides. When a pastor assesses a care seeker's capacity for repentance, a perceived *lack* will call for pastoral focus on strengthening that capacity. Conversely, a perceived propensity for *excessive* or *inappropriate* repentance will require focus on the gifts of grace, including how these might more readily be recognized and appropriated. The pastoral goal here is to help the care seeker cease to bear an undue burden with respect to his "sin."

The pastor might explore the care seeker's capacity for repentance with these kinds of statements and questions:

- I'm wondering what you understand your role to be in reconciliation.
- It's clear that "Joe" has hurt you, and, as you say, it would help if he owned up to his responsibilities. Fair enough. Let's hope that happens soon. Until then, what do you see as your responsibility in this?

26. Pruyser, *The Minister as Diagnostician*, p. 73.

- What will you yourself do now to promote the solutions you seek?
- How might you think about altering your behavior as a means for moving closer to what you say you want?

These questions get at whether the care seeker has considered his own role — and perhaps negligence — in a given problem, and likewise, the extent to which he tends to embrace opportunities presented to him for repentance. In other words, these types of questions allow the pastor to gain more insight into the care seeker's awareness of his own responsibility for a problem or difficulty, but also his agency and power in the process of change.

In a case where a pastor suspects that the care seeker will benefit from becoming *less* inclined to repent, in that she tends to do so excessively or unnecessarily, the following statements and questions may prove helpful:

- Help me understand more about how you see this as your responsibility.
- What role might others have played in this problem?
- How much of the problem stems from you and your actions, and how much stems from others and their actions?
- What is possible for you to control here, and what is not?
- You seem more than ready to take the lion's share of responsibility here. Why do you think this is the case?
- How and when do you tend to say "I'm sorry"?
- How and when is it appropriate for you to say "I'm sorry"?

When used sensitively and prudently, these kinds of statements and questions can elicit responses that may prompt the care seeker to see her overly active propensity for repentance in a new, more constructive, and even more faithful light.

A Person's Capacity for Communion

Pruyser describes a sixth organizing principle for pastoral assessment as a person's capacity for communion. At base, this has to do with one's level of connection with other individuals and groups of people.

As Pruyser puts it, "It has to do with embeddedness, reaching out, caring, and feeling cared for," its most "basic sense" being "the individual's disposition to see himself either as continuous or discontinuous with the rest of mankind and nature."[27] While this disposition manifests itself in numerous ways, Pruyser thinks that a principal one is the ability to recognize that all of us travel in the same boat when it comes to being "poor sinners" making the best of life that we can. Essentially, this disposition is demonstrated in one's capacity for saying "There but for the grace of God go I."

Pruyser suggests that the pastoral concern here, the "diagnostic task," centers on assessing the care seeker's basic life orientation. Of particular interest is whether his "general attitude" toward life would be described as "embedded" or "estranged," "open to the world" or "encapsulated," "in touch" or "isolated," "united" or "separated."[28] The pastor will want to keep the following kinds of concerns in mind as she listens to the care seeker's story and assesses his propensity for communion:

- the degree to which he views his life and the lives of others as fundamentally fused, as part of one another and members of a larger web of life and relationships
- the tendency to think of life in terms of requiring some kind of common "life thread," one that weaves its way through all of life and all of humanity, binding both together in essential, even sacred ways
- alternatively, the tendency to see disjunction, fraction, and discontinuity all around and to assume that is ordinarily the way things are

More than mere optimism or pessimism, a propensity for communion has centrally to do with one's basic stance toward others, toward life and its events, and toward the world itself. Thinking about communion in terms that the psychoanalyst Erik Erikson proposed means focusing on a person's feeling or sense of "at-homeness" in the world, a confidence that his place in the world matters and remains more or

27. Pruyser, *The Minister as Diagnostician*, p. 74.
28. Pruyser, *The Minister as Diagnostician*, p. 74.

less in synch with life around him. This sense of "at-homeness" serves to build and maintain his capacity for trust and hope.

While listening to a care seeker's story, the pastor may gain insight into his sense of communion or "at-homeness" in the world by offering these kinds of comments and questions:

- You seem to be dealing with lots of difficult issues right now. I hope that you have some people in your life who can offer support.
- I can sense that you feel overwhelmed with worry right now. Whom will you be able to share that with when you leave my study?
- Tell me about your family and your support system.
- What was it like for you growing up when you faced a difficult problem or were worried about something?
- Where do you find peace, solace, and hope?
- On whom will you lean during this journey?
- How might members of the congregation support you?
- How might I support you?

These comments and questions facilitate the pastor's exploration of the degree of connectedness (or disconnectedness) with which the care seeker lives, and also of whether he has a network of support that may provide ongoing care and nurture. Disquieted souls tend to require a degree of connectedness lacking in their lives, a connectedness that serves as grounds for assurance that "everything will be OK." The pastor does well to remember this need and to assess it in her pastoral care.

The pastor cannot and should not attempt to be all things to all people. The pastor alone cannot provide sufficient care in a faith community, and when she attempts that, she risks providing inadequate care, eventually burning out, and usurping the gifts that others in the community have for caring ministries. Good stewardship of care calls for the minister to share the responsibility for care with others, in the faith community and beyond. Assessing the care seeker's capacity for communion provides clarity concerning how amenable he is to connecting with and drawing from a community of care. Helping the care seeker to rely upon the larger faith community helps him become more reliant on others, something the Christian story prizes, and fosters the kind of stewardship of care that holds spiritual and practical benefits, for the care seeker himself and for the larger community.

It is important to note that a person who generally feels a sense of connection with others, and for whom communion is a more or less natural state of being, may experience alienation or disconnection at certain times and with respect to certain events. For example, going through a divorce can be quite alienating, particularly when relationships change not only with a former spouse but also with family, friends, colleagues, the faith community, and other close associates. This scenario involves what could be called a situational lack of communion, as compared to a more comprehensive or pervasive lack of communion. In other words, before the divorce the person who now seems disconnected and alienated from others embodied an observable capacity for communion. Thus the key to assessing this capacity remains the pastor's discerning whether the care seeker's feeling of disconnection dominates his way of being in the world or is temporary and due to particular problems in his life. If a lack of communion characterizes his general orientation toward life, the pastor does well to look for opportunities to demonstrate that strength can be found in relationship with others. The relationship between pastor and care seeker should serve as a model.

A Person's Sense of Vocation

Pruyser's seventh organizing principle fixes upon a person's sense of vocation. This concept has less to do with one's career choice or goals (though that may be part of it), and more to do with "a person's willingness to be a cheerful participant in the scheme of creation and providence, so that a sense of purpose is attached to his doings which validates his existence under his Creator."[29] Pruyser likes the term *vocation* because it allows the pastor using it to work between "high-level theological positions" on the one hand, and "the pedestrian details of everyday life" on the other. Viewing vocation in this way provides opportunities for pastors to discern the extent to which care seekers "make their work fit into a set of values and tend to endow it with almost cosmic significance, no matter how lowly the task."[30] The primary pastoral in-

29. Pruyser, *The Minister as Diagnostician*, p. 76.
30. Pruyser, *The Minister as Diagnostician*, p. 77.

terest here lies in finding out more about how the care seeker's work, whether formal or informal, paid or volunteer, fits with his operative values and broader sense of the cosmos.

Pruyser adds that vocation may be thought of too as "heartfelt participation in constructive work that is cued to divine benevolence and assiduously shuns alignment with malevolence."[31] Keeping in mind this focus on "participation," "purpose," "validation by one's creator," and work "cued to divine benevolence," I would suggest that we think of vocation as referring at base to one's sense of working with God on behalf of oneself, others, and the world. This shared labor serves as the basis for how one views life and engages it in all its facets. The pastor attuned to the care seeker's sense of vocation will want to discover more about the following:

- the manner and degree to which he views his life as part of God's plan and activity in the world
- the tendency to interpret life, with all its joys and trials, in light of God's providence and God's claim on all of creation
- not only how he views what he does in life, but also whether that has significance beyond his own life, for the benefit of others and of God

The focus on vocation grows out of the other principles cited and may be thought of as the overarching one into which all the others feed. Vocation may thus be viewed as a convergence of one's views of *the holy, providence, faith, grace, repentance,* and *communion.* Many theological traditions understand the meaning of vocation in terms of "life's meaning and purpose" by virtue of God's presence and claim upon God's people.

The pastor may explore the care seeker's sense of vocation with these kinds of comments and questions:

- Tell me what all of this means to you.
- What purpose have you found in what you're describing?
- Help me know more about who you understand yourself to be in light of what has happened.

31. Pruyser, *The Minister as Diagnostician,* p. 77.

- Where does your relationship to God fit into the decision you're trying to make?
- How have you prayed about this matter, and what have you discovered in doing so?
- How do you discern God's accompanying you in this journey?
- How does your life seem to fit with what you envision God wanting for you?

These queries bring the issue of vocation to the fore and, once again, draw attention to the inherent strengths of connection, to God and to others, which vocation thus conceived provides.

Conclusion

It may prove difficult and unwise for a pastor to attempt to use all seven of Pruyser's diagnostic categories, whether in one or several pastoral conversations. Indeed, the pastor should not feel obligated to make such an attempt. Donald Capps suggests a more likely way to use these categories: by focusing pastoral listening and conversation on three of the seven categories or "themes." These include (1) a major theme, (2) a minor theme that has bearing on the major theme and how the care seeker is experiencing it, and (3) a theme that is conspicuous by its absence from the conversation.[32] Furthermore, while all seven themes are potentially relevant for pastoral conversation about anxiety-related concerns, it may be helpful to view the themes in terms of two distinct but related sets.[33] The first set of themes captures the emphasis on cognitive processes and their role in anxiety. Specifically, *providence, faith,* and *grace or gratefulness* tend to fit more with the cognitive focus and efforts toward becoming more aware of how and what one thinks. The second set of themes emphasizes behavior or agency, including faith practices. Specifically, *awareness of the holy, repentance, communion,* and *vocation* fit with the focus on anxiety-reducing behaviors and agency that faith practices promote. The relationship between the two sets of themes may be viewed as follows:

32. See Donald Capps, *Pastoral Care: A Thematic Approach* (Philadelphia: Westminster Press, 1979), esp. pp. 108-36.
33. I am indebted to Donald Capps for this insight.

Cognitive Focus Themes	Behavioral Focus Themes
Providence	Awareness of the holy
Faith	Repentance
Grace or gratefulness	Communion
	Vocation

The pastor may listen to the care seeker's story and suggest particular strategies for changing the way she thinks or behaves related to her anxiety, according to how these themes divide in their principal focus, along cognitive and behavioral lines. In other words, when the care seeker's queries or statements organize around the themes in the first set, then the pastor may be cued to pay closer attention to how and what the care seeker *thinks* and how that informs her disquieted soul. Likewise, when a care seeker's queries or statements organize around themes in the second set, the pastor may want to attend more closely to the care seeker's agency (or lack thereof) and how it informs her disquieted soul. A word of caution must be added. These themes dovetail with one another and share common qualities, so the goal is not to think in rigid ways about what may or may not be contained in a given theme, or to make pastoral assessment mechanistic with respect to any diagnostic category. Thinking along the lines of two sets of themes simply offers one way to make use of Pruyser's thought in ministry with disquieted souls. Whether or not a pastor chooses this approach, Capps's suggestion to focus on a major theme, a minor theme, and an absent theme should nonetheless be strongly considered.

In advocating the use of Pruyser's categories, I am not encouraging the pastor to resort to any sort of labeling as he listens to and assesses a care seeker's story. Simplistic or reductionistic explanations for complex life problems have little if any value, as Pruyser himself recognizes. In point of fact, most human problems prove far richer and more layered than any label or diagnostic category will fully capture. Furthermore, Pruyser does not claim that his categories should necessarily be shared explicitly with the care seeker. Rather, these diagnostic criteria aim to assist the pastor in listening to the care seeker's story in a way that leads to identifying theological, spiritual, or faith-related questions, concerns, or struggles. These criteria remain valuable because they offer a sound and user-friendly interpretive framework for encouraging the pastor to listen and think in more spiritually oriented terms, to assess a situation or a problem from what Pruyser calls "a pastoral perspective."

With respect to disquieted souls, Pruyser's framework for assessment, coupled with attention to the four concerns that I have posited (theo-centric, theo-relational, vocational, and mortal), fosters needed focus on matters that contribute to anxiety and what holds potential for relieving it. Making use of Pruyser's categories and the four concerns keeps the pastor mindful of the anxious care seeker's vulnerability, of her connection or disconnection from God and others, and particularly of how a way of thinking about God and understanding God — the operative cognitive set — informs her disquieted soul. Both of these interpretive frameworks, Pruyser's and my own, remain grounded in the language and perspectives of faith. Both interpretive frameworks facilitate this language and these perspectives taking hold in the pastoral conversation, providing a way to sharpen focus on and understanding of personal struggles tied to the disquieted soul. At the same time, these frameworks provide a place to begin mapping out, in partnership with the care seeker, a plan for help.

Nevertheless, none of these categories or variables, Pruyser's or mine, should be viewed as a simple checklist. Nor should they be viewed as a one-size-fits-all tool for the pastor's work. Rather, these categories and variables, and the language of faith in general, should simply "linger in the pastor's mind, functioning as guideposts to his diagnostic thinking and as ordering principles for the observations he makes."[34] Assessing the care seeker's situation in this manner serves to foster an ongoing pastoral perspective. These frameworks inform care in ways consistent with the Christian story and, very likely, with the care seeker's hopes and expectations, without becoming a canned checklist that makes for good theological window-dressing but offers little in the way of substance.

These frameworks are meant to help the pastor with hearing, interpreting, understanding, and discussing experiences of anxiety in *spiritual* terms. These frameworks draw attention to how anxiety relates to God and God's presence in the care seeker's life, including who she understands herself to be in relationship to God in both life and death.

34. Pruyser, *The Minister as Diagnostician*, pp. 95-96.

Because the way we think shapes how we feel, a primary goal in making use of these frameworks involves learning to embrace a different type of cognitive set than one prompting anxiety. This new cognitive set will carry different perspectives on various matters relating to God, including perspectives that offer assurance that, by virtue of God's love and concern, "everything will be OK."

In the next two chapters I suggest how pastors may help anxious persons to restructure their cognitive sets, so that in thinking, feeling, and acting differently they change their personal stories shaped by disquieted souls.

Chapter 6

LEARNING A DIFFERENT STORY

Why Disquieted Souls Need the Church

I maintain that anxiety's roots may be found in the soul, in the relationship of the whole person to God, which makes anxiety a spiritual condition requiring spiritual means for its relief. Spiritual replenishment of disquieted souls requires a greater sense of connection, to God and to others, which counters the vulnerability that anxious persons feel, particularly with respect to their standing before God and what it means for their lives. In the next two chapters I want to focus on how the Christian faith holds the power to affect souls and to foster spiritual replenishment. Specifically, I focus on the power of the Christian story and its faith practices to refashion the personal stories and practices of disquieted souls.

The Power of Stories

Considering, learning, embracing, telling, retelling, and living stories, which human beings have done from the beginning of time, serves to orient us in the world. As the South African theologian John W. de Gruchy suggests, this orientation occurs because stories allow us "to make sense of our place in the world," which includes providing an understanding of "our origins, who we are, why the world is like it is, and how we should live," by "shaping who we are, informing our values, and directing our paths." Moreover, "the stories we tell, whether about ourselves or about others, reveal how we see life and understand what it means to be human."[1] These obser-

---

1. John W. de Gruchy, *Confessions of a Christian Humanist* (Minneapolis: Fortress Press, 2006), pp. 4-5, 8.

vations lead de Gruchy to suggest further that stories hold at least two additional powers: to break open a new reality and to provide hope. He writes, "Stories told with honesty, like all genuine works of art, break open reality, helping us to see things differently, to see ourselves differently and hopefully to live differently," for "stories evoke hope, whether personal or communal, without which we cannot be truly human."[2]

A central idea at work here is that we human beings necessarily "story" our lives. Doing so provides a framework for meaning and understanding, and for the norms and values we adopt. Across time and experience, we make use of language and the various traditions that touch our lives as we record, organize, link together, attempt to make sense of, ascribe meaning to, shape and are shaped by our experiences, relationships, and social interactions. As theologian William C. Placher puts it, "The language we use and the tradition in which we have lived shape the way we experience things and indeed the kind of experience we can have."[3]

Language, then, particularly as used to consider, construct, tell, and retell stories, serves as the principal means for understanding our world and, in turn, for telling ourselves and others about it. The language we make use of, not only for communicating with others but also for communicating with ourselves (what we think, feel, experience), informs our view of how things are — our reality. Our language also allows us to make sense of our lives and to find meaning. The pastoral theologian Charles V. Gerkin describes the role that language plays in meaning-making:

> Language constructs world. To have a world, to live in a world, means, for humans, to inhabit a time and place in which a certain language is connected with experience to give meaning to that experience. More than anything else, the capacity to make meaning marks the human as human. Whenever any event occurs in our lives, be that so small an event as stubbing one's toe on a crack in the sidewalk, or so "large" and significant an event as entering into a marriage or contracting a dread disease, it

2. De Gruchy, *Confessions of a Christian Humanist,* p. 7.

3. William C. Placher, *Unapologetic Theology: A Christian Voice in a Pluralistic Age* (Louisville: Westminster John Knox Press, 1989), p. 158.

does not become an experience to us until language is attached to the event and it is given meaning.[4]

Gerkin adds that meaning-making occurs automatically, even unconsciously, and that while reflection on our experience may create new meanings, the connection between life and language, and especially stories, remains.

This process of connecting life and language informs not only our personal narrative, *our* story, but also how we understand *others'* stories. We often say and hear said things like "What's her story?" or "Tell me your story" or "I could tell you some stories" — which get at this narrative quality of human existence. Storying our lives takes place continually within the context, or against the backdrop, of multiple narratives that we and others constantly create, recreate, and share. In fact, we could go so far as to say that our lives are storied largely through *our own* experiences as we encounter, learn, and either embrace or reject the stories crafted by others through *their* experiences.[5]

These stories that we tell and encounter include individual, familial, and larger social and cultural ones. Personal stories get created by virtue of living in relationship to the stories of parents, siblings, grandparents and extended family members, friends, neighbors, teachers, schoolmates, colleagues, and supervisors. Personal stories get created too by virtue of things like one's nationality, regional locale, race, ethnicity, gender, sexual orientation, and other qualities that human beings claim, are claimed by, and into which they live. For some people, the story provided by their religious tradition plays a particularly important role in the formation of their personal story. Their religion or faith story may very well be among the most powerful shapers of their perceptions and understandings of life, as well as their participation in it.

In a sense, we encounter and borrow from many stories that others tell on the way to creating our own story over the course of a lifetime. Some of the stories we come across have existed for a long time. Others

---

4. Charles V. Gerkin, *The Living Human Document: Re-Visioning Pastoral Counseling in a Hermeneutical Mode* (Nashville: Abingdon Press, 1984), pp. 39-40.

5. Martha Nussbaum, "Narrative Emotions: Beckett's Genealogy of Love," in *Why Narrative? Readings in Narrative Theology*, ed. Stanley Hauerwas and L. Gregory Jones (Grand Rapids: William B. Eerdmans, 1989), pp. 216-48.

are newer. But all of them evolve across time, being shaped and re-shaped in fresh ways as they interface with one another through lived experience: as they are told and retold, lived and relived. This ongoing process precipitates new stories being formed. Although earlier narratives remain part of us and influence us throughout life, in their telling and retelling over time they may be understood differently and shape both the tellers and the hearers of those stories in new and different ways. This phenomenon suggests that as our web of relationships grows, our social environment expands or changes, and our exposure to new narratives increases throughout life, new stories continue to present themselves. As a result, these new stories prompt a reworking of our personal narratives. Inevitably, we locate and relocate ourselves and others in relation to these multiple stories that we encounter and participate in throughout life. In so doing, we find meaning, understanding, purpose, value, and feeling in our lives.

We also tend to think of the Christian faith and life in storied terms. The Bible consists largely of a collection of stories. They recount the experiences of individuals and groups of people with God, and also people's relationships to one another and the created order in light of their relationship to God. Many of us learn these stories as children. We come to know about our faith by means of hearing, learning, and telling the stories over and over again. These stories shape how we understand and live in relationship to God, Jesus, our faith, and other people. The Christian story thus becomes part of us, or, more accurately, we become part of it. The Christian story takes our personal story into its story, so that our personal story is never the same again. Consequently, as the refrain in the well-known hymn declares about the Christian life, we come to say about the Christian story "This is my story. . . ."

The power of stories prompts us to think about and understand ourselves, others, and God fundamentally in terms of narratives that we craft over time and through lived experience with others who themselves are storying their lives. At least two things follow from the power that stories hold. First, the stories that we craft and live out make us who we are. Second, as these stories change — as our lives are restoried — we change too.

The Christian Life:
Embracing and Enacting a Particular Story

The Christian life entails living intentionally in relationship to a *particular* story, the Christian story. I have described that story in this way: God's creative, transformative, and redemptive acts throughout history, which Christians have most frequently recognized in the history of Israel; the life, death, and resurrection of Jesus; and the ongoing work of the Holy Spirit. This story has been told in the Bible and brought to life through shared beliefs, passions, and acts among Christian persons for approximately two millennia in the community called "church."

The Christian story makes particular claims about the way things are, what holds the greatest value and importance, and what qualifies as moral, ethical, and just. This story also lays down normative ways of being in relationship to ourselves, other people, the created world, and ultimately God. Furthermore, the Christian story summons its adherents to commit their lives to its claims and norms, which involves locating their personal stories within its story so that it molds, guides, and sets boundaries for their personal stories. When we commit to it in this way, the Christian story claims us and makes claims upon us; it offers promises to us and informs how we make meaning of life, including how *we view* the world, our relationships, ourselves, and ultimately God. We could go so far as to say that the Christian life *is* a lived story. Giving us our identity, constituting our selfhood, and commissioning our way of being and acting, this story makes us who we are.

To claim that Christian faith entails living intentionally in relationship to a particular story has an additional implication. The church, which cannot be separated from the story it espouses and calls upon its adherents to live out, may be the best context for quieting the disquieted soul. By virtue of its custom of having adherents engage in various faith practices, the church offers particular ways of thinking, acting, and feeling in relationship to the Christian story. Routine and even habitual actions that faith practices involve serve to break open a new kind of reality for those who take part in them as they draw participants further into the Christian story and engulf them with its reality. This new reality, one inseparable from the Christian story and actually created by it, may lead to at least two things happening in and among the persons who embrace the story. The new reality may evoke hope in ways that otherwise would be absent, just as de Gruchy suggests, and the new reality may alter, if not replace, a current reality tied to the story of the disquieted soul.

Embracing the Christian faith means that its story forms, guides, and sets boundaries for the storying of its adherents' lives, as individuals and as faith communities. As it becomes the central story in our lives, the Christian story serves as the grounds for other stories, including ones that we fashion ourselves and ones fashioned by others that we encounter and accept or reject as part of our own story. Why? The Christian story invites and incorporates other stories into its narrative. This is because, as Gerard Loughlin has suggested, for the Christian church, and thus for the person of faith, one particular life-story comes first. This life-story belongs to God in Jesus Christ. It "has always been a life-story that comes first, against which all other things are to be matched. . . . The story is imagined for us before it is re-imagined by us: the story is *given* to us."[6] In being given to us, this story fashions our identity, our selfhood, and our understanding of the world, others, ourselves, and God.

Consequently, this story frames how we live our lives. Specifically, we live in concert with this story or we do not. In either case, the story *contains* our lives and living. The story demarcates an approach to life. Located in the Christian story, we become persons who claim and are claimed by God's creative, transformative, and redemptive acts throughout history, which Christians have most frequently recognized in the history of Israel; the life, death, and resurrection of Jesus; and the ongoing work of the Holy Spirit. As a result, we learn to think, act, and feel about all manner of things having to do with ourselves, others, and God *in harmony with this story.*

From Story to Perspective

Stories inform *perspectives* on life. When we hear, consider, embrace, tell, retell, and live out stories, we develop ways of thinking, seeing, hearing, feeling, relating, and living in accordance with these stories. Stories give us points of view, particular outlooks or perceptions. In terms

6. Gerard Loughlin, *Telling God's Story: Bible, Church, and Narrative Theology* (Cambridge, U.K.: Cambridge University Press, 1996), p. 32.

used by practical theologian Craig Dykstra, stories give us an "angle of vision" with which we look upon, and *see,* all sorts of things.[7] How we live cannot be separated from what we see or fail to see.

We may consider anxiety from within the context of various "stories" that inform different perspectives on the condition. These include stories that individual persons tell about their lives or the lives of others, which inform an experiential perspective on anxiety, and stories that inform various frameworks for understanding anxiety (theological and psychological), which provide a conceptual perspective. In either case, the story to which one's perspective is tied — or the story that contains one's perspective by setting its boundaries and limits — goes a long way toward determining how anxiety will look and feel, and how one understands it and seeks to alleviate it. Why? Because the story produces the "angle of vision" by which matters are seen and understood. The story shapes our perspective.

Consequently, just as how one tells the story of healing shapes one's perspective on what is normative with respect to disease and health, how one tells the story of "getting right with God" informs what one considers normative for living in relationship to God. How we consider and live out the story of God and ourselves affects the state of our soul, just as how we consider and live out the story of health and disease affects the state of our healing. If we see anxiety as psychopathology that requires psychotherapeutic and medical cures, we will seek to relieve it accordingly. In the same way, if we view anxiety as a condition of the soul, the whole person's relationship to God, we will seek ways to relieve it that center on soul work.

Pastoral caregivers often need to work within various types of stories and from various perspectives, relating them to one another in pastoral care. Caregivers necessarily draw on multiple ways of looking at anxiety in seeking to gain familiarity, clarity, and acumen with respect to this condition and its care. But I contend that the *predominant* perspective or "angle of vision" that the caregiver holds and employs at any given point in time remains crucially important. The "lens" through which one peers into anxiety has a shaping effect on what one sees, both in how one understands anxiety as a condition and how one

---

7. Craig R. Dykstra, *Growing in the Life of Faith: Education and Christian Practices,* 2d ed. (Louisville: Westminster John Knox, 2005), p. xx.

finds solutions for it. I advocate a pastoral care of disquieted souls that promotes and relies upon the Christian story, making use of *its* perspectives and practices for understanding anxiety and seeking to assuage it.

In touting the place of the Christian story in pastoral care with disquieted souls, I am advocating the embrace of what postmodern thinkers refer to as a "grand narrative." By "grand narrative" I have in mind a larger story that serves as a "container" for these other stories being crafted. The Christian story serves as the grand narrative that contains our personal stories and thus shapes the way that we experience life.

Grand narratives have been suspect for a number of years, appropriately so. They are suspect because they can have the effect of discounting differences among persons and needs. They can impose values and perspectives on individuals and groups that may not want them but remain powerless to refuse them. As de Gruchy points out, grand narratives have produced numerous "offspring" that have done great damage to countless lives, including racism, sexism, ageism, tribalism, imperialism and religious intolerance, homophobia, and numerous kinds of xenophobia and their own progeny. Furthermore, grand narratives may oversimplify — if not homogenize — human experience. We must be careful, therefore, when advocating appeal to any kind of grand narrative, just as postmodern thinking teaches.

But as de Gruchy also notes, not all grand narratives are destructive or problematic. Moreover, he says, "despite the justifiable antipathy towards grand narratives, it does seem that we cannot easily live without them."[8] The question, therefore, is not whether we will live with stories that set parameters for thinking about, understanding, and living our lives. Rather, the question is what the larger story, the grand narrative, will be. In the case of disquieted souls, a grand narrative marked by particular questions, concerns, and struggles having to do with God is already operating. This grand narrative informs anxiety and causes a great deal of harm — physically, emotionally, behaviorally, relationally, and spiritually. Hence my claim that pastoral care of disquieted souls needs to focus on helping anxious persons *change their stories.* This change may occur by replacing one grand narrative — the story of the disquieted soul — with another one: the Christian story.

8. De Gruchy, *Confessions of a Christian Humanist,* p. 11.

Another possible critique of this approach, which I sought to answer in Chapter 2, is that "the Christian story" means different things to different people. As a result, we do not know precisely what we have in mind, nor can we be sure that we agree on what we mean, when making an appeal to its narrative. Fair enough. As de Gruchy himself suggests, the way that persons think about, understand, and make appeal to the Christian story will change over time as that story gets lived out in different contexts and eras. In fact, "each of the many Christian traditions is an interpretation of that story, the way in which its adherents relate to the 'grand narrative' of the Christian tradition as a whole."[9] I have kept these critiques in mind when defining the Christian story as I have, and I believe that my definition honors the fact that it will be understood and lived differently with respect to contextual and temporal factors. Furthermore, the power of the Christian story persists in its *varied* understandings and traditions.

I wish to stress the following point. When the Christian story serves as a basis, limit, and principal angle of vision for our lives, regardless of our particular tradition we see, think, feel, relate, and act in particular ways — namely, those that find harmony with the story and its claim on us. We also allow ourselves to be drawn deeper into this story's world and its reality, and only then does our current reality begin to change. As George Lindbeck has pointed out with respect to biblical texts, among those immersed in the Christian story, "no world is more real" than the world it creates. This world of the Christian story has the capacity "to absorb the universe" and thus other worlds.[10] The world created by the Christian story serves as the basis for believers to understand reality and live their lives. Moreover, Craig Dykstra makes this powerful observation: "As we hear, tell, think about, interpret, use, and appropriate this story, its world more and more becomes our world. Our thinking, believing, and behaving become shaped by it, so that we come to think, believe, and behave by means of it. It is no longer a world outside of us, which we look at, but that world from which and by means of which we see at all."[11]

---

9. De Gruchy, *Confessions of a Christian Humanist*, p. 11.

10. George A. Lindbeck, *The Nature of Doctrine: Religion and Theology in a Postliberal Age* (Philadelphia: Westminster Press, 1984), p. 117.

11. Dykstra, *Growing in the Life of Faith*, p. 59.

Breaking Open a New Reality by Changing One's Story

Pastoral care of disquieted souls requires assisting anxious persons with exchanging one world, the anxious one, for a world that offers more peace. This exchange, which pastors and faith communities can and do facilitate, occurs as the anxious person begins to replace her dominant story and the reality it informs, both of which are anxiety-laden, with an alternative story and reality, one that enlists trust in a God who promises peace that quiets the soul. In changing the grand narrative that governs her life, she changes her way of seeing the world. Why? Because when we change our story, we introduce a new kind of reality.

There may be no better way to speak of relieving anxiety than in terms of de Gruchy's image — *breaking open a new reality*. As noted previously, anxiety is a thinking disorder that creates and fosters a reality — a world — pervaded by anxiety's qualities. Anxiety grows out of distortions in a person's sense of the way things are based on erroneous thoughts, ideas, and concepts. How one *thinks* — that is, out of anxiety-laden cognitive sets — makes one *act* and *feel* anxious.

Chiefly important for the anxious person's reality are assumptions about God and one's standing before God, and how one's thinking about these informs one's personal life story, including how one considers and approaches death. I have suggested that anxiety among persons in the church often links with some combination of the following: misguided or confused thinking about God's nature or character; thinking that one lacks an appropriate relationship to God, including devotion or fidelity to God or to God's claim on oneself; thinking that one's life is in need of grounding, meaning, or purpose; and thinking that one's death (and place before God in eternity) is something to fear.

Noting what philosopher Martha C. Nussbaum says concerning the nature of emotions, that they are learned responses tied to the way we think, I have suggested further that anxiety may also involve judgments (reflective and evaluative thinking) about one's well-being and status in relationship to things one values but does not fully control. This lack of control includes having to acknowledge one's incompleteness and neediness.[12] I want to return here briefly to Nussbaum's

12. Martha C. Nussbaum, *Upheavals of Thought: The Intelligence of Emotions* (New York: Cambridge University Press, 2004).

claim. Her philosophical take on the narrative quality of emotions relates closely to what Aaron Beck and Gary Emery claim regarding cognitive sets.

Drawing on the thought of Stoic philosophers, Nussbaum argues for what she terms "a strong cognitive view of emotions." She conceives of "the major human emotions" in this way:

> They are not simply blind surges of affect, stirring, or sensations that arise from our animal nature and are identified (and distinguished from one another) by their felt quality alone. Instead, they themselves have a cognitive content; they are intimately related to beliefs or judgments about the world in such a way that the removal of the relevant belief will remove not only the reason for the emotion but also the emotion itself. The belief is the necessary basis and "ground" of the emotion. It might even be said to be a constituent part of the emotion itself.[13]

She adds to this her endorsement of the claim of Chrysippus, "the most profound thinker on emotion in the entire philosophical tradition," that "the emotion is itself identical with the full acceptance of, or recognition of, a belief."[14]

Nussbaum suggests that how one feels remains strongly tied to what one thinks or believes. Feeling always involves judgments, or reflective thinking, about what we believe. Her idea bears close resemblance to Beck's observation concerning the cognitive basis for emotions, particularly as demonstrated in the relationship between emotions and behaviors. Recall Beck's view that while a person starts to feel anxious when encountering a situation that he thinks may be dangerous, how he feels, his emotional state, does not lead directly to any particular behavioral response. Rather, what he feels has to be *thought of again* (appraised or judged) in the cognitive process. Only then does he decide how to respond behaviorally. Consequently, to the extent that we change the way a person thinks about any given matter, we change not only the way he feels about it but also how he behaves in light of how he thinks and feels. Relieving anxiety — quieting the soul — thus requires not merely breaking open a new reality; that reality must also be tied to a cognitive set that

13. Nussbaum, "Narrative Emotions," p. 223.
14. Nussbaum, "Narrative Emotions," p. 223.

informs thinking and judgment differently than the reality and cognitive set to which anxiety is joined.

For anxious persons, a new, more peaceful reality depends upon relearning both their way of thinking (*how* they think) and the content of their thinking (*what* they think), particularly about God. I return to this claim later in the chapter, suggesting how one may go about breaking open a new reality by engaging in various faith practices in the context of the faith community.

Cognitive Restructuring and
Learning to Think Differently about God

Before discussing those faith practices and making suggestions for their use in the pastoral care of anxious persons, I want to return to my previous discussion of what cognitive therapy terms "cognitive restructuring." I do so because, in essence, I am suggesting that faith practices engaged in the context of the faith community serve to restructure our cognitive sets, and that in doing so they have the capacity for altering, even transforming, not only how we think but also how we act and feel.

Because anxiety grows out of disordered thinking tied to faulty cognitive sets, relieving anxiety requires learning how to think differently, including *how* one thinks and *what* one thinks. This cognitive restructuring involves educative work around at least five matters. These include (1) enhancing self-awareness; (2) modifying negative imagery, including replacing it with more positive and presumably realistic imagery; (3) modifying the affective component tied to anxiety (how it feels), so that when one becomes anxious, one experiences one's anxiety differently and less severely than before; (4) modifying the behaviors linked to anxiety, which tend to involve avoiding situations, people, and other matters that produce anxiety; and (5) restructuring assumptions about three major life concerns: acceptance, competence, and control.[15]

15. Gary Emery devotes a chapter to each one of these facets of cognitive restructuring. See Aaron T. Beck and Gary Emery, *Anxiety Disorders and Phobias: A Cognitive Perspective* (New York: Basic Books, 1985), Part II, pp. 167-322.

In Chapter 4 I noted how these components of cognitive restructuring serve to alter the way we think, act, and feel, and thus how they may serve to relieve anxiety. I revisit part of that discussion here, specifically in terms of how one thinks, acts, and feels about matters pertaining to God and one's relationship to God. Having noted several cognitive-based strategies for relieving anxiety, I consider two of those strategies again — enhancing self-awareness and point/counterpoint — in order to set the stage for suggesting how faith practices may serve to quiet one's soul by facilitating these very strategies of cognitive restructuring.

Becoming More Aware of How and What One Thinks about God

Cognitive therapy with anxiety-related concerns begins with helping an anxious person become more aware of her thought processes. The therapist educates the client on several matters so that she may do the work of cognitive restructuring, not only during therapy but also at other times as well. Education focuses on enhancing a client's ability first to identify her thoughts and then to "catch" them as early as possible in her thought process. Of particular concern are thoughts in her chain of automatic thinking that eventuate into anxiety.

To illustrate how this process works, I want to recall the previous example of a man who gets anxious when he hears a siren blare in the distance. Because he is an anxious person, he does not stop with "I hear a siren." He automatically begins to string together a series of linked thoughts: "That sounds like a fire truck. It must be on the way to a fire. It sounds awfully close to my neighborhood. It must be in my neighborhood. I bet I didn't turn the iron off before I left. That must have caught on fire. My house is on fire. The fire truck must be on its way to my house. My wife and children are there. They must be in danger. They are going to be harmed." In this scenario, an initial thought leads to a series of other thoughts in a seemingly instinctive or involuntary way. Such linked thinking derives from the kind of cognitive set with which the man operates. The man quickly moves from an initial thought ("I hear a siren") to one that prompts anxiety ("My family will be harmed") with little ability to stop and reflect on whether a given thought in the chain of thinking is realistic, accurate, or makes sense.

The therapist using a cognitive approach would seek first to help this man become more aware of his thought processes, including the way he routinely links thoughts together automatically and unreflectively.

Consider another person who makes use of a similar kind of thinking process. Let us suppose that as she drives past a church on her way to work, her thinking proceeds like this: "I'm not feeling good about myself or about God. I feel this way because I haven't been faithful to God. Because I'm not living up to what God expects of me, I have failed God. I actually fall short of meeting God's desires all the time. Going to church doesn't seem to help. I still don't understand God or myself. Try as I may, I can't figure out what my life is supposed to be about. That's not what God wants — I do know that. No matter what I try, I can't get past feeling this way. I know that God will not forgive me or accept me. I'm afraid to die because God will punish me."

Like the therapist working with cognitive restructuring, a pastor caring for this woman would seek to provide support and education that assist with discovering and understanding how she got from "I'm not feeling good about myself or about God" to "I'm afraid to die because God will punish me." Like the primary therapeutic goal, the goal of pastoral care would be to assist her in several ways.

First, the pastor might help this woman to become more aware of her thought *process* as early in the chain as possible, beginning with "I'm not feeling good about myself or about God." Included here would be raising awareness of this thought being tied to the woman's relationship to God (a theo-relational concern). Once she becomes aware of this thought, she may stop there and reflect further on it rather than moving on to the next thought. After becoming more aware of her thought process, she may attend next to the *content* of her thinking. This would involve considering what exactly about her thoughts troubles her and how this makes her feel.

In reflecting on why she feels the way she does, and especially on the thoughts related to how she feels, she may ask herself questions like these: "Why am I feeling unfaithful to God?" "What specifically troubles me?" "What's prompting my feeling this way right now?" These questions and others like them help hone awareness of *how* she thinks and feels and *what* she thinks and feels about God and her relationship to God.

Second, the pastor could seek to help this woman learn to catch herself as she begins her automatic thinking process. This "catching" would involve finding a mechanism to point out to herself when this process begins or likely will begin. She could say to herself (preferably out loud, because actually hearing ourselves speak often leaves a more lasting impression on us), "Here I go" or "I've started this process of thinking anxious thoughts that relate to God and my faith." Catching her thoughts would also include learning how to remind herself of what tends to happen to her when she thinks this way. She could learn, for example, to say to herself (preferably out loud), "When I'm not feeling good about my relationship with God, I tend to feel unsettled, even anxious. Feeling that way tends to involve thinking that I've failed God or been unfaithful in some way. I also tend to think of worst-case scenarios, like 'God will not forgive me,' and I start thinking about and fearing my own death. All of that causes me great pain. There's a better way to respond."

A third way the pastor could assist this person would be to help her discover how to stop the automatic thinking process once she has "caught" herself. One way to do this would be to help her learn to say to herself (preferably out loud), "I remember what I've learned in church. I've learned through being a part of the church, worshipping, praying, reading the Bible, serving others, and confessing my shortcomings [additional faith practices that she finds meaningful could also be noted here] that God loves me in spite of what I have done or failed to do. Regardless of how I'm feeling about myself, God, or our relationship, God loves me and always will." Here the woman draws on what she's learned about God and herself, which has not yet become a significant enough part of her cognitive set to inform her automatic thinking process, to remind herself of a different way of thinking about what makes her anxious.

A fourth way to assist this woman, closely related to the one just mentioned, would be to help her learn how to change her operative cognitive set. Specifically, the pastor would want to help her change from a cognitive set that informs anxiousness to one that informs more peaceful calm. This change happens by virtue of intentionally substituting positive, calming thoughts for the more negative and anxiety-laden ones currently prevailing. Repeatedly and consistently reminding herself of what she has learned about God and her standing before God — recalling the Christian story — may serve to change her operative cognitive set and automatic thinking process. This change may lead to a change in what she thinks about her relationship with God. Furthermore, she may change how she acts and feels by virtue of having learned to think differently about her relationship with God.

Here the goal of pastoral care would be to reinforce, through frequent recollection of the Christian story and its claims about God, the new, more peaceful way of thinking. For example, this woman could learn to say to herself regularly, "God loves me in spite of how I'm feeling about myself, God, or our relationship. The gospel promises me that." Similarly, she may be helped to think differently by saying to herself (preferably out loud) something like this: "I am loved and valued for who I am, even if I'm not perfect or close to perfect. I can benefit from feeling anxious if I focus more intently on my relationship with God and my place in the community of faith, but I don't need to dwell on this to the extent that I become severely anxious. Why? Because God's promises in the gospel sustain me, drawing me closer to God and to others as I continue in my faith journey." Learning to think differently, with respect to thought process and content (the "way" and "what" of thinking), serves to change the way she feels.

Of course, various anxious persons would describe their thinking (its process and content) and their associated feelings differently, whether having to do with God, themselves, or something else. I offer this example simply as an illustration of how this thinking could proceed and, just as important, how a pastor might consider assisting such a person by paying closer attention to her thoughts *and* helping her to pay more attention to them as well. Helping an anxious person learn to observe how she thinks and what she thinks, while focusing too on how her thinking leads to a series of thoughts that eventuate in an anxious response, is a necessary first step for pastoral care. This process helps the anxious person learn to respond differently to her thoughts when they arise and, consequently, helps her to feel different.

Engaging in faith practices provides a means for facilitating precisely this kind of cognitive restructuring. Why? Because faith practices help to reinforce the kinds of understandings of God that anxious persons require for living with quieter souls. Faith practices facilitate a process of interiorizing the Christian story. This interiorizing happens as those engaging these practices are drawn further and further into the Christian story, and its realities engulf them and become their own.

Over time, with repetition, faith practices serve to shape and reshape operative cognitive sets. To put it differently, drawing an actor into a different story than presently governs her understanding of herself and her experiences helps to change that story.

Three Questions to Enhance Self-Awareness

A strategy that enhances self-awareness entails reflecting on one's experience in light of Gary Emery's three guiding questions: (1) What's the evidence? (2) What's another way of looking at the situation? and (3) So what if it happens? Emery notes that a person may respond better to one of these questions than the others, but that she will benefit most from developing an ability to utilize each one.[16] How might pastors make use of these questions in ministry with disquieted souls?

What's the Evidence? A person who senses that she feels bad about herself or God needs to learn to ask herself (preferably out loud), "What's the evidence for my feeling this way? How do I know that what I feel really has to do with God, as opposed to having to do with someone or something else?" She may ask too, "If I really am feeling bad about myself or God, what's the evidence for that having to do with my failing God or not living up to what God expects of me? Further, if I have disappointed God, even failed God, what evidence do I have for thinking that I do this all the time, or even most of the time?" Likewise, she may ask, "Why do I assume that going to church provides no help? What evidence do I have for that? And furthermore, even if I don't understand God or myself, and even if I haven't figured out what my life is all about, and even if that isn't what God wants, what makes me think this means that God will not forgive me, that God will punish me eternally, and that I must therefore be afraid to die? What evidence do I have for any of that?" These kinds of self-questions provide a useful way for the anxious person to examine the logic of her initial (automatic) thinking and its alignment with what is accurate and real. These kinds of questions and reflection on them help curb the tendency to

16. Beck and Emery, *Anxiety Disorders and Phobias*, p. 201.

move toward minimization, selective abstraction, magnification, and catastrophizing responses, all of which anxious persons typically fall prey to.

What's a Different Way of Looking at the Situation?   This is another beneficial question for the anxious person to ask herself. Or, stated differently, "What's an alternative, perhaps more likely scenario than the one that's causing me so much anxiety?" These questions seek to expand her operative cognitive set by encouraging her to think about her experience in different ways. We sometimes use the term *reframing* to denote this kind of change in the way someone looks at something. As Donald Capps has illustrated, helping a parishioner reframe a problem or situation tends to result in her responding differently to it.[17] A person responds differently because she now thinks about and understands the situation in a different way. The anxious person in our example may be helped to reframe her situation, to consider a different perspective, by saying to herself (preferably out loud) something like this: "How I feel may have little, if anything, to do with my perception of God or my relationship to God. It may be the case that I'm feeling bad about something else. And even if my feeling bad has to do with God, the gospel tells me that all of us fall short of God's expectations, that none of us fully understands God, and that God's pledge of forgiveness and presence in my life will sustain me, whatever I do or fail to do." She may continue, "The gospel calls this 'grace.' As one who embraces the Christian story as my own and who follows Jesus, I enjoy the benefits of that grace." Learning to consider alternative perspectives on her experience, such that she thinks differently about God and her standing before God, tends to result in her feeling different as well.

So What If It Happens?   A third question that promotes self-awareness and the restructuring of one's thinking is this: "So what if what I'm anxious about actually happens?" Making use of that question encourages the anxious person to consider a "worst-case scenario." While considering this may seem ill-advised, the pastor encourages it for two reasons. First, he wants to help "decatastrophize" what the anx-

17. Donald Capps, *Reframing: A New Method in Pastoral Care* (Minneapolis: Fortress Press, 1990).

ious person has envisioned will take place ("I have failed God . . . God will punish me"), a scenario that is pervaded by anxiety. Second, he wants to help the anxious person imagine how she would cope with a worst-case scenario if that in fact came about. The goal is to encourage her to imagine that her greatest concern ("God will punish me") has come to pass, that what she's anxious about has happened, because doing so actually serves to reduce its power. If we avoid our anxiety, it tends to become more powerful, to take on added qualities and complexities, thus gaining more control over us. On the other hand, confronting our anxiety in light of a worst-case scenario tends, somewhat paradoxically, to lessen its power and control.

In our example, the anxious person would likely find it extremely difficult, if not impossible, to imagine what it would be like if God were to punish her, especially if that punishment meant "going to hell" or otherwise being cut off from God eternally. Of course, the pastoral goal would be to help her trust more in God's ability and desire in Christ to forgive her and remain present with her always, even "to the end of the age" (Matt. 28:20). Nevertheless, cognitive therapy principles suggest that simply entertaining this worst-case scenario, especially if it is followed by alternative scenarios — in this case, reminders of God's promise to do otherwise than punish eternally — may help to lessen the power that the worst-case scenario holds. Occasions of anxiety that revolve around less catastrophic matters may be better suited for using this third approach. As Emery reminds us, different persons with different anxieties may call for different approaches. Even so, anxious persons benefit from making use of each one of these three questions to the best of their abilities with respect to their particular anxiety-laden concerns.

Recall too Emery's use of another approach, "point/counterpoint," which tends to capture the essence of the "So what if it happens?" question. The point/counterpoint approach involves the therapist and the client working together to rebut or falsify the client's anxious thoughts and scenarios. This falsification works as the therapist presents statements or scenarios that the client finds troubling (the point), and the client then rebuts the point or offers evidence to the contrary (the counterpoint). When the client runs out of rebuttals, the roles change, and the therapist provides the counterpoints. This strategy tends to focus particularly on four concerns: (1) the feared event's likelihood or probability; (2) its degree of awfulness or horror; (3) the person's capability to prevent it from occurring; and (4) the person's ability to cope — that is, to accept and deal with the worst-case scenario.[18] In making use of this strategy for pastoral care with disquieted souls, the pastor would draw explicitly, repetitively, and intensively on the Christian story's claims and promises to help "rebut" in counterpoint the woman's concerns about God, her standing before God, and God's punishment. In time, and through engaging various faith practices I will detail in the next chapter, she may learn to enlist this strategy by means of *internal dialogue,* so that eventually she "automatically" produces a pleasant, more assuring thought (counterpoint) when becoming aware of a problematic or painful one (point).

Pastors do well to keep in mind the role that cognitive restructuring and its techniques can play in changing an anxious person's perception of reality, and thus her story, by helping her think differently. I encourage pastors to look for opportunities to facilitate cognitive restructuring in their offers of care, so that disquieted souls may begin to change their personal stories. When making these attempts, pastors — and all caregivers, for that matter — should remember that a radical restructuring of how one thinks often will require extensive work. It would not be surprising if a handful of attempts at learning to think differently prove insufficient. At the same time, it would not be surprising to discover that one or two pastoral conversations that make use of some of the strategies discussed here prove to be adequate, particularly when these are followed up by the care seeker using these strategies consistently on her own. As Donald Capps has noted, a great deal may be accomplished in a few pastoral conversations provided the caregiver takes those conversations seriously and knows how to maximize the time spent together.[19]

I want to attend next to the power that various faith practices hold for facilitating cognitive restructuring. Along with pastoral care that happens in the form of one-on-one conversations between pastor and parishioner, in which some of the strategies of cognitive restructuring may be utilized, faith practices, when routinely engaged, may provide

18. Beck and Emery, *Anxiety Disorders and Phobias,* p. 209.

19. Donald Capps, *Giving Counsel: A Minister's Guidebook* (St. Louis: Chalice Press, 2001), pp. 3-4.

the best ongoing means for helping to calm the disquieted soul. The power of faith practices lies in their capacity to alter one's perception of reality and thus change one's story. Most of these practices may be enlisted individually and corporately, formally and informally, both in and out of church. Because faith practices maintain a central place in the life of the typical congregation and the pastor charged with its care, they present opportunities for facilitating new realities and changing personal stories. In order to understand this power that faith practices hold, we first need to consider the role that patterns and habits of thinking, relating, acting, and feeling play in our lives.

The Role of Patterns and Habits in Our Lives

Donald Capps attends to how pastoral ministry may involve the creation of new realities when he suggests that a principal role that pastors can play is helping persons in their care change the ways they typically respond to life's various situations.[20] Capps recognizes that human beings develop *patterns* of relating and acting. These patterns, what he calls "themes," inevitably influence how we respond to the situations we encounter in daily living. For example, we have a tendency to respond to the irritating behavior of a family member or a colleague in more or less the same way, across time and individual episodes. Perhaps we raise our voice as we express disenchantment. Maybe we ignore the other person and send more subtle signals that we are angry or displeased. Perhaps we seek out the person for a calm but direct conversation in which we articulate our feelings and concerns. Whatever the case, we respond in routine and predictable ways by virtue of the patterns of thinking, acting, and feeling that are operative in our lives. Most of these patterns are learned. Beginning in childhood, we learn them through the interplay of our significant relationships, our own personality and constitution, and the social conventions and mores that touch our lives and contexts.

Capps's view of the central role that patterns play in our lives relates to what William James claimed with respect to what he called "the

20. Donald Capps, *Pastoral Care: A Thematic Approach* (Philadelphia: Westminster Press, 1979).

laws of habit." In his "Talks to Teachers," delivered in 1892, James detailed what could be termed "a psychology of habituation."[21] He claimed that "all of our life, so far as it has definite form, is but a mass of habits — practical, emotional, and intellectual — systematically organized for our weal or woe, and bearing us irresistibly towards our destiny, whatever the latter may be." He thought that almost all of our activity in life — by which he meant thinking, acting, and feeling — is "second nature" and derived from "habits":

> Ninety-nine hundredths or, possibly, nine hundred and ninety-nine thousandths of our activity is purely automatic and habitual, from our rising in the morning to our lying down each night. Our dressing and undressing, our eating and drinking, our greetings and partings, our hat-raisings and giving way for ladies to proceed, nay, even most of the forms of our common speech, are things of a type so fixed by repetition as almost to be classed as reflex actions.[22]

James goes on to say that while established habits play a prominent role in our lives, we have the ongoing capacity to discard these habits and develop new ones. This capacity applies not only to habits of action or behavior, but also to our "thinking and feeling processes." In other words, we can learn to think, act, and feel by virtue of the kinds of habits we embrace and internalize. Consequently, much of life consists of being educated with respect to the habits that we have acquired and also those that we have yet to cultivate.

With Capps's and James's insights in mind, and taking a cue from Beck and Emery's view of cognitive restructuring, I suggest that anxiety follows from a *patterned* or *habitual* way of thinking. This way of thinking informs disordered thoughts that shape reality in ways that lead to one acting and feeling anxious. One's habits of thinking impact one personally and relationally, informing life in both the private and the public spheres. The previous example of "automatic thinking" — of the woman who progresses quickly in her thoughts from "I'm not feeling good about myself or about God" to "I'm afraid to die because God will

---

21. William James, *Talks to Teachers on Psychology; and to Students on Some of Life's Ideals* (New York: Literary Classics of the United States, 1987), pp. 705-887.
22. James, *Talks to Teachers on Psychology*, pp. 750, 751.

punish me" — illustrates a patterned thinking process that eventuates in a predictable (habitual) way of acting and feeling. An initial thought leads to a succession of other thoughts in a prefigured manner that, more often than not, produces the same result.

Pastoral care should help an anxious person alter or replace current thinking patterns and habits with alternative ones, so that new results follow. This goal is similar to what cognitive therapists attempt through the techniques previously discussed. But how does a *pastor* do this? How might a typical pastor draw from the insights of cognitive restructuring to assist disquieted souls in the congregation? Along with offers of presence, attention, and nurture through pastoral conversation and care, which may include attempts at the kind of cognitive restructuring discussed, means for altering or replacing anxious persons' patterns and habits are found in the Christian life, which itself involves espousing and appropriating a particular *life pattern* and set of habits. That pattern and those habits entail believing, acting centrally in relationship to, and feeling passion for the Christian story. Following James, we might call these the intellectual (believing), practical (acting), and emotional (feeling) qualities of Christian existence. Inviting its adherents to locate their lives, their personal stories, within its larger, encompassing narrative, the Christian story offers them particular understandings, values, goals, norms, commitments, priorities, hopes, dreams, and expectations. All of this becomes the content for meaning-making, and that, in turn, establishes patterns of relationship, behavior, and feeling. Among other benefits, attempting to live more intentionally out of the patterns and habits that the gospel narrative puts forth allows us not only to make sense of things in new ways — namely, with respect to a different view of God, our relationship to God, and related matters — but also to locate ourselves in relation to something larger than our own solitary existence, something beyond merely our own story. In so doing, we find our personal story affected by, even altered by the Christian story.

If anxiety links especially with feeling disconnected and vulnerable, then pastoral work does well to focus its efforts on helping disquieted souls find ways to locate themselves, not only emotionally but physically as well, in relation to others' stories *and* the Christian story in more explicit and routine ways. This promotes a deeper, more meaningful connection to others and to God that tends to soothe disquieted souls. For those who claim the Christian story — or, perhaps better said, for those claimed by it — this story's patterns and habits become the principal ones that inform, organize, and shape others, including those that make up their own personal stories. In Capps's and James's terms, the Christian story becomes the theme or pattern for our lives by virtue of particular habits of believing, acting, and feeling that are formed and practiced in the life of faith. That, in turn, affects the state of the soul. We turn now to how faith practices can help us locate our personal stories in relation to the Christian story.

Chapter 7

CHANGING THE SOUL'S STORY

The Power of Faith Practices

In the last chapter I noted the power that stories hold in our lives, and how claiming and being claimed by the Christian story affects how we think, act, feel, and live. In this chapter I want to focus on how particular faith practices hold power for shaping the stories by which we live, and especially how those practices may help to change our personal stories in light of the Christian story.

The Importance of Engaging in Faith Practices

Faith practices may provide the disquieted soul that performs them with at least three essential things: (1) deeper connections to God, others, and oneself; (2) routine and explicit exposure to and facility with the Christian story; and (3) a manner of taking part in that story *and* being drawn deeper into its world, intellectually (thinking), practically (acting), and emotionally (feeling). Christianity's beliefs and practices cannot be separated, much like body, soul, and spirit cannot be separated. Furthermore, our beliefs, practices, thoughts, judgments, spoken words, and actions collectively fashion us into the persons we are, including how we understand the world and our place in it, and what we find valuable and meaningful. We believe and understand *as* we speak and act, and we speak and act *as* we believe and understand — each informs the others. Moreover, how we think and act has a significant impact on how we feel. Using William James's terms, our *intellectual* and *practical* facets of life deeply influence our *emotional* life. Moreover, our thinking, acting, and feeling *in relation to* the Christian story have a profound influence on *how* we think, act, and feel.

Of course, in acting we may very well have our understandings and feelings altered. There remains a kind of reciprocity between understanding (believing) and feeling on the one hand, and acting on the other. The point to underscore is that in acting on what we understand or believe, we become who we are — that is, we become ourselves.

I learned from the fine Kierkegaard scholar David J. Gouwens that my view on the narrative qualities of personhood, including how the Christian narrative may shape persons through engaging them in its stories and practices, relates closely not only to Kierkegaard's thoughts about the self but also to those of Augustine. As Gouwens points out when discussing the work of Vincent McCarthy, Kierkegaard views emotions "in terms of their relationship to beliefs, attitudes, actions, and feelings, that is, in terms of broad patterns of a person's life that are observable and describable," as opposed to being located in some kind of psychic structure or something else. Moreover, "for the Augustinian tradition, the self is to be seen in terms of a temporal narrative of one's journey from and to God. The project of self-understanding is to gain clarity about oneself by rehearsing the narrative of one's own life, not in isolation, but in terms of two additional factors: the 'ordinary experience' of daily life and also the relation of the self to God as the source and goal of one's happiness: in Augustine's famous words in his *Confessions,*'You made us for yourself, and our hearts are restless until they find rest in you.' "[1] Kierkegaard and Augustine agree that becoming oneself can never be separated from one's *agency,* so that who we are remains inseparably linked with what we do. The "broad patterns" of living that we enlist — our actions — have a great deal to do with shaping who we are and will become. Jesus seems to have recognized as much too, having pointed out to his followers: "You will know them by their fruits" (Matt. 7:16).

By virtue of being embedded in the Christian story, constantly informing and being informed by it, faith practices have the capacity to help anxious persons learn to perceive things differently, to think about life in alternative ways, to respond to life's questions and situations dif-

1. David J. Gouwens, *Kierkegaard as Religious Thinker* (New York: Cambridge University Press, 1996), pp. 90-91.

ferently, and thus to feel another way — less anxious. Faith practices have this power because they present us with new realities as they invite us into a particular kind of world and story. They invite us into the story of God's creative, transformative, and redemptive acts throughout history, which Christians have most frequently recognized in the history of Israel; the life, death, and resurrection of Jesus; and the ongoing presence of the Holy Spirit. As we live deeper and deeper within this story, so that it has more and more influence on our personal stories, a new reality increasingly takes hold. In that new reality we draw closer to God, we come to know God differently, and we believe particular things about God's character and God's desire for relationship with us. Significantly, we believe that God seeks us unceasingly, regardless of our merits, and that God directs and empowers our living. We call this grace. Living more fully in awareness of that reality, which faith practices foster and maintain, eventually may result in replacing a current reality marked by the soul's disquiet with one marked by the promises of the Christian story and its more peaceful, grace-filled reality.

Faith practices hold this power because they promote the development of a distinct cognitive set that nurtures the soul's quiet. Engaging in faith practices contributes to learning how to think in particular ways about God, one's relationship to God, one's life purpose or calling, and also God's activity in the world — whether in life or in death — in accord with what the Christian faith reveals. As these practices become habitual and deeply a part of those who perform them, so do the cognitive sets that accompany them. As a result, faith practices influence how we see the world, think, act, and feel about life and all that it entails. Not only that, but faith practices also have an effect on how we live out, through our actions, our most significant relationships, with other persons and with God.

Those who engage regularly the practices of church membership, worship, the reading of Scripture, prayer, service, and confession have their lives impacted and shaped by the Christian story in ways that otherwise would be lacking. To say it differently, in touching the intellectual (believing), practical (acting), and emotional (feeling) qualities of persons living the Christian story, faith practices foster the formulation and internalization of more accurate (faithful) and less troubling ways of thinking about, understanding, and being in relationship to God, other persons, oneself, and life as it is lived. This new way of thinking includes how one approaches the end of one's life. Faith practices help individual persons and larger communities to cultivate and impart particular assumptions about God, the world, and human life and relationships that *differ* from the assumptions that inform anxiety. Consequently, faith practices may serve to quiet souls.

I would suggest another reason that faith practices may lend themselves to the needs of disquieted souls. Because anxious persons tend to experience a good deal of shame about their "disorder" — so much so that they go to great efforts to mask, hide, and even deny its grip on them — they often are reluctant to seek help from a mental health professional. As indicated in the portraits of disquieted souls previously presented, many anxious persons suffer in silence because of an unwillingness, or an inability, to share their struggles and needs with others. A deep concern for how one appears to others often lies at the heart of anxiety and also serves to exacerbate it. The possibility that he will be judged negatively by others remains one of the greatest stressors for the anxious person. Recall the story of José. His experience is one shared by typical disquieted souls: "I just fought the anxiety. I was able to hide it. No one knew . . . because I didn't want anyone to know about my condition."

Consequently, disquieted souls may be helped more readily by opportunities to meet their needs in ways that require less of them in the way of public acknowledgment or drawing explicit attention to themselves and their condition. Donald Capps identifies this possibility in his book on the condition of social phobia, a form of anxiety. He recognizes that "researchers note that social phobics are more likely to attend church services than to become involved in more personally demanding social gatherings. This is because churches allow for rather marginal or restrained participation. Thus, church leaders would do well to know that there are social phobics in their congregations, and that their personal, social, and religious needs are not the same as those of non-social phobics."[2] The same may be said about disquieted souls and their needs. While I will try to make a case for the importance of anxious persons *not* remaining at the margins of church life, suggesting potential benefits of holding formal membership in a congregation and participating actively in its life and work, it remains true that anx-

2. Donald Capps, *Social Phobia: Alleviating Anxiety in an Age of Self-Promotion* (St. Louis: Chalice Press, 1999), p. xi.

ious persons may be more attracted to participating in faith practices as a means for quieting their souls than they are to meeting face-to-face with a pastor to talk about their condition and their struggles. Although I do not want to minimize the role that direct pastoral conversation and care may play in helping anxious persons, it may be the case that a significant number of them will be helped as much, or more, by pastors encouraging them to engage in these faith practices.

The last fifteen years have brought much attention, especially in practical theology, to faith practices, the role that they play in the life of faith, and to advocating that faith communities and their leaders reclaim a central place for these practices in ministry. At the center of these efforts has been the work of Craig R. Dykstra, Dorothy C. Bass, Miroslav Volf, and their associates. A series of books in which these thinkers have been involved demonstrates not only that faith practices hold distinctive — if not unique — power for shaping the lives of those who perform them, but also that such practices are both biblically endorsed (if not mandated) and occupy a long-standing place in Christian tradition. In her work with the Valparaiso Project, Dorothy Bass has written about twelve practices, and various other scholars have subsequently produced book-length treatments of them. The work of Bass and her associates, in turn, has generated yet more work on faith practices by still others. The twelve practices that Bass highlights include honoring the body, offering hospitality, promoting prudent household economics, saying yes and saying no, keeping Sabbath, giving testimony, practicing discernment, shaping communities, offering and accepting forgiveness, seeking healing, dying well, and singing our lives. I commend the work of Dykstra, Bass, Volf, and their colleagues that focuses on faith practices and their value for pastors.[3]

In his influential book *Growing in the Life of Faith: Education and Christian Practices*, Craig Dykstra clarifies the power that Christian faith and its practices hold. He recalls Bonhoeffer's advocacy for both in his book *Life Together*. That book recounts Bonhoeffer's experience of heading an underground seminary in Finkenwalde, Germany, during Nazi

---

3. See Craig R. Dykstra, *Growing in the Life of Faith: Education and Christian Practices*, 2d ed. (Louisville: Westminster John Knox, 2005); *Practicing Our Faith: A Way of Life for a Searching People*, ed. Dorothy C. Bass (San Francisco: Jossey-Bass, 1997); and *Practicing Theology: Beliefs and Practices in Christian Life*, ed. Miroslav Volf and Dorothy C. Bass (Grand Rapids: William B. Eerdmans, 2002).

rule, when he and his students engaged regularly in particular faith practices for the purposes of formation and sustenance in the Christian faith. Dykstra points out that "these practices, when engaged in deep interrelation with one another, have the effect of turning the flow of power in a new direction. . . . They become arenas in which something is done to us, in us, and through us that we could not of ourselves do, that is beyond what we do."[4] Stated differently, engaging in faith practices fosters a kind of God-centered, community-grounded, external assurance, and in so doing actually cultivates an ongoing *awareness* of that assurance, just as psychotherapy tends to foster and cultivate a more internally based and self-centered assurance. Both kinds of assurance, which may over time become an internalized and more self-aware *reassurance,* hold value and offer anxious persons a measure of what they need, a sense that everything is going to be OK.

In this book our interest lies principally in the kind of reassurance that comes from the Christian faith and its practices. Located in and arising from the Christian story called "good news," this reassurance stems from none other than God's promise to abide by God's people, come what may! The Christian story and the reassurance it offers remain the pastor's purview and forte, as does cultivating that reassurance and sharing it with others. This kind of cultivation and sharing tends to be what those seeking out pastors and faith communities want and need.

I want to attend now, briefly, to six faith practices that hold promise for fostering and sustaining the soul's quiet. These practices include membership in the church; regular participation in worship, Scripture reading, and prayer; serving others in mission and outreach; and practicing both public and private confession. Some of the practices that I mention have been identified and reflected on by Dykstra, Bass, Volf, and their associates, and I draw on their work in my remarks here. However, in identifying and discussing these practices, I have chosen to rely particularly on Bonhoeffer's understanding of how Christians may experience "life together," and also on the notions of patterns and habits put forth by Donald Capps and William James. I hope that this approach will provide a deeper understanding of how faith practices may be a central part of ministry with disquieted souls in particular, and also that my reflections will, at least in some small measure, add to the

4. Dykstra, *Growing in the Life of Faith,* p. 56.

important work of Dykstra, Bass, Volf, and a number of others who continue to champion faith practices and their necessity for the Christian life and ministry.

I provide merely a sketch of what each practice involves and also how it may foster the soul's quiet. On the one hand, significant work on faith practices has been done already, and there is not a great deal that I can add to those offerings. On the other hand, the persons most qualified to figure out how best to make use of these suggested practices will be pastors and other church leaders who consider and engage them routinely in their ministry. These practices will take on different forms and content depending on the contexts in which they are utilized and also who makes use of them. Consequently, my remaining remarks will be more suggestive than prescriptive.

Nevertheless, each of these practices merits the pastor's close attention in ministry. Why? Because each fosters what many disquieted souls need: a different understanding of God, an alternative view of their own relationship to God, a deeper sense of vocation in light of these matters, and a stronger sense of connection — to God, others, and themselves — that assuages their uneasiness about life and death. To say it differently, faith practices encourage us to think, act, and feel differently with respect to *theo-centric, theo-relational, vocational,* and *mortal* concerns. In doing so, they serve to assuage our concern for disconnection and vulnerability, in both life and death, which may drive the soul's disquiet.

Engaging faith practices serves to assuage these concerns in that faith practices create a "space" in which to work out one's anxiousness. What I have in mind here relates to what Harry Stack Sullivan and Sigmund Freud suggest about therapy with anxious persons. Specifically, anxious persons require a "safe space" where they may explore, identify, and attend to the roots of their anxiety. They need to revisit their patterns and habits — of thinking, feeling, acting, and relating — and their associated qualities in a place of "core security," a context free of the threat of judgment, rejection, abandonment, or harm, whether on the part of God or others. In other words, engaging these faith practices creates a psychological and spiritual "space" in which new patterns and habits of thinking, feeling, relating, and acting may form and develop. This development of new patterns and habits may lead to living in the midst of new realities tied to a different story.

My contention that pastors may model the engagement of these faith practices, while encouraging the same on the part of others, hinges on two things that I believe. First, anxious persons can and must change their habits associated with anxiety. These changes include the ways in which they think, act, and feel. Second, the Christian faith and its practices hold unique power to foster these changes — these practices hold the power to help those who perform them learn a different story about God, others, and themselves. This different story becomes the basis for thinking, acting, and feeling different, and thus for quieting the soul.

The Practice of Habitual Membership in the Church

Since disquieted souls tend to experience sustained feelings of vulnerability, disconnection, and isolation, whether from others, from themselves, or from God, caring for them pastorally should include finding ways to mitigate those experiences. A principal way to do that involves encouraging disquieted souls' membership in the faith community — and I mean formal membership.

As Bonhoeffer recognizes, Christ unifies individual Christians, connecting them in ways that otherwise would be impossible. In doing so, Christ provides them peace: "'He is our peace,' says Paul of Jesus Christ (Eph. 2:14). Without Christ there is discord between God and man and between man and man," for "through him alone do we have access to one another, joy in one another, and fellowship with one another."[5] We might add here that without Christ there is discord within ourselves as well. Christ unifies us *in ourselves*. He connects us in the totality of our being, in our souls, *as* he connects us to God and others. One thinks here of Jesus' words to his disciples concerning the peace that he offers: "Peace I leave with you; my peace I give to you. I do not give to you as the world gives. Do not let your hearts be troubled, and do not let them be afraid" (John 14:27).

In siding with Paul, Bonhoeffer concludes that we experience the peace that Christ offers, which includes a kind of "inner" peace or lack of internal discord ("Do not let your hearts be troubled, and do not let

5. Dietrich Bonhoeffer, *Life Together* (New York: Harper & Row, 1954), pp. 23, 29.

them be afraid"), *by virtue of* our unity with Christ and one another. Bonhoeffer recognizes that living the Christian faith, following Christ and partaking of his peace, does not — indeed, cannot — happen in isolation. Rather, the Christian life must be lived with other followers of Christ, in the community that we call the church. Bonhoeffer goes so far as to call it a "privilege" to live "in visible fellowship" with other Christians, noting further that "the physical presence of other Christians is a source of incomparable joy and strength to the believer."[6]

This presence is required because all of us need support. Sooner or later, we struggle, experience hardships and strife, and we stand in need of comfort, assistance, and companionship. We need encouragement in life. Bonhoeffer has in mind a particular type of encouragement: "truth-telling" according to God's Word with the goal of "meeting one another as bringers of the message of salvation." He writes, "The Christian needs another Christian who speaks God's Word to him. He needs him again and again when he becomes uncertain and discouraged, for by himself he cannot help himself without belying the truth."[7] This view suggests that Christians, particularly those who live anxiously, benefit from being part of the church. They benefit from the connections, including physical, psychological, and spiritual ones — to others, themselves, and God — that the faith community provides. The "privilege" of church membership offers ongoing opportunities for connections, but also for the giving and receiving of support and encouragement, for "truth-telling" according to God's Word, and for bringing and receiving the message of salvation, a message that, among other things, assures us that everything is going to be OK. All of this promotes ever-deepening connections to God and others, a greater sense of inner peace, and, as a result, a way to mitigate the kind of vulnerability that anxious persons tend to experience.

While establishing church membership will entail different things in different traditions, including baptism, a public profession of faith, or the transfer of a letter of membership from another congregation, when advocating *formal* membership I have something particular in mind. I am referring to a personal (one's own) and public (the community's) recognition and endorsement of one's presence in, contribu-

---

6. Bonhoeffer, *Life Together,* pp. 18-19.
7. Bonhoeffer, *Life Together,* p. 23.

tions to, and belonging not only among the church universal, to which all Christians belong, but also within a particular, local, demarcated congregation of Christ's followers. Formal membership provides the opportunity for a particular kind of investment, "ownership," and accountability among Christians that provides something essential to disquieted souls. Specifically, formal membership adds quality and depth to the connections that we form and maintain, whether to God, others, or ourselves.

At first glance this claim may seem rigid, overly prescriptive, and unnecessary. It may also appear as if I am suggesting that yet another demand be placed on an already burdened group of persons. Let me be clear. We would never treat those who are not church members differently from members with respect to pastoral care needs, never require that individuals formally join the church in order to participate in its ministries or means of grace. Jesus doesn't seem to have been concerned with formalities anyway. Nevertheless, formal membership offers some particular things that anxious persons may urgently require. First, it provides a recognized and sanctioned structure for promoting the kind of connections that anxious persons long for and struggle to secure. In other words, when holding membership in a particular congregation, anxious persons (and others) can make appeal to that membership. Such an appeal, in essence, involves recalling an officially recognized belonging that encourages members to make a claim for their place in the community and its shared story — the Christian faith — in more definitive and confident ways. Joining a local congregation brings a two-fold newfound commitment. Those who join commit to the requirements and expectations of church membership, which tends to involve opportunities for serving God, one another, and the world. But their commitment also entails a more explicit obligation to seek connections and to maintain them by virtue of their decision to become church members. When their belonging becomes official, they tend to make a more lasting and in-depth investment of themselves in the life of the community and its ministry. They typically feel as though they are more accountable to others and others to them. Consequently, they tend to immerse themselves more fully in the faith community's world and all that it entails. This kind of deep involvement can help disquieted souls find the connections and support that they need.

Second, as I will discuss further below, formal church membership and the connections it fosters set the stage for engaging regularly in particular activities like worship, Scripture reading, prayer, confession, and service to others, in the church and beyond. As Bonhoeffer recognizes, the church and its adherents take up the charge of truth-telling and of bringing the message of God's saving acts not only among one another, but also (as Bonhoeffer's own life and witness made clear) among all people through a public, "worldly" witness. This truth-telling and bringing the message of God's salvation may serve to assuage the soul's disquiet.

I do not mean to suggest that church membership brings only pleasant, nurturing, and faithful experiences one's way. The institutional church has its share of flaws. Moreover, when its membership behaves badly it serves to promote precisely the kind of disconnection, isolation, vulnerability, and "untruth-telling" that all persons, disquieted souls included, need *less* of in their lives. I am instructed by Douglas John Hall's reminder that "when we think of the church, we should try to avoid being idealistic, romantic, and utopian."[8] Moreover, as a former pastor, I recognize that a significant number of people who maintain active involvement in congregational life, and who contribute generously with their time, energy, passion, and gifts, may not welcome formal membership. In fact, if pressed for more formal membership, many persons will not only resist or decline it but may also be put off by such an overture and give less of themselves to the church as a result. More than once I've heard the responses of people who have been encouraged to make their membership in the congregation more formal: "I see no need for that"; "I'm not a 'joiner'"; or "I'm not interested in being a member. I like things the way they are!" Nevertheless, if formal membership in a congregation holds import for all adherents to the Christian faith, anxious persons and those who offer them care do well to take it particularly seriously. Pastors may want to gently but firmly encourage anxious persons to increase their investment in congregational life in the ways that formal membership provides, with the assumption that it may very well be good for their souls.

8. Douglas John Hall, *Why Christian?* (Minneapolis: Augsburg Fortress Press, 1998), p. 122.

Karla (whom we met earlier) described her experience with the church, which seems to support encouraging church membership among disquieted souls:

> Fairly recently it dawned on me that being in a sanctuary — all the sanctuaries I've been in — feels like I'm at home. And interestingly, I've never had a problem talking in front of people in sanctuary. I know — I'm weird. But I think it's because I figure if there's any place you can be who you are and mess up, it's the church, because I assume that there's acceptance there. I know there isn't always, but that's my perception of what should happen there. I think if you are who you are, you have a lot better chance of acceptance than if you're trying to be who you're not.

While Karla may have a similar experience without formal church membership, one can imagine that its benefits would promote the feelings of being "at home" and accepted that Karla wants and needs.

The Practices of Habitual Worship, Scripture Reading, and Prayer

With church membership comes the opportunity for engaging routinely in particular activities associated with the Christian faith and life that bring adherents into a direct encounter with the Christian story and its world. I have in mind particularly the activities of worship, reading the Bible, and praying.

As they perform these activities, these faith practices, adherents form distinct habits associated with the Christian story. In terms that William James and Donald Capps might endorse, worshipping, reading the Bible, and praying intentionally and routinely foster habitual, patterned ways of thinking, acting, relating, and feeling. Specifically, as we perform these practices, we experience learning how to think, act, relate, and feel in relation to the Christian story, including its claims and promises concerning God, others, and ourselves, in both life and death.

Bonhoeffer's reflections again prove instructive. He suggests that each day in the Christian life should begin with some form of common worship or devotion that includes Scripture reading and prayer.[9] He writes, "For Christians the beginning of the day should not be burdened and oppressed with besetting concerns for the day's work. At the threshold of the new day stands the Lord who made it. . . . All unrest, all impurity, all care and anxiety flee before him. Therefore, at the beginning of the day let all distraction and empty talk be silenced and let the first thought and the first word belong to him to whom our whole life belongs. 'Awake thou that sleepest, and arise from the dead, and Christ shall give thee light' (Eph. 5:14)."[10] Bonhoeffer recognizes that beginning the day in a posture of worship and devotion brings us into an encounter with God and the Christian story. An encounter with both may quiet the soul.

Furthermore, the scriptures in particular draw those who read them into the Christian story because they draw them into the scriptural world and its stories. Bonhoeffer goes so far as to say that the scriptures "set the listening fellowship in the midst of the wonderful world of revelation of the people of Israel with its prophets, judges, kings, and priests, its wars, festivals, sacrifices, and sufferings. The fellowship of believers is woven into the Christmas story, the baptism, the miracles and teaching, the suffering, dying, and rising again of Jesus Christ. It participates in the very events that occurred on this earth for the salvation of the world, and in doing so receives salvation in Jesus Christ."[11] At stake for Bonhoeffer is the way that particular faith practices — in this case, the "consecutive reading of Biblical books" — link us to the Christian story, invite us into its world and realities, and thus serve as means of grace. Ongoing encounters with the scriptures, Bonhoeffer claims,

> force everyone who wants to hear to put himself, or to allow himself to be found, where God has acted once and for all for the salvation of men. We become a part of what once took place for our salvation. Forgetting and losing ourselves, we, too, pass through the Red Sea, through the desert, across the Jordan into the promised land. With Israel we fall into doubt and unbelief

9. Bonhoeffer, *Life Together,* p. 44. Note that Bonhoeffer also included singing as part of morning devotions.

10. Bonhoeffer, *Life Together,* p. 43.

11. Bonhoeffer, *Life Together,* p. 53.

and through punishment and repentance experience again God's help and faithfulness. All this is not mere reverie but holy, godly reality. We are torn out of our own existence and set down in the midst of the holy history of God on earth. There God deals with us, and there He still deals with us, our needs and our sins, in judgment and grace. It is not that God is the spectator and sharer of our present life, howsoever important that is; but rather that we are the reverent listeners and participants in God's action in the sacred story, the history of the Christ on earth. And only in so far as we are *there*, is God with us today also.[12]

While the practices of worship, Scripture reading, and praying provide all of what Bonhoeffer suggests, they especially present those who perform them with the opportunity to develop new kinds of habits. In the case of anxious persons, they may develop habits that differ from those associated with anxiety. For example, rather than continuing to ruminate about whether or not God loves her and accepts her, which can manifest itself in the avoidance of God and others and thus promote disconnection, a person could be helped to make it her habit to read particular Scripture passages that confirm God's faithfulness and desire for relationship. She could also be encouraged to learn to pray in ways that prompt her to recall the nurturing qualities of God, God's promises, the care and kindness of Christ, and other matters relating to the Christian story that mitigate her sense of vulnerability and accompanying anxiety. Through habitual worship, Scripture reading, and prayer, she could also learn to take what she experiences when engaging in these practices — intellectually, emotionally, and practically, but also spiritually — beyond the practices themselves, so that what she experiences becomes more deeply part of her broader life.

To cite one more example: this woman might experience in the practice of celebrating the Lord's Supper a sense that Jesus is with her, in her, and part of her, such that she thinks, acts, and feels in ways that are comforting, assuring, and relaxing. If so, then she may learn how to carry a similar experience with her beyond Sunday-morning worship and into the rest of her week. She could do this by thinking about what

12. Bonhoeffer, *Life Together,* p. 53.

she thinks about during the Eucharist, reflecting on her thought processes and the content of her thoughts. She could also reflect on how she feels during the Eucharist — comforted, assured, and more relaxed — so that eventually this thinking and feeling inform her operative cognitive set. Over time, the practice of being with Jesus in the Lord's Supper may become a pattern that she takes beyond that experience, so that it becomes part of her other experiences as well.

Recall how José noted that his faith in God, and especially the practice of Scripture reading, had helped him with anxiety: "My belief in God has helped me through the struggles. Some years back, Scripture reading would help. I think reading, you know, some poem . . . or there was a psalm. . . . 'Be still and know that I am God.' I came across another, where Paul says, 'We're perfect in our weakness.' Those would bring me some comfort."

I want to reiterate the point that persons who perform faith practices are exposed to particular ways of thinking, behaving, and feeling that grow out of an ongoing encounter with the Christian story. As Bonhoeffer suggests, these practices bring us to where God is, into an encounter with the One with whom we need to experience connection, provision, and care. It matters little whether these practices are done on Sunday or at other times of the week, done with others in a more public setting or alone in solitude. And it matters little what particular forms these activities take — high or low liturgy, *lectio divina* or *lectio continua,* worship-book prayers or extemporaneous prayers. As these practices become habits, they foster new patterns for thinking, feeling, relating, and acting. They promote the formation of new realities tied to a different story.

Potential benefits that habitual worship, Scripture reading, and prayer present to those who practice them include stronger and more numerous connections, a decreased sense of vulnerability, and a new and different reality that fosters a quieter soul.

Stronger and more numerous connections include connections with God, with others in the faith community, and within oneself. While church membership provides a structure for such connections, these are formed and strengthened *as* faith practices draw us deeper into the Christian story and its realities and patterns become our own. Why? This story assures us of God's promises in Christ to be faithful, present, and also to remain in relationship with us, in life and in death, regardless of our merits. This story also calls upon us to reach out to others in relationship, even as we look for them to reach out to us. Consequently, the Christian story binds in deeper communion those who embrace it and live it together, alleviating the alienation and isolation that anxious persons often feel.

Another potential benefit of these practices is a decreased sense of vulnerability. This follows first from having formed stronger connections with God, others, and within oneself, and then from the reassurance of God's fidelity, provision, acceptance, care, and concern that the Christian story includes and faith practices convey. Perceiving that one is less vulnerable by virtue of who God is and what God provides may mitigate the uneasiness that anxious persons tend to feel, especially as it relates to matters of God and their relationship to God, but also to matters of acceptance, competence, and control. Remember, anxious persons want and need to be assured that everything will be OK.

A new and different reality that fosters a quieter soul becomes possible as these faith practices help anxious persons learn to perceive their current reality differently, and then to change it, by virtue of internalizing the reality put forth by the Christian story. As they are confronted by the reality of the gospel, they can learn to identify their thoughts that lead to anxiety and *stop* them, so that they prevent the automatic chain of anxiety-laden thoughts from forming. Moreover, as they think about God, others, themselves, and the world in a different way, in light of the gospel's claims and promises, and as they begin to live differently in light of how they think, by virtue of what they glean from their faith and its practices, they begin responding to the situations they face in life differently, and they feel different because their reality has changed. Their personal story, at one time shaped largely by the reality of the disquieted soul and its story, has been altered by the Christian story and its reality. This new reality continues to alter the sources of the disquieted soul and thus serves to assuage anxiety.

Of course, worshipping God, reading Scripture, and praying, like any other faith practice we might consider, always remain ends in themselves. We practice these in order to give thanks and glory to God for God's presence, gifts, and promises. Nevertheless, these practices edify and build up, they form and re-form persons intellectually, emotionally, relationally, and spiritually. They nurture the soul. As a result, they provide preparation for and sustenance in the Christian life.

The Practice of Habitually Serving Others

The Roman Catholic theologian Lucien Richard, O.M.I., begins his book *Living the Hospitality of God* with these words: "Christianity is above all a vision and therefore a way of seeing. Christianity offers a peculiar and distinct take on reality, on what is really real. I am suggesting that such a vision and such a take are well expressed in the scripture's affirmation: 'I was a stranger and you welcomed me' (Matt. 25:35). To be a Christian, a disciple of Christ, is to see the stranger the way that Christ saw the stranger and by implication the way God sees the stranger."[13] Similarly, Ana María Pineda, a member of the Sisters of Mercy, notes that "to welcome the stranger is to acknowledge him as a human being made in God's image; it is to treat her as one of equal worth with ourselves — indeed, as one who may teach us something out of the richness of experiences different from our own."[14] Richard and Pineda view living hospitably as a faith practice and a central part of the Christian story, its world, and its claim upon its adherents.

While we extend hospitality for many reasons, not the least of which involves faithfulness to the gospel, serving others as a faith practice holds particular importance for anxious persons. One reason is that extending hospitality helps them to get their minds off of themselves and their condition. Anxious people tend to find this difficult not because they are particularly selfish or egotistical, but because their condition brings with it an overwhelming urge to pay attention to the details of their lives. They find it difficult to resist fixating on the concerns that inform their anxiety. They feel consumed by the matters that trouble them, which involves needing to sort those matters out, to understand them more fully, including where they come from and why they are so powerful, and certainly to find solutions for the struggles they bring. Charles (whom we met earlier) describes his own experience with anxiety in these terms — and explains how helping others helped him:

> [Anxiety's] by-product is that you get very self-absorbed because you're analyzing yourself so much, and when you start getting

13. Lucien Richard, O.M.I., *Living the Hospitality of God* (New York: Paulist Press, 2000), p. 1.

14. Ana María Pineda, "Hospitality," in *Practicing Our Faith*, p. 38.

into deep anxiety, having trouble functioning and getting . . . sliding into depression, your world is so small, you really just are focusing on yourself at that time. "How do I get healthy?" "I need to get out of this." "What are other people thinking about me?" You think it's noticeable. So all of a sudden, you slide into this very self-absorbed manner of thinking and that's why, if you can . . . one of the best things you can do is just start helping other people . . . to break the cycle and to think outside of your-self. It's one of the things I did that helped me. I decided to take a risk in terms of what I was choosing to do to help other people, and that became the prison ministry I got involved in.

We may help anxious persons feel better by attending to that "by-product" of anxiety. Specifically, we may provide them with opportuni-ties for turning their gaze more outward, beyond themselves, so that their "world" grows larger and they enjoy a physical, emotional, and spiritual break.

Of course, anxious persons should not cease paying attention to themselves and their condition altogether. Even if that were possible, they would still need to remain "self-centered" to some degree. Why? Because in order to learn to live less anxiously, with a quieter soul, they must spend a good deal of time and energy learning to think, act, and feel differently. Paying attention to themselves and their needs, there-fore, remains appropriate and necessary. Nevertheless, they also need to find ways to take a break, to engage that "safe space" and nurture that "core security" required to assuage the disquieted soul. Serving others and their needs offers anxious persons needed rest.

Serving others tends to help disquieted souls in another way. Ex-tending hospitality results in a visible reminder of at least two things: first, how vulnerable many, if not all, people are to life's vicissitudes; and second, how it is precisely our connections to one another *and* to God that provide a way to compensate for those vulnerabilities. We have noted how anxious persons often have the sense that they are all alone in their struggles. They assume that others would not under-stand their pain, but also can assume that no one else lives with the de-gree of risk, threat, or vulnerability that they do. Consequently, they suffer in isolation and, typically, in silence. Whether or not such as-sumptions would prove accurate, they often inform the perspective, the *reality,* of anxious persons. Therefore, ongoing reminders of the widespread nature of human vulnerability and struggle may themselves serve to lessen the burden that comes with anxious persons' feeling like they suffer uniquely or alone.

In light of the ways that Richard and Pineda speak about the relationship between hospitality and the stranger, I would suggest that disquieted souls tend to feel like strangers, not only to others but also to themselves. Often they feel a kind of *internal* disconnection, cut off from who they truly are or want to be, and isolated from life as they envision living it. If the heart of the Christian faith and life involves learning to see the stranger beyond us differently — that is, as Christ and God see her, so that we then welcome her hospitably — serving others may also provide a new way of seeing and welcoming the stranger *within.* In welcoming the stranger, we live faithfully toward Christ's claim on us while, presumably, providing for another's real need. Moreover, welcoming the stranger beyond may serve to remind the anxious person that she really is more connected that she realized, connected to God, to others for whom God also cares and loves, and to herself. As a result, welcoming the stranger beyond may serve to "normalize" the anxious person's experiences of vulnerability, of feeling threatened by or uneasy with life and its demands. Spending time with persons who struggle fosters solidarity in suffering. Even when another's struggle seems different from one's own, sharing in the other's experience may leave one saying to oneself, "I am not alone. Others suffer too, maybe even more than I do." While this newfound perspective likely would not remove one's own pain entirely, it might serve to alleviate "the suffering in suffering" that Moltmann identified — the sense that one suffers outside the awareness of other persons and of God, or that one suffers alone because no one else suffers. As Pineda recognizes, the stranger may have something to teach all of us about himself, about other strangers, about God, and about ourselves.

The Practice of Habitual Confession

An additional faith practice to consider is confession. For almost every Christian tradition, confessing our sins against God, others, ourselves, and the created order holds a central place in the Christian life. This practice typically takes place in the context of worship, usually in the form of a corporate prayer of confession. Corporate confession does not take the place of confession outside of worship, which adherents to the Christian story are also encouraged to practice. Corporate confession simply provides an opportunity, when one gathers with fellow pilgrims in faith, to search oneself, to identify one's sin, and to confess before God and others ways that one has missed the mark for which God desires human beings to aim, so that one may begin living differently.

For traditions that trace their roots to the Protestant Reformation, the corporate prayer of confession also has served to correct what the reformers saw as a theological error. Specifically, they disagreed with the notion that Christians need an intercessor, a priest, to offer their confession to God and, in turn, to administer God's blessing of pardon, often called absolution. The reformers held that the church consists of "a priesthood of all believers," such that all persons who follow Christ have access to God and may confess and receive pardon from God without the need for another person, whether ordained clergy or not. Consequently, the ancient practice of "private," one-on-one confession was abandoned in most Reformation churches.

While there may be valid theological reasons for leaving this practice behind, I believe that something was lost when the practice of confessing directly before another person largely ceased. I have in mind here the value of intimacy tied to meeting alone with another person, searching one's heart for what might need to be confessed, and then sharing it with that person in whom one trusts and has confidence. When we relate to another person in this way, even if a screen or other type of physical barrier lies between us — as is the case still in the Roman Catholic Church — we have the opportunity to be vulnerable in safety. We can dare to open ourselves and our lives up to another, an act that disquieted souls find so challenging. We can view our vulnerability as something embraced and welcomed by God, daring to be more honest with ourselves as we seek greater honesty with another. Occasions for honesty foster a deeper self-awareness and self-understanding that anxious persons require in order to live more peacefully. Furthermore, vulnerability and honesty in confession foster more profound connections, with other persons and with God, who hear our prayers and our attempts to search our hearts, and, in learning of our desire to go forward living differently, hold us accountable for doing so.

Incidentally, most of these benefits of so-called private confession that I describe are, more or less, found in various kinds of counseling and psychotherapeutic relationships. At their best, therapists provide a "safe space" — emotionally, relationally, even physically — in which a client may open himself, explore his vulnerabilities, seek honesty with himself and others, become more self-aware, cultivate greater self-knowledge, and in so doing make stronger connections with others and himself. This poses the possibility that a more routine practice of confessing to another person in the context of a shared living of the Christian story might result in church members making fewer visits to counselors or therapists.

Disquieted souls do well to consider the potential benefits of confessing their sins, their struggles and needs, and especially their experiences with living anxiously to their pastor. Likewise, pastors do well to encourage this practice. Such confession is good for the reasons already mentioned, and also because we know that one of the best ways to relieve anxiety is simply to share the fact that one is anxious with others. One of the things taught in public-speaking courses, for example, is that it can be very helpful when one feels particularly anxious to admit this at the outset and then move on. Behind this suggestion lies the fact that the more we seek to hide anxiety, the more powerful its grip on us tends to become. Regrettably, hiding it feels most natural. Deeply afraid of being discovered, afraid that others will think even less of them than they already fear if their anxious feelings become known, anxious persons go to great measures to mask, conceal, or otherwise deny their condition. As they do so, anxiety takes on more power and more of a life of its own, building in complexity and degree.

Charles recognizes how confession has played a positive role in quieting his own soul. Conveying that he was an anxious child who tended to have "a guilty conscience," he says, "I'd have a lot of anxiety build up until I could vent it . . . get out of my mind what I was carrying, the guilt I was carrying." Moreover, as an adult, he now finds it helpful to share his struggles with anxiety, believing that as painful as his condition has been to live with, it also provides a certain kind of gift. Much like Kierkegaard recognized, Charles believes that anxiety can and does draw one closer to God, as it keeps one aware of the need for Christ. Moreover, by sharing his own experiences, Charles invites others to do the same:

I need to allow myself the ability to say, "You know what? God gave me this anxiety for a reason, and I'm not sure why, but let's look at it as a way to draw closer to him."

And I'm trying to do that. As painful as it is, I'm trying to give myself the permission to do that, to really sink my teeth into it and believe in it — that God made me for a reason uniquely in this way. I look for every opportunity I can, in small group situations, at retreats, when asked, to give my testimony. I include the anxiety and depression, and I do it for a reason. It's to combat the stigma on mental health that's out there, and because I know there's somebody out there who needs to hear what I have to say. Each time I share my story, someone will come up to me afterwards and seek counsel and seek advice and tell me how glad they are to hear me share because they suffer from the same thing.

By advocating the practice of confessing to a pastor, whether one struggles with anxiety or something else, I encourage those who *do* struggle with this condition to spend less time and energy trying to conceal it, which only makes it worse, and more time and energy sharing their struggles more publicly. Sharing anxiety with another person tends to ease its burdens, for anxious persons themselves and for others around them.

Conclusion

Pastoral care of anxious persons requires locating, or perhaps relocating, the story of the disquieted soul within God's encompassing, grace-full story of redemption. Helping anxious persons learn to hear, consider, embrace, and ultimately tell, retell, and live *this* story of God's grace, even as they locate themselves and their struggle in it, may lead to a new word being lived and spoken: the disquieted soul does not have the final say. To an extent, engaging the faith practices that I have outlined here also may offer benefits similar to those found in various cognitive therapy approaches: the "turn-off" technique, the repetition technique, the technique of substituting contrasting imagery, and the "as if" technique. Specifically, as anxious persons routinely take part in practices of formal church membership, worship, Scripture reading, prayer, serving others in mission and outreach, and public and private confession ("repetition"), they may find themselves able to "turn off" anxiety-laden thoughts, images, feelings, and behaviors, and "substituting contrasting imagery" that informs feeling less anxious. Consequently, they may find themselves living more and more "as if" they were not so anxious after all.

Locating and orienting one's life story within the Christian story, which occurs as faith practices are engaged habitually and in community, provides an alternative to the disquieted soul's dominant, destructive story. Because of anxiety's spiritual nature, its grounding in *theo-centric, theo-relational, vocational,* and *mortal* concerns, and because anxious persons sojourning in congregations may very well be experiencing precisely this kind of anxiety, I encourage pastors to make it their priority to offer care steeped in the Christian story and its practices. A pastoral perspective will be guided by how Christian faith understands the disquieted soul's condition, and how faith practices may foster the soul's quiet against the backdrop — the story — of God's creative, transformative, and redemptive acts throughout history, which Christians have most frequently recognized in the history of Israel; the life, death, and resurrection of Jesus; and the ongoing work of the Holy Spirit.

A PERSONAL NOTE

My investment in this project and subject derives from my experience in ministry with anxious persons, which has been rich and instructive. However, my interest in anxiety stems from something else as well. Anxiety has been my own experience. I know how perplexing, stifling, and painful this condition can be. I have witnessed intimately, both in my own life and in others', its impact on relationships, decision-making, moods, dreams, vocational clarity, church life, and many other facets of daily living. Furthermore, since beginning work on this book, I have heard from many more people — including students, friends, colleagues, and family members — that anxiety has marked their lives too. While their accounts are anecdotal, I am convinced that they illustrate well, in very personal ways, what impersonal statistics increasingly indicate. Anxiety is a widespread phenomenon that people need to understand and, in many cases, from which they require immediate relief.

Through my experiences in social work, parish ministry, and seminary teaching, I have been privileged to listen to more people than I can recall recount painful struggles with anxiety, even as I have sought to assist them with finding ways to minimize anxiety's destruction. Anxiety has never been unbearable for me. But I do know and love people who *have* experienced unbearable anxiety. Some have been friends and family members. Others have been part of congregations, institutions, and agencies that I have served. Indeed, I have witnessed anxiety's incapacitating pain in too many close associates. In numerous cases, I have journeyed with them along the path of gaining greater insight into their struggle and coming to terms with it. These journeys have been a privilege and a gift from God. To be invited into another's life, particularly in more dark and uncertain moments, often involves a stunning kind of sacredness. At times, we see in these occasions a glimpse of the Divine that many of us — maybe most of us — ordinarily gloss over, if we don't miss it altogether.

My struggle with anxiety has not been insignificant, however. In fact, much of my adult life has involved trying to understand and live better with my own "disquieted soul," its difficulties and potentials, while supporting others' efforts to do the same. I have found my share of comfort, and even joy, in this journey. In fact, my experience with anxiety, though painful, has provided a richness and a depth to life that may very well be lacking otherwise. Distressing experiences have the potential to promote enhanced understanding, empathy, and even solidarity with others who struggle, all of which may serve as a relational balm to soothe one's own pain and promote the healing of one's own wound. At the very least, learning to speak more openly, and less shamefully, about my disquieted soul has eased its power and effects. This is because sharing experiences, especially those that entail suffering, help to remove the "suffering in suffering" that Moltmann identifies. Moreover, learning that numerous others — more than I ever imagined — know firsthand the struggles and shackles that accompany the anxious life has itself proved curative.

The principal source for quieting my own soul has been my faith. I do not mean to suggest that it has offered an instant, unlabored cure-all, one that a pathologically optimistic North American culture *and* church both envy and propagate. Luther would have associated that with a *theologia gloriae* (a theology of glory), which, as Douglas John Hall so aptly describes it, "offers people a perfected and already-redeemed state — so long as they can keep their eyes shut."[1] Rather, my anxiety, and I think others' too, seems to give as much evidence to the mysteries of God and the paradox of faith remaining alive and well as it does to faith's promise of healing, happiness, and harbor, as desirable as these remain.

I have found particular comfort and assurance as well as challenge when recalling Jesus' words to his disciples in Matthew's Gospel: "Be

---

1. Douglas John Hall, *Bound and Free: A Theologian's Journey* (Minneapolis: Fortress Press, 2005), p. 68.

not anxious" (6:25, ASV). At minimum, these words convince me that when anxiety dominates one's life, it does so against God's wishes. Though I think that Kierkegaard shows wisdom when noting anxiety's gift to the person of faith, the reminder that we need Christ to sustain us, I also believe that Jesus' plea "Be not anxious" confirms that chronic and severe anxiety impedes life as God would have us experience it. Kierkegaard's insights notwithstanding, too much of a good thing, or a gift that "keeps on giving," may in the end be anything but a gift. Engaging in the faith practices that I have discussed, whether as a pastor or as a "pew sitter" (more common for me these days), has served to remind me of two truths. Painfully disquieted souls are not God's desire, nor are they are ever beyond God's deep concern. Furthermore, faith practices have shaped and reshaped me in ways that continue to curb my tendency toward anxiety and support my seeking a quieter soul — and I believe that they can do the same for others.

Along my journey's way, and with the help of faith practices, I have learned to find new and more profound meaning in my struggle. This has allowed me to embrace my own disquieted soul, and to live more fully and faithfully with it. Finding more meaning in my experience has also allowed me to claim anxiety as simply a *part* of who I am, perhaps even a necessary part that, while mysterious and at times painful, is nonetheless valuable in its own way. With Kierkegaard, I have come to view anxiety as a kind of adventure and gift that need not be burdensome, at least not entirely so.

William James pointed out that at least two things inform religious faith: a "sense that there is *something wrong about us*" (an uneasiness) and a sense that "*we are saved from the wrongness* by making proper connection with the higher powers" (its solution).[2] James's insight describes well my own experience with uneasiness and solutions for it. The disquiet of my soul has proved to be a profoundly spiritual condition that calls for faith practices. Those that I have detailed remain centrally important for my own journey, even when I grow lax in performing them. They remain a soothing, curative balm for my "dis-ease."

Perhaps such can be the case for other anxious persons too. Some individuals' experiences may call for more. If so, resources from psy-

---

2. William James, *The Varieties of Religious Experience* (New York: Literary Classics of the United States, 1987), p. 454.

chotherapy or psychiatry may prove invaluable. But disquieted souls continue at the very least to call for what the Christian faith and its practices have to offer. After all, Jesus urged his people, "Be not anxious!" In doing so, he offered them an alternative way of thinking about and living with God, themselves, and others. I pray that this book will help disquieted souls, and those who minister with them, to live more fully into Jesus' plea and his desire that they rest in him.

For Further Reading

Beck, Aaron T., and Gary Emery, with Ruth L. Greenberg. *Anxiety Disorders and Phobias: A Cognitive Perspective.* New York: Basic Books, 1985.
Brantley, Jeffrey. *Calming Your Anxious Mind: How Mindfulness and Compassion Can Free You from Anxiety, Fear, and Panic.* New York: New Harbinger Publications, 2007.
Capps, Donald. *Agents of Hope: A Pastoral Psychology.* Minneapolis: Fortress Press, 1995.
———. *Social Phobia: Alleviating Anxiety in an Age of Self-Promotion.* St. Louis: Chalice Press, 1999.
Gerzon, Robert. *Finding Serenity in an Age of Anxiety.* New York: Bantam Books, 1998.
Kierkegaard, Søren. *The Concept of Anxiety.* Edited and translated by Reidar Thomte. Princeton, N.J.: Princeton University Press, 1980.
———. *The Sickness unto Death.* Edited and translated by Howard V. Hong and Edna H. Hong. Princeton, N.J.: Princeton University Press, 1980.
Lester, Andrew D. *Hope in Pastoral Care and Counseling.* Louisville: Westminster John Knox Press, 1995.
May, Rollo. *The Meaning of Anxiety.* Rev. ed. New York: W. W. Norton, 1996.
Restak, Richard. *Poe's Heart and the Mountain Climber: Exploring the Effects of Anxiety on Our Brains and Our Culture.* New York: Harmony Books, 2004.
Salecl, Renata. *On Anxiety.* London: Routledge, 2004.
Strauss, Claudia J. *Talking to Anxiety: Simple Ways to Support Someone in*

Your Life Who Suffers from Anxiety. New York: New American Library, 2004.

Tillich, Paul. *The Courage to Be.* New Haven: Yale University Press, 1952/ 1980.

Wicks, Robert J. *Living Simply in an Anxious World.* Mahwah, N.J.: Paulist Press, 1988/1998.

Wybrow, Peter C. *American Mania: When More Is Not Enough.* New York: W.W. Norton, 2005.

Index